Literature,
Performance, and
Somaesthetics

Literature, Performance, and Somaesthetics:

Studies in Agency and Embodiment

Edited by

Anna Budziak, Katarzyna Lisowska and Jarosław Woźniak

Cambridge
Scholars
Publishing

Literature, Performance, and Somaesthetics:
Studies in Agency and Embodiment

Edited by Anna Budziak, Katarzyna Lisowska and Jarosław Woźniak

Refereed by Dorota Koczanowicz, Wojciech Małecki

This book first published 2017

Cambridge Scholars Publishing

Lady Stephenson Library, Newcastle upon Tyne, NE6 2PA, UK

British Library Cataloguing in Publication Data
A catalogue record for this book is available from the British Library

ISBN (10): 1-4438-8281-X
ISBN (13): 978-1-4438-8281-1

TABLE OF CONTENTS

Part II: Literary Reception, Canon, and History

Part III: Literary Interpretations: Soma and Text

ACKNOWLEDGEMENTS

This book is the result of the conference *Performance Studies, Literary Studies, Somaesthetics* which was held at the University of Wrocław in December 2014. We owe special acknowledgment to the keynote speakers of the conference: Professor Richard Shusterman (Florida Atlantic University), Professor Adam Chmielewski (University of Wrocław) and Dr. Kacper Bartczak (University of Lodz). We are also grateful to the academic staff, Ph.D. students and friends who helped to organize this event.

We would like to thank: the Faculty of Letters of the University of Wrocław for their financial and practical support in preparing this publication; The Wroclaw Mime Theatre (Pantomima Wrocławska) for their permission to use a performance image from "BATORY_trans" for the cover of this book; and Dr. David Schauffler from the University of Silesia, who proofread the manuscript.

Jarosław and Katarzyna wish to thank the Institute of Polish Studies for their assistance. They are particularly grateful to Professor Anna Gemra, Professor Wojciech Soliński and Dr. Wojciech Małecki for their continued support. Finally, thanks to our colleagues from the University of Wrocław—Jakub Krogulec and Michał Wolski—for their help with technical issues and graphic design.

INTRODUCTION

ANNA BUDZIAK

This book views textual and extra-textual worlds as intimately connected, as forming a continuum, in fact. The collected essays—on literature, philosophy and art—which it contains derive their theoretical inspirations from two realms where embodiment and agency are particularly stressed: philosophical somaesthetics, a discipline proposed by Richard Shusterman in 1999, and performance studies, remarkable for its current expansion. The studies of performativity and performance, which originate in the philosophy of language and theater studies, began in the mid-1960s to permeate a host of other disciplines. Morphing into performance studies in the 1970s, they also drew inspiration from cognate domains, such as anthropology, cultural studies, sociology, ethnography, psychology, cognitive science, and neurolinguistics. This interdisciplinary development —described as the performative turn—is now in full swing, spreading not only within humanities, but also far beyond. However, performance studies has also a tradition reaching back to the nineteenth century. Its key term, "performance," comes from John Austin's theory of performatives; and it has now been used for more than fifty years in a number of contexts ranging from theater studies to anthropology. But the meaning of the term "performance" is constantly changing and expanding in various directions. Today, primary subjects of performance studies are aspects of performativity, agency and acting, both on stage and in everyday life. At the same time, the research done in this broad field combines diverse methods and methodologies without forcing them into a single perspective.

Jon McKenzie, one of the most celebrated advocates of the performative turn, predicts that, in terms of the organization of knowledge in the twenty-first century, the idea of performance will replace the idea of discipline, which is a legacy of the eighteenth and nineteenth centuries (2001, 176). McKenzie's hypothesis—locating the studies of various types of performances and performativity at the center of disciplines that have an ambition to explain the human condition in post-modern reality—is certainly a daring prediction. But contemporary performance studies began modestly. In his *Drama: Between Poetry and Performance* W. B. Worthen

(2010) associates their rise with the resistance to the New-Critical—that is, purely literary, or textual—approach to the drama as exercised by theoreticians and practitioners of theater. To Worthen, thus, the field of performance studies was formed as a result of the conflict between, on the one hand, literary studies emphasizing the drama's textual dimension and, on the other hand, the theoretical approaches that focused on performance that was unrelated to any previously scripted form.

Born of this discord, performance studies found their place among the intellectual tendencies that challenged the long-lasting supremacy of textuality in the humanities and social sciences. Theoreticians and practitioners worked to find alternative models of cognition to instate in the place of frameworks which had been predominantly linguistic. The linguistic paradigm—established at the beginning of the 1960s with recourse to Ludwig Wittgenstein's philosophy and to Ferdinand de Saussure's work in the field of linguistics, and under the dominance of structuralism, poststructuralism and deconstructionism—reasserted its authority within sociology, anthropology, and history. From the radically textualist perspective, reality was considered as mediated exclusively by language, unstable, indeterminate, flickering, a matter only of the games played within various discourses. The world came to be seen as a text: human experience was reduced to a story, the logic of history became replaced by the appeal of rhetorical figures—such are the four master tropes of Hayden White's historiography—and the self, after Richard Rorty, assumed the shapes of varying sets of vocabularies, descriptions and re-descriptions.

However, this tendency was also counterpointed by the recognition—appearing in various fields—that neither the world nor selfhood were texts and contexts all the way down. Resistance against body-mind dualism within neuroscience, inaugurated by Antonio Damasio's works (beginning with his *Descartes' Error: Emotion, Reason, and the Human Brain* published in 1994), has been long rising also within humanities. The counterturn in the humanities stressed the significance of corporeality and proposed to break out of the prison-house of ideality into the physical world. Both in linguistics and in philosophy, the textualist, narrative pattern was eventually deemed insufficient. In linguistics, the view of language as a site of ideality has been challenged by cognitivists who argue that we do not explain the surrounding reality by relying solely on a narrative paradigm. The cognitivists have queried whether and how language—and, even more importantly, thought—can be a product of corporeality and of our embodied existence in the physical world. Mark Johnson and George Lakoff, the major luminaries of this approach, have sought to answer this question by exploring metaphors underlying the ways of sense-making; and they have shown that meaning arises as something visceral, that is starts with the way we orient ourselves in the surrounding physical environment.

In philosophy, for that matter, Rorty's stance has been challenged by Richard Shusterman's emphasis on the embodied self. Shusterman questions the assumption that the human subject connects with the external world only through stories and acquires self-understanding exclusively in the course of interpretation. Understanding, to Shusterman, is a category broader than that of interpretation; and the self becomes significant if restored to its somatic dimension, rather than only re-storied. It is performance studies and Shusterman's somaesthetics—a discipline which, as Christopher J. Voparil and John Giordano (2015) state,[1] is a momentous inspiration behind the somatic turn—that the authors of the essays presented in this book engage with. Shusterman defined somaesthetics as a disciplinary proposal in 1999. But substantial philosophical explorations of the embodied (aesthetic) experience can be found in his *Pragmatist Aesthetics: Living Beauty, Rethinking Art* (1992), culminating, as of today, in *Body Consciousness: A Philosophy of Mindfulness and Somaesthetics* (2008) and *Thinking Through the Body: Essays in Somaesthetics* (2010). Over nearly twenty years, somaesthetics has exceeded disciplinary boundaries by growing into a broad discourse and attracting scholars from the realms of both humanities and sciences. At present, it provides a framework for combining philosophical, literary-critical and theoretical concerns with the findings of neurophysiology, feminist studies, studies of affectivity, and theories of reception and performance.

In the most general terms, the point of convergence for somaesthetics and performativity is their stressing the agency of the embodied and sentient human self. Admittedly, in their preoccupation with the embodied *esse*, the explorations presented in this book reflect Michel Foucault's concern with disciplining discourses, even his apprehension of their punishing and limiting impact on the body. But, on the other hand, they share Judith Butler's conviction that the body can become a site of rebellion against such discursive and textual regimes; and they also engage with Shusterman's hope that the recognition of the implications of the body and corporeal dimension within the humanities will have ameliorative effects, liberating the self from discursive paradigms and empowering the embodied human self to alter them. This latter assumption—of the human subject's agency—has, among its corollaries, the supposition that as the texts influence the reader on a somatic level, so the sentient reader can affect the meaning of the text. The relationship is one of reciprocity.

The authors of the essays brought together in this book explore the question of agency through its various manifestations. They examine the construction of literary characters, with the emphasis on the representation of their corporeality and affectivity. They look into the problem of the formation of the literary canon as enacted rather than established, and into literary history as retold rather than re-written. And they focus on the problems of literary reception, considering it on the visceral, physical level. In these explorations the reading subjects are considered to be capable of shedding their passive attitudes, viewed as actors and performers involved in literary communication. The reader, then, is recognized neither as a function of the text nor, as Derek Attridge has it, the archive of idioculture (or the individual version of the culture as a whole), but as a sentient psychosomatic subject: an embodied active self. In *Literature, Performance, and Somaesthetics*, the agency of this embodied sentient self is regarded as it is outlined in philosophy—in somaesthetics and in the ethics of emotions—and as it manifests itself in these arts which follow Dewey's call to abandon the shelter of the museum glass case. It should be noted that art, as approached in this collection of studies, is energy and, as in Richard Shusterman's (post-Deweyan) philosophical reflection, a distinctly emotive and somatic experience. It is also a locus where the self can be liberated from its discursive confinement and the sphere where the audience's taboos and prejudices can be exposed and challenged.

Thus, by stressing agency and the embodiment of the human subject—in philosophy, the arts, and literature—the essays in this volume engage with the performative and somatic turns to counterpoint the textual tradition. But providing a counterpoint to textualism does not mean opposing it blindly. The essays collected in *Literature, Performance, and Somaesthetics: Studies in Agency and Embodiment* acknowledge the inspiration of performance studies and follow the somaesthetic proposal to attend more closely to the world stretching beyond the text; nevertheless, they also rely on the interpretative strategies developed under the aegis of structuralism and poststructuralism. Such inclusiveness seems to be suggested by Richard Schechner. Whilst Schechner warns that literature and performance are fundamentally different phenomena and that, as such, they require different research methods, he also asserts that the fundamental feature of performance studies is their openness to other fields. The essays presented in this book—discussing the problems of narrativity and performativity, and textuality and corporeality as closely connected—demonstrate this openness. They stress the embodied and agent status of the human subject in philosophy, underline the corporeal and affective appeal of art, and highlight the performative and somaesthetic aspects of literary texts and readings.

***

The book is divided into three parts concerned with philosophy and art (I), literary reception (II), and literary interpretations (III). Part One opens with Urszula Lisowska's study of performance and perception considered in the light of Martha Nussbaum's ethical philosophy. Her essay stresses art's role in cultivating human emotions. By bringing together Nussbaum's multifarious philosophical concerns—including the theme of political liberalism, the dilemma of plurality and collectiveness, Nussbaum's insistence on the attitudes to the body, her philosophy of emotions, and her position on the function of art—effectively, Lisowska arrives in her discussion of Nussbaum at the point where Shusterman's and Nussbaum's philosophies converge. Martha Nussbaum—like Richard Shusterman, who for that matter revives the Deweyan tradition in philosophy—emphasizes that art should be moved from the stultifying space of a museum into social space and insists on art's capacity to arouse in its recipients a sense of wonder and delight. While considering Nussbaum's moral and aesthetic philosophy in a broader philosophical context, Lisowska finds in it a solution to the dilemma of plurality and collectiveness, which John Rawls, she says, failed to provide. She indicates that Nussbaum offers this solution by applying her variety of the capability approach, insisting, at the same time, on the embodied nature of human experience and on the significance of affectivity. Following Nussbaum, Lisowska juxtaposes the negative feelings of an individual with a sense of gladness which art can evoke: specifically, she contrasts the socially disruptive emotions of shame and disgust, which come from denying the animality of human bodies (anthropodenial), with the emotions of compassion and wonder seen as conducive to a respectful recognition of other humans, of their autonomy and dignity. These positive emotions, she argues, are induced through aesthetic experience; thus art—especially the art performed in the public space—performs a socially meliorative role. Accordingly, in her essay, Lisowska puts an emphasis on the arts involving social participation, such as theater performance and design of public spaces; and she interprets particular projects—including the Vietnam Veterans Memorial in Constitution Gardens in Washington and Anish Kapoor's Cloud Gate in Millennium Park in Chicago—by paying attention to the corporeal and intersubjective aspects of space design.

Alex Ciorogar in his essay "From Somaesthetics to the Stylistics of Existence" is also concerned with the ameliorative function of art. In his paper, Ciorogar brings together two disciplines: on the one hand, he outlines the characteristics and aims of Shusterman's philosophy, on the other hand, he looks at a branch of studies that has recently arisen within the field opened and outlined with Shusterman's explorations—Marielle Macé's Anthropology of Practices, or a Stylistics of Existence. Their affinity is noted in their approach to the notion of style as embodied and in their engagement with literature. Shusterman uses literary examples when describing various styles of living, which, Ciorogar claims, function as "worksheets" for self-improvement. Literature, on this view, can help us to develop "a sense of harmony" and improve the quality of our interpersonal relations; thus, art inspires life. Macé, in turn, views the act of reading as artistic: she elaborates the theory of the reading practice as an aesthetic process, as a part of the stylistics of existence. Ciorogar compares the two approaches, showing that they come together in their concepts of the non-essentialist, relational self and through their involvement with literature, though they differ in their emphases on the social and individualist aspects of the self, respectively. However, most importantly, Ciorogar seems to suggest, both Shusterman's somaesthetics and Macé's stylistics of existence are concerned with the ethical project of shaping the relational self through various stylistic practices, and they both are concerned with finding a correlation between the styles of living, reading and writing, or between soma and text.

While Lisowska's essay stresses affectivity and corporeality in performative art, and whilst Ciorogar expands on the somatic aspect of style, Konrad Wojnowski engages with a broader problem of returning to physicality. In his "Thermo-performatics: Energy and Performance Studies," Wojnowski focuses on the idea of energy as the material aspect of communication; and he reinterprets the issue of energy in the sphere of performance studies. By viewing communication, on the one hand, and performance, on the other hand, in terms of energy flow, he proposes to change the understanding of both. His approach is interdisciplinary, also in that it goes beyond the traditional realm of humanities in the direction of hard science. Significantly, Wojnowski offers an overview of the changing emphasis in the realm of hard science: from the affirmation of the physical mode to the assertion of the mathematical abstract model which, he says, leads to the new Platonism. However, he recommends the re-conceptualizing of humanities in terms of physical science dealing with tangible objects, rather than along the lines proposed in information studies and in computation. The inspiration for his theoretical model of performance and communication comes from the physical, rather than mathematical sphere. Consequently, he claims, there should occur a metaphorical shift in the understanding of performance: a change from the mechanic to the organic metaphor. Wojnowski proposes to explore speech acts in terms of energy flow and with reference to thermodynamics. Specifically, he considers the problem of energy in relation to three other notions—context, system, and energy distribution—and, while analyzing various types of energy-distribution systems, he argues that a particular emphasis should be placed on the examination of the ways of freeing and channelling energy during communication. Thus, Wojnowski underlines the materiality of communication, and proposes that the analysis of the energy flow which takes place in the course of performing and communicating can be useful in performance studies. He proposes to name this type of analysis with the neologism introduced in the title of his essay, "thermo-performatics," a term encouraging the cooperation of the humanities and sciences, performance studies and physics.

Concerns with physicality, corporeality and performance are creatively employed in the fourth essay in this book, in Sabina Macioszek's interpretation of Thomas Bernhard's play *The Ignoramus and the Madman* and of its adaptation as an opera under the same title, composed by Paweł Mykietyn and directed by Krzysztof Warlikowski. Whilst Wojnowski's essay is preoccupied with the energy-invested materiality of performance, Macioszek's article—discussing complexities of the literary text, theatrical play, and operas (she also refers to Mozart's *The Magic Flute*, an intertext for *The Ignoramus*)—likewise, explores the ambivalence of the simultaneous ephemerality of voice and its materiality. The essay's focus is on the character of the diva, "the coloratura machinery," but it also shows a very dense network of relationships between the characters, themes and genres. Macioszek discusses the problem of patriarchal power wielded over the female artist, the aesthetization of the self and its reduction to an artistic asset (the voice), the consequent disembodiment of the female artist (metaphorically reinforced by the passage in which a male character discusses autopsy, the dissembling of the body) and, finally, the female artist's rebellion against being limited to her gender role and reified as an object d'art. The two-sided nature of the voice—both a physical fact and immaterial phenomenon—is paralleled in Macioszek's interpretation by another ambivalence, that of power relations: the female artist is controlled as a diva, but at the same time she controls men through her voice. Macioszek's interpretation also shows a working paradox: while the opera as a genre exposes its vulnerability to a critique—for its decline and its exhaustion—simultaneously, it demonstrates its potential and creativity by using its exhaustion imaginatively. In her interpretation of those ambivalences, Macioszek uses notions which capture instabilities: of presence, being and duration, activity and action, disappearance and fading (borrowed from Catherine Clément and Mladen Dollar) and of negative performativity (taken from Joanna Jopek, Bojana Kunst and Judith Halberstam). Having discussed these troubling variabilities in the text, the opera, and the play, Macioszek indicates an interesting parallel between the contemporary plight of the opera and the position of the female artist. Whilst the opera, by exposing its limiting conventions, rebels against the limitation of the genre, the female artist, by employing her disembodiment *ad absurdum* (and against those who require it of her)—by literally disappearing on the stage—rebels against the limitations of her gender role. Thus, in the course of performance and through playing with embodiment and disembodiment, the limitations of both gender and genre are transgressed.

The issues of corporeality and performance are also discussed in "How to Work with the Body—Theory and Practice: Karol Radziszewski's Works Regarded in the Context of Merleau-Ponty's Philosophy." Paulina Tchurzewska regards them as interwoven with the problem of sexual taboo and its appearance in the public space, and as creatively explored in the exhibition *The Prince and the Queens*: *The Body as an Archive* by Karol Radziszewski, a Polish painter, photographer, video-artist, writer and performer. Tchurzewska's major focus is on art as performance and on film as documentary. Considering the modes of representing the body in Polish contemporary art, Tchurzewska specifically presents the ways in which Radziszewski's art enters a dialogue with some of the most significant Polish performers (including Jerzy Grotowski, Ryszard Cieślak, Natalia LL and Ryszard Kisiel). She explores the meaning of art located at the intersection of the artistic, erotic, sexual and social, and outlines the creative ways of experimenting with the altering of perception. Tchurzewska highlights the fact that the exhibition to which she refers, in fact, discloses the ways in which the audience perceives art located in the social space: it *exposes* the dependence of the audience's response on their prejudices and desires and on social taboos. Thus, like other authors in this book, she stresses the social function of art. As noted in the title, the theoretical background of this essay is constituted by Merleau's Ponty's philosophy of the body. But Tchurzewska not only views Radziszewski's art in the light of Merleau-Ponty's philosophy, she also views this art as both animating and testing the concepts of Merleau-

Ponty's phenomenology of perception and of anti-dualism in the understanding of the self.

The essay closing Part One of *Literature, Performance, and Somaesthetics*, Gloria Luque Moya's "The Mysterious Force of *Duende*: A Dialogue between Federico García Lorca and Richard Shusterman," engages with the idea of heightened emotion, a passion which is moving, stirring, abysmal, tinged with a sense of the daemonic and permeated with an awareness of death. It is the all-encompassing emotion of flamenco. The concept of *duende*, Luque Moya notes, entered the realm of aesthetics in 1933 through a lecture which Federico Garcia Lorca delivered in Buenos Aires. This notion, which Lorca took from the Spanish folklore and transformed into a category of aesthetics, is discussed by Luque Moya in the context of the essay with which Shusterman officially inaugurated his somaesthetics: "Somaesthetics: A Disciplinary Proposal" from 1999. The *duende*, in Luque Moya's essay, is probed as an aesthetic category, as a creative force, and as a deeply felt somatic emotion. She explores the idea of *duende* by referring to traditional Spanish songs and Lorca's poems and plays, and with a particular emphasis on the expression of grief and the artistic command of mourning. But she also regards the notion of *duende* within the framework which Shusterman introduced when presenting his project of somaesthetics—through its analytic, pragmatic and practical dimensions.

Part Two of this book—with a particular focus on literary reception, canon, and history—starts with Jarosław Woźniak's essay on "Performance of Narrative Fiction," a comprehensive attempt to bring together the narrative and performative approaches to literature (as suggested in the title) and to combine three domains—performance studies, somaesthetics, and the theory of intersubjectivity—into a rich single interpretative perspective. Woźniak's article moves across the fields of philosophy and literary studies, but it engages most closely with the work of Polish theoreticians: Anna Krajewska's proposal to view writing, reading and interpreting as a dramatic, even theatrical, act, and Arkadiusz Żychliński's idea of fictional narration as *anthropoficiton*, a label for stories which help us to understand better what it means to be a human being. For Woźniak, the reader is an embodied and active subject, no longer reduced to a construct, to an "implied" reader of a text, and no longer aloof—but rather viewed as capable of emotionally identifying herself with a literary character. The readers' somatic self-awareness helps them, Woźniak claims, to understand other humans, and hence, to better appreciate literary characters. This latter conviction has its theoretical inspiration in Shusterman's somaesthetics: namely, in his consideration of the idea of *anthropofiction*, Woźniak prioritizes the notion of "understanding" over pan-textualist "interpretation," engages with the anti-Cartesian view of the mind as embodied, and highlights the post-Foucauldian concern with the reader's agency as opposing what, after Foucault and following Shusterman, he terms "discursive determinism."

The reader's experience also remains at the center of Lilla Farmasi's study of a novel by Don DeLillo. In her "Kinetosis in Don DeLillo's *The Body Artist*: Tracing the Somatic Experiences of the Reader," Farmasi explores the material aspect of an aesthetic experience. The essay's focus is on the physical experience of space, encoded in the literary text and decoded by the readers guided by their own sensorimotor experience. To conceptualize the reader's bodily experience, in her paper Farmasi combines narratology and cognitive theory: she regards bodily physical experience of space—pre-conceptual and non-propositional—as reflected not only at the level of metaphor, but also, and indeed predominantly, at the level of plot. Deploying cognitive narratology in her approach to *The Body Artist*, she demonstrates how DeLillo's narrative technique—relying for its effect on many-leveled narrative, fragmentary accounts, and the blurring of the border between the imaginary and the retrospective—reflects a confusion typical of the state of trauma. DeLillo's main character, suffering from trauma after a loss, is confused in body and mind, which shows in the disruptions and fragmentation of the plot. But, then, Farmasi argues, if the plot reflects the confused mental and sensory state of the main character, it also affects the reader in a sensory way. It creates in the reader a mental state equivalent to the bodily feeling of *kinetosis*, a feeling of physical discomfort and unease evoked by conflicting sensory data. Thus, to Farmasi, reading is a process of interaction which happens at the pre-conceptual level, with the reader affected not only by metaphors but also by the structure of the plot. Interpretation, consequently, depends not only on the logical conclusions but also on the senso-motor inferences. In this way, the reader's body participates viscerally in the sense-making.

In its concern with the somatic response to art, Zuzanna Kozłowska's essay closely connects with Farmasi's paper. However, while Farmasi's focus is on the sensorimotor feeling which all humans share, Kozłowska's point of reference is the more exclusive experience of synesthesia: that which is effected by the mingling of the senses, or by the crossing of the sensory pathways. In her article, Kozłowska provides examples of various instances of synesthetic appreciation of art (for instance, by considering the emotional appeal of alliteration). She also outlines the features of the somatic synesthetic experience. On her account, it involves hypersensuality, heightened sensitivity to formal properties of artworks, and an accompanying feeling of approval or aversion. Engaging in her study with the sensual, proprioceptive, "syn-aesthetic" experience of art—and acknowledging inspiration from neuroaesthetics and somaesthetics—she claims that the visceral experience of art should not only receive more attention but also be systematically studied within the field she proposes to call a somato-poetics of reading. Kozłowska believes that a somato-poetics of reading would provide a way of enlivening, or "reinventing" the traditional reader-response criticism. It would also lead, she states, to the redefining of the concept of beauty. Possibly Kozłowska's hypothesis about the general, or universal, mechanisms underlying any aesthetic judgment may lead to a heated and protracted debate between the essentialists and non-essentialists, but in its far-reaching proposals, her article also reflects the energy of the expanding field.

The essay by Joanna Maj offers yet another perspective on the somatic reception of literature. It engages with this specific response to literature which results in the outlining of literary history and establishment of the literary canon. But, significantly, in the literary history that Maj examines—Stanisław Bereś's *Polish Literary History in Conversations: 20th-21st Centuries*—the view of literary history is presented as embodied. Bereś's history of Polish contemporary literature includes transcriptions of interviews recorded for the Polish television; thus, in a sense, it is a transcript of oral literary history, if such a genre could be said to exist. This possibility Maj explores. She investigates the aspects of performative literary historiography by focusing on conversations with two authors, Czesław Miłosz and Kazimierz Brandys, and regards the performative significance of the pictures included in Bereś's *History*, and of the written record of gaps, silences, and repetitions which occurred in the course of the dialogues. But she also indicates the elements of the originally videoed interviews, which could be noted by the viewers, but are lost to the readers of the text: gesture, pose, facial expression, prosodic qualities of words, their tone and tune (Miłosz sings). The history of literature in a dialogic form, Maj indicates, relies heavily on personal insight and on anecdotes recounted by the speakers; it also causes an affective engagement in the viewer. But, most of all, it reveals the intersubjective and performative character of literary tradition—literary history is created during a meeting of two embodied individuals, and it is invested not only with their ideas but also with their emotions.

The discussion of the embodied and dialogic nature of literary history is extended in this volume into the consideration of the literary canon viewed in the performative context. This problem is central to Aleksander

Trojanowski's consideration of Ricardo Piglia's novel *Artificial Respiration*. Trojanowski's approach to the question of the literary canon, as revealed in his reading of Piglia, also ties in with Jarosław Woźniak's insistence on the reader's agency and the intersubjective nature of the act of reading and writing (which appears in the essay opening Part Two of this book). A literary text, in Trojanowski's interpretation of Piglia's novel, is an integral element of the social world, and it can cause things to happen. Besides, it is a locus of experience: a place where the experience of the other can be unjustly confined, but then, it can be also recreated and restored. The reading of literature, in turn, is a shared performance rather than a silent perusal. Trojanowski, relating himself to Eric Hobsbawm's theory of tradition formation, and viewing the novel from the perspective of performance studies, shows how the narratives of literary history (the canons) are established and how they can be reformulated and undermined in the course of a subversive act of dialogical reading. Considering *Artificial Respiration*, Trojanowski demonstrates the mechanisms of exclusion, appropriation, and identity construction that were employed in the canon formation in Argentina under the military regime. Specifically, he explores the mechanisms represented in the novel: the exclusion of the "barbarians," the romanticizing of the gaucho, and the two contrasted projects of a new language formation in the works of Roberto Arlt and Leopold Lugones. His essay not only shows how Piglia reveals the ideologies underpinning canon construction but also how Piglia-the-author becomes a performer by staging for the reader the experience of living under the military regime, rather than by merely describing it. But Trojanowski also stresses the dialogic nature of literary history as suggested by the very form of Piglia's novel: he emphasizes that the novel comprises letters, diaries and conversations, and that, from these various forms, the readers of the novel, as well as its protagonist, must unravel the meaning of the literary canon. This meaning, Trojanowski's essay suggests, is not there, written down for the readers, but is performed in front of them.

Part Three of this volume—featuring literary interpretations which, in their concern with the soma, go beyond the problem of reception—opens with András Berze's study of staged violence. Embedded in philosophy, and drawing on the conclusions of cognitive theories and the studies of theatricality, Berze's essay turns to Thomas Harris's novel *The Red Dragon*, its film adaptation by Brett Ratner, and the television series *Hannibal*. Besides violence, its subject is empathy and the lack of it. Empathy in Berze's essay is not a psychological aptitude, but a theatrical faculty. It is an ability to imagine oneself (or "theatricalize" oneself) in the body of the other. The imaginary protagonist of Harris's novel, and of its adaptations, in whom such empathy is absent, is described as a "theatrical serial killer." The concept of theatricality is central to Berze's considerations. After Samuel Weber, Berze reasserts that, paradoxically, while the popular appeal of the theater seems to be declining, the idea of theatricality—as a way to describe reality—is on the rise. Thus, for the purpose of his analysis, Berze uses reformulated concepts of the audience and stage. He deploys Benjamin's idea of a "grouping," stressing the non-institutionalized, accidental nature of spectatorship; and he conceptualizes the notion of the stage as any environment in which an intervention has taken place. Whilst the idea of empathy in Berze's essay is understood as an ability to "theatricalize" oneself in the body of the other, it is also explained within the frameworks of phenomenology and cognition theory. The Heideggerian Being-with, Berze says, is insufficient—a quality of detached spectatorship; only Being-in-the-world can provide the ground for empathy. Empathy, then, depends on human beings' shared corporeality. Heidegger's terms are used by Berze in discriminating between different types of experience. The killer's existence is described as "Being-with," whereas the "Being-in-the-world," or an empathic sharing with others of his experience of the body as the source of agency, remains beyond his sensibility. Body and corporeality, Berze insists, following Mark Johnson's theory of cognition, also structure our cognitive patterns. Mind is embodied—and only as such does it participate in the world. In his analysis of Harris's protagonist and his motivation, Berze argues that the killings can be viewed as resulting from the Cartesian mistake. His essay, then, remains firmly embedded in the tradition of critiquing the Cartesian split between the body and mind. Berze sees this split as enacted in Harris's imaginary killer's decision to murder his victims and to re-animate their bodies as a puppeteer would. According to the killer's criminal logic, whose workings Berze persuasively explains, the victims are only inanimate corpses to be arranged as the audience watching the spectacle of the killer's (Dolarhyde's) transformation. Their living "souls"—or their will and agency—Berze explains, are seen as separable from their bodies, to be removed and then replaced by the tricks of Dolarhyde's aesthetic inventiveness. Berze not only studies the protagonist's motivation but also outlines the stages in which violence is enacted. He ends his essay by placing his conclusions in meta-perspective: the readers of the novel and the audience watching the film, he claims, are violated, too. Violence initiated by displaced empathy (the killer's sociopathy) spreads through he channels of extra-sensitive empathy (the detective's) and normal empathy (the audience's and the readers'). But

Harris's novel and the films, he notes, also critique the mass-media reliance on violence for commercial success.

The concept of theatricality is also employed by Matthew Biberman in an exploration of the combined notions of affectivity and the self in his "Archeologies of Affect: Shakespeare's Phantasm of Love in *Romeo and Juliet.*" Engaging with Frederic Jameson's idea of affect, Biberman explains that, to Jameson, the "spiritualized" body of the pre-modern epoch is replaced by the "affective body" of the modern era. To Jameson, as stressed by Biberman, the rise of affectivity depends on the "waning," or "repression," of the spiritual; affect, then, occupies the empty space from which the spiritual has been removed, in fact, relegated to the realm of the purely theological or metaphysical. Hence, Biberman stresses, affect is synonymous with a lack of the spiritual, or with melancholia. Biberman suggests that the postmodern self, following the Jamesonian modern affective self, can be seen as resulting from the return of the repressed: the melancholic taking the place of the spiritual. The emphasis in his article, however, falls on this stage which emerges between the Jamesonian epochs of the spiritual and affective selves. Biberman posits that there exists an intermediary phase between these two periods: between the epoch which proffered the spiritualized body and that which produced the affective self, comes the one which features a form of embodiment he proposes to call theatricalized or performative body. Biberman expounds his hypothesis of the theatrical body and self by analyzing passages from Shakespeare and referring to Marsilio Ficino. He posits that within the sphere of the theater—with the individual that is exposed, staged, isolated ("monadic"), and towering above the community of spectators—the "waning of the spiritual" was delayed. In Shakespeare, for that reason, Biberman notes, the sensibility is still pre-modern. The Shakespearean self represents an intermediary hybrid, its spiritual aspects being rendered in a strikingly physical way. This midway stage is illustrated by Biberman in his examination of the concept of love in Shakespeare, when he shows that this apparently spiritual state is understood with recourse to concepts and paradigms that render love as a quasi-material, semi-physiological phenomenon and that nowadays might occur in the discourses of optics and neuroscience.

The idea of performance in Katarzyna Lisowska's "The Re-evaluation of Female and Queer Bodies in Selected Works of Contemporary Polish Literature" is explored with reference to gender identity. The literary-analytical focus in her essay is on contemporary Polish authors, whilst the theoretical background for her considerations is derived from the work of Judith Butler and Richard Shusterman. She engages with Butler's concept of gender performativity, convinced that by highlighting the performative aspect of gender identity, literature participates in the process of liberating individuals from normative and confining social and ideological paradigms. She also invokes Shusterman's somaesthetics with its emphasis on the cultivation of body consciousness, which leads to the deepening of self-understanding and advances self-improvement. In her paper, she reads works representing various genres, but connected through their preoccupation with the uncovering and disputing of the ostracized and downgraded position of those whose corporeality does not represent an ideological mainstream. In particular, she discusses selected works of Polish contemporary literature—including a short story by Szczepan Twardoch, Ewa Schilling's novels, and Izabela Filipiak's drama—to expose the ways in which they undermine and reinterpret the dominating narratives of the body and the images these narrative impose, thus re-evaluating the marginalized corporeality. Lisowska concludes her interpretive-theoretical essay by stressing literature's socially transformative role: she notes that, by naming marginalized phenomena and by materializing them in discourse, literature participates in the transformation of images and beliefs that dominate in a given culture and society.

In the essay presented by Iulia Maria Rădac the idea of performativity is, once again, probed within the perspective of somaesthetics. Rădac investigates the complex relationship between soma and text or, more specifically, the way in which Mircea Cărtărescu's prose reduces "the distance between the body and the letter." Rădac's essay has an important informative role in introducing the work of contemporary Romanian theoreticians and artists into the realm of somaesthetic discourse. But this essay also offers an analysis of Mircea Cărtărescu's *Travesti* (*Disguise*), with particular attention paid to the representations of the body, of somatic experience, and of the correlation between the somatic experience described in *Disguise* and the structure of the text. In her reading of Cărtărescu's work, Rădac stresses an interesting paradox: she observes that even if Cărtărescu focuses on his character's mental states, then, by deploying visceral metaphors, he draws the reader's attention to the character's corporeal status. Rădac studies the narrative tactics in this novel and shows that, effectively, its narrator functions as a performer who uses various strategies to seduce the reader. She characterizes these narrative tactics and strategies by referring to the work of contemporary Romanian author and theoretician Gheorghe Crăciun; and after Crăciun, she calls them somatographic.

The essay closing this book, Ágnes Bató's "Unimmortal Men and the Body of Death: The Somatic Experience of Death in Milton's *Paradise*

Lost"—in demonstrating the sense of corporeality as heightened by the awareness of death—echoes the theme of Gloria Luque Moya's "The Mysterious Force of *Duende*" (from Part One). However, while Luque Moya speaks of corporeality and the awareness of death as the aspects of the vital force of *duende*, Bató, considering Christian theology in Milton, highlights embodiment as necessary for the overcoming of death. In her essay, Bató discusses the four kinds of death in Milton's writings (in *Paradise Lost* and the prose work *A Treatise on Christian Doctrine*): the death of innocence (or guiltiness), the spiritual death of Satan, the corporeal decline and death of Adam and Eve, and death as eternal damnation after the Judgment Day. The third kind, then, is bodily. But Bató notes the great complexity in Milton's rendering of corporeality and death, which cannot be exhausted through this fourfold paradigm. For instance, she observes that sin and death in Milton's work are not only abstract entities but also, as epic characters, corporeal beings; they are not only allegorical personification of univocal concepts, but characters—such as a personal vice and the death overcoming an individual—partaking in the embodied human experience. In this respect, Milton's epic cosmology is also compounded by the fact that, in Christian theology, corporeality and death are signs of both sin and redemption. Indeed, corporeality is inalienable from the Economy of Christian Redemption: Christian theology and the Bible speak of the God who assumed a human body, died in the body and was risen in the body, thus overcoming mortality. If death comes to humans in the form of the dying body, so Redemption is delivered through the corporeal death of the sinless Redeemer. Significantly, in Milton, as Bató notes, the only figure that remains beyond the Economy of salvation is Satan. A purely intellectual, spiritual being, Milton's Satan is incorporeal.

The aim of this book, if it may be restated, is to return literature to the physical world of corporeal beings and to stress, beside the activity of an artist, the agency of the reader and of the art recipient. Then the question of agency appears as equal in importance to the problems of corporeality and embodiment. The contributors to this book read and "performed" their essays during the International Conference at the Faculty of Letters of the University of Wrocław in December, 2014. While showing a keen interest in performance studies and somaesthetics, the authors of these essays bring in, at the same time, the expertise gained in their primary fields of research. They draw ideas from philosophy, musicology, literary theory and cultural studies; they venture into psychology and hard science; and they concern themselves with various literary genres and forms, including epic literature, lyrical poetry, tragedy, the experimental novel, thrillers, literary history, theological treatises, documentary, flamenco and opera. They also represent various national backgrounds: Hungary, Poland, Romania, Spain, and the United States. But, as they came to Wrocław, in 2014, they discussed their shared concerns with embodiment, agency and affectivity, seeking ways to correlate soma, text and performance and to explore the physical aspect of art perception. And while they talked, they tried to adjust their vocabularies and to outline the field in the humanities where the three disciplines can meet and where literary studies can benefit from the approaches offered by performance studies and philosophical somaesthetics.

References

McKenzie, Jon. 2001. *Perform or Else: From Discipline to Performance.* New York: Routledge.

Worthen, William B. 2010. *Drama: Between Poetry and Performance.* Oxford: Wiley-Blackwell.

Voparil, Christopher J., and John Giordano. 2015. "Pragmatism and the Somatic Turn: Shusterman's Somaesthetics and Beyond." *Metaphilosophy* 46 (1): 141–61.

Notes

[1] Voparil and Giordano's article is an omnibus review of Richard Shusterman's *Thinking Through the Body: Essays in Somaesthetics* (Cambridge: Cambridge University Press, 2012); *Shusterman's Pragmatism: Between Literature and Somaesthetics.* Ed. by Dorota Koczanowicz and Wojciech Małecki (Amsterdam: Rodopi, 2012); and Wojciech Małecki's *Embodying Pragmatism: Richard Shusterman's Philosophy and Literary The*ory (Frankfurt am Main: Peter Lang, 2010).

PART I

ENACTING PHILOSOPHY, PERFORMING ART

Chapter One

Perception and Performance in Martha Nussbaum's Reasonable Moral Psychology[1]

Urszula Lisowska

Martha Nussbaum's philosophy is a constantly evolving, flexible and varied system of ideas applied in various contexts and for various purposes. Therefore, when approaching it, an interpreter should be careful lest she imposes an artificial systemic structure on Nussbaum's rich store of insights. And yet, as becomes a philosophical work of the highest quality, there is a great degree of coherence between different aspects of Nussbaum's *oeuvre* to date. In what follows, I want to explore the intellectual intersections that exist in Nussbaum's work, at the same time remaining aware of the non-monolithic character of Nussbaum's inquiries.

My point of departure will be the most recent development of Nussbaum's philosophy. In her book *Political Emotions. Why Love Matters for Justice* (2013) Nussbaum takes up the question of the stability of political liberalism, which was first raised by John Rawls. I propose to look at this issue in more detail in the next section. At this point, however, it is worthwhile to indicate its complexity. To put it briefly, the problem involves the challenge of securing the maintenance of common political principles in view of a reasonable pluralism of comprehensive (religious, metaphysical or ethical) doctrines. Thus, there has to be a way of, first, defining such sharable values and, secondly, of nurturing commitment to them, in both cases without referring to one particular comprehensive doctrine. My focus in this paper will be on this latter issue: the cultivation of the values that can be held in common without sacrificing respect for pluralism.

To find a method of cultivating attitudes supportive of political principles we need first to be equipped with a non-comprehensive account of how we reason morally. According to Rawls, this is the object of a reasonable moral psychology, which he himself, however, never developed. Nussbaum (2013, 8–9) offers to fill this gap. Since she presents her own political philosophy as a variety of political liberalism, she, too, faces the challenge of stability. On the basis of her reasonable moral psychology, the solution to this problem depends largely on the nurturing of proper emotional responses, which form the core of her reasonable moral psychology. Importantly, the crucial means of such cultivation turns out to be the arts. The aim of this paper will be to demonstrate that, because of the specificity of Nussbaum's political philosophy (capabilities approach), which underlies her inquiries about stability, one of the major tasks of artistic activities is to change the perceptions of our own and others' bodies. And, given Nussbaum's idea of perception developed in her earlier ethical writings, this can be most fruitfully realized within one field of the arts in particular, namely performative arts such as theater, dance and the arts in urban space.

On the whole, then, my objective will be to interpret Nussbaum's philosophy so as to point to the political significance of our attitudes to bodiliness and the role of performative arts in their reconfiguration. Most of the paper will be theoretical, offering an approach to Nussbaum's project and developing a conceptual framework which can be put together on the basis of her writings. Towards the conclusion, however, certain practical implications will be presented. Thus, along with suggesting an interpretation of Nussbaum's philosophy, an equally important intention of this paper will be to argue for the need of the ongoing presence of the arts in public life.

The Problem of Stability and a Reasonable Moral Psychology

Let us briefly define liberalism as a political stance based on the values of freedom, equality and individuality. On this account, society is essentially a system of cooperation between citizens, who pursue their goals on equal terms. In his groundbreaking work *A Theory of Justice* (1971), John Rawls attempted to define the terms of such cooperation by means of the two principles of justice arrived at in the situation of fairness. Although Rawls never changed the content of his theory, he later realized that a liberal approach requires a different justification than the one provided in his 1971 publication. This is because the liberal account of society sketched above allows for a diversity of often incompatible life projects. In other words, it embraces the fact of reasonable pluralism, i.e. a plurality of reasonable comprehensive doctrines.[2] Therefore, as Rawls highlighted in his second seminal book, *Political Liberalism* (1993), a liberal theory of justice cannot be founded on any specific conception, as was the case with the strongly Kantian premises of the early version of Rawls's theory. Instead of being comprehensive, liberalism and, hence, a theory of justice which it offers should be political—grounded in several basic ideas implicitly present in the political culture of democratic societies and shared by citizens, whatever their respective comprehensive doctrines might be (Rawls 1993; 1996, xiii–xxxv).

Otherwise a liberal theory of justice will not meet the criterion of stability, i.e. it will fail to effectively motivate citizens' behavior in a time span spreading over generations. For, in view of the plurality of reasonable comprehensive doctrines, we cannot expect all citizens to endorse principles based on only one of those doctrines. *Political Liberalism* offers a different solution. Firstly, given that the principles which it proposes are based on ideas implicit in democratic political culture, they can become the object of an overlapping consensus between reasonable comprehensive doctrines. That is, a theory of justice functions as a an element which can be attached to any such set of beliefs, so that each citizen embraces it on the basis of his or her own doctrine (Rawls 1993; 1996, 11–15). Secondly, however, the idea of overlapping consensus has to be supplied by a moral psychology. This means that we have to account for the thin agreement on the basic political ideas by demonstrating how people come to acknowledge and internalize them. In other words, we need a psychological explanation of how we learn these core values, which can later form an overlapping consensus.

This, however, Rawls never provided. Although *A Theory of Justice* contains a rich and insightful account of moral development, which, unlike much of (male) liberal tradition, recognizes the value of family and emotions in this process (Okin 1989, 229–49; Nussbaum 2003, 488–520), Rawls later bracketed this part of the book for revision, probably wary of its comprehensive underpinnings. In *Political Liberalism* he sketched only a rough outline of moral psychology, signaling the need to provide such a supplement (Rawls 1993; 1996, 81–88). As noted, Martha Nussbaum takes up this challenge in her recent publication, *Political Emotions*. Although she disagrees with Rawls in many important respects, she has embraced political liberalism as well and sets out to provide it with a reasonable (i.e. non-comprehensive and potentially sharable by all citizens) understanding of moral development (Nussbaum 2013, 9). She attempts to demonstrate how our practical reasoning can be cultivated in accordance with a politico-liberal theory of justice—that is, how political principles promoted by such a theory come to be included in our own schemes of goals.

Arguably, Rawls and Nussbaum were not the first philosophers to have noticed that the exercisability of political values requires proper attitudes on the part of citizens. The projects of civic education which we can find in the history of philosophy, however, often draw on comprehensive doctrines. Two which are particularly prominent, Rousseau's idea of civic religion and Comte's religion of humanity, consist in the inculcation of a specific set of beliefs and therefore are at odds with politico-liberal respect for reasonable pluralism (Nussbaum 2013, 44–49, 54–81). A reasonable moral psychology has to proceed with greater care so as not to violate people's right to hold their own comprehensive doctrines. Therefore, the task which Nussbaum sets out to carry through is a very demanding one. She offers to find a way to arrive at common values without erasing differences between citizens.

Nussbaum's Capabilities Approach as a Variety of Political Liberalism

What is important, Nussbaum (2013, 118) declares that she is inquiring about the stability of political liberalism in general, i.e. a family of conceptions which share the same basic values. It does seem, however, that her account of political liberalism is in fact influenced by her own variety of this perspective—a version of the capability approach. The contents of the principles whose stability should be secured reflect certain normative assumptions characteristic of her theory. Therefore, even if Nussbaum deliberately does not reiterate her capabilities approach[3] in *Political Emotions*, a short overview of it appears nonetheless to be advisable.

Nussbaum's account of politico-liberal values is centered around the idea of human dignity, "dignity" being understood along Kantian lines, as the right to be treated as an end in itself, not a mere means, which, in turn, implies the recognition of agency (striving)[4] in each person. So far, this is in keeping with the rough outline of political liberalism sketched above. To accept the fact of the reasonable pluralism is to acknowledge that all citizens have equal moral worth (call it dignity), which entitles them to pursue their own ideas of a good life. However, Nussbaum then further specifies this basic assumption by observing that striving—the active pursuit of the self-chosen goals—cannot be separated from "vulnerability." That is, in the very exercise of our agency, we are nonetheless dependent on external factors. Not only can the ill fortune impede our activities, but also we need support from without to carry out our plans (Nussbaum 2013, 121–24).

Now, these assumptions are not incompatible with the idea of equal human dignity. Yet they do not logically follow from this basic premise either. In fact, the emphasis on human vulnerability is one of the main points of divergence between Nussbaum and Rawls and their respective versions of political liberalism (Nussbaum 2007). Therefore, a reference to Nussbaum's account of justice seems in order. As I have mentioned, she has been advocating a variety of the capability approach. This broad perspective extends well beyond Nussbaum's own philosophical inquiries and has been adopted in such fields as, among others, development economics, education and healthcare. The notion of capabilities was introduced by the economist and Noble Prize winner Amartya Sen, who understood a capability as an actual possibility of acting (2001, 5). This concept of a capability has been used both in a narrower, descriptive sense—as the proper measure of the quality of life—and in a broader, normative meaning—as the guiding idea of public policy planning, the aim of development or the criterion of justice (Crocker and Robeyns 2009, 60–61).

On the whole, by focusing on people's real opportunities, the capability approach recognizes the relevance of external factors to human lives. What we are able to do is to a significant extent determined by our surroundings (which can, for example, either impede or facilitate the exercise of our rights, thus determining the actual scope of our agency). The emphasis on human dependency characterizes the entire family of capability approaches, then, and makes its way into Nussbaum's understanding of political liberalism through her affiliation with this paradigm. Her capabilities background resonates in her insistence that striving is inseparable from vulnerability.

This generic feature, however, is particularly amplified in Nussbaum's project. Her understanding of capabilities is Aristotelian in spirit, in that she sees them as the components of the good lives of humans as rational animals.[5] On her interpretation, the notion of a capability encompasses these two aspects of the human condition, pertaining to both ability and neediness. Thus, capabilities are our possibilities for functioning which we develop in the process of the constant struggle against internal and external limitations which stem from our bodiliness (Crocker 2007, 173; Nussbaum 1990b, 365–91). Combining this perspective with the Kantian idea of dignity, Nussbaum has worked out a minimal theory of justice articulated in the form of ten central capabilities, which need to be provided in order for citizens to live dignified lives. The capabilities included in the list are all combined capabilities, i.e. inner abilities coupled with facilitating external conditions,[6] and the content of the catalogue refers to both rationality and animality, suggesting their inseparable nature.[7] Thus, Nussbaum's capabilities approach highlights the "embodied" character of human dignity and the resulting human neediness.

Hence the set of values that she sees as the proper object of political stability should take into account human bodily conditions, as suggested by her including striving and vulnerability in the politico-liberal agenda. In this sense Nussbaum's own theory of justice influences her understanding of political liberalism. The aim of the reasonable moral psychology is, roughly speaking, to explain how citizens can come to acknowledge that mutual respect requires, among other things, acknowledging one's own and others' neediness.

Political Emotions

Such a general outline of politico-liberal values, with its focus on human animality, determines Nussbaum's understanding of the means which lead to stability of political principles as well. As its title suggests, her basic assumption in *Political Emotions* is that the key role in this process belongs to emotions. Although Rawls had already noted their importance for moral development, he not only refrained from providing a politico-liberal interpretation of this observation, but also, Nussbaum suggests, failed to fully confront the potential of emotions. For Rawls allowed only for their abstract forms, such as the love of just institutions, and was wary of their more particularistic types. Nussbaum argues that any emotion directed at a general principle needs to be supported and supplied by more specific emotional attachments. Our commitment to political principles always has an emotional dimension to it (Nussbaum 2013, 115).

In *Political Emotions* Nussbaum turns to contemporary psychological research on emotions to justify her claim. However, scientific evidence serves her rather as a source of examples, which, in order to be instructive, should be placed against the background of the theory of emotions that she has provided elsewhere (Nussbaum 2009, 2001). In this account, emotions are judgments (or, to use a less demanding terms—thoughts [Nussbaum 2013, 142]) in which a person expresses the belief that, *because of its intrinsic value*, a certain good is important to her good life (*eudaimonia*). Each type of emotion is further specified by the particular observation which it makes about its object—that it has been lost (grief), is endangered (fear) or pleasing (joy), etc.—but their common feature is their eudaimonistic character. In emotions, we evaluate reality from the perspective of our ideas of flourishing. Now, for the Stoics, whose philosophy has been a major source of inspiration for Nussbaum, all emotions were directed at external and, therefore, vulnerable goods. Nussbaum does not want to build this condition into the definition of emotions. However, her capabilities-based idea of the human good points to our strong reliance on external factors. This suggests that our judgments about the intrinsic value of certain items usually refer to, or at least presuppose the support of, external goods. Therefore, emotions are in most cases acknowledgments of our incompleteness and the need to accept help from without.[8]

Such a conception of emotions, backed up by the scientific evidence which Nussbaum presents (see below for examples), has two consequences for the question of political stability. First of all, it demonstrates that we do, in fact, use emotions in our practical reasoning. Therefore, a reasonable moral psychology will have to take this feature of our rationality into account. Secondly, when considered in conjunction with Nussbaum's capabilities approach, it suggests that our emotions reflect our neediness. We respond emotionally as human animals, expressing commitment to external goods in the form of such judgments. What is important, the "embodied" nature of emotions means that they tend to be particularistic. Concrete, bodily persons develop emotional relationships with specific goods. Therefore, as I have already suggested, a reasonable moral psychology cannot abstract from the local character of emotions. On the contrary, it has to employ for its purposes whatever positive potential particularistic emotions may have, at the same time curbing the danger which they may pose.

Thus, we have first learned that the object of political stability is the principles that are based on the idea of the equal dignity of human animals. Now we have found that among its major prerequisites are the development of emotions supportive of, and the prevention of emotions inimical to, the political values which such principles represent (Nussbaum 2013, 3). Emotions, in turn, appear to be marked with the sense of neediness which stems from our bodiliness. All this suggests that political stability strongly relies on the cultivation of proper attitudes to one's own and others' bodies (Nussbaum 2013, 133). If Nussbaum's political liberalism is to become a viable, effectively internalized theory of justice, we have to come to terms with our animal nature. That is, we have to recognize the dignity in our bodiliness, which, given that the awareness of our vulnerability finds its outlet in emotions, requires the development of certain emotional responses and the containment of others. It is this connection between political stability and our approach to our animality that I want to explore.

Emotions and Moral Development

Different types of emotions reflect different ideas of bodiliness. Thus, the aim of a reasonable moral psychology is, first, to define those that are desirable and undesirable from the perspective of political stability. This is a descriptive task, which involves sketching an account of our moral development. Secondly, this conception will be used to serve as a basis for practical implications. Drawing on a reasonable moral psychology, Nussbaum wants to find the methods of cultivating emotions supportive of political liberalism (and of preventing those inimical to it) that would be in keeping with the spirit of this variety of liberalism, i.e., a political philosophy that is respectful of people's right to hold whatever comprehensive doctrine they may choose. As we shall see, this is where the arts step in.

In order to meet the first objective, a reasonable moral psychology has to say more about the role of emotions and their relationship to bodiliness in the development of moral attitudes. Here Nussbaum relies strongly on psychoanalytical accounts, mostly derived from object relations theory, which underline the basic experience of dependency characteristic of early infancy. Donald Winnicott, for example, speaks of the ambivalent sense of omnipotence in infants, who expect their needs to be fully catered for (as was the case before their birth). This demand, however, is combined with an utter inability to fend for oneself typical of human animals. Unlike those of other creatures, our bodies are poorly equipped. Thus, when an infant starts to differentiate herself from her surroundings, she experiences extreme neediness. She is entirely dependent on the environment, which, she begins to realize, is not centered on her needs. The development of the self consists in the constant balancing of one's claims for support against the recognition of the external world's autonomy (Nussbaum 2001, 174–90; 2013, 168–77; Winnicott 1990, 21–38).

Nussbaum embraces this general image of a budding human self. The task of a reasonable moral psychology is to show how we achieve the state that she, paraphrasing William Ronald Dodds Fairbairn's original term, describes as reciprocal interdependence. For, given that external help most often comes from other persons, the aim of moral development is to acknowledge the network of dependencies between oneself and the people around one. That is, an individual has to realize that other human beings are subjects just like herself—dignified and entitled to autonomy, yet in the pursuit of their goals reliant on support, which it is sometimes up to her to provide (Nussbaum 2001, 224–35). In other words, the state of mutual interdependency involves the recognition of the equal dignity of human animals (in the sense presented above). Therefore, psychological insights cited by Nussbaum back up her politico-liberal ideal. The dynamics of the human self seem to comply with her normative model (Winnicott 1990, 239–59).[9]

We can expect that emotions will feature prominently in the process of moral development thus understood. As the recognitions of the boundaries of one's control, emotions constitute one of the basic forms of relating to the external world. They have to be cultivated so that they become compatible with the state of mutual interdependency. One of the most important emotions which should be developed in this process is compassion. Nussbaum (2001, 297–327; 2013, 137–60) devotes a lot of space to this emotion, referring both to psychological research and philosophical texts. Contemporary studies show that many non-human animals display compassion-like responses in that they can sympathize with other animals' pain. Humans, in turn, appear to be capable of compassion already in early infancy, this emotion being at the root of their moral development (Bloom 2005, 109–22). Combining the scientific data with her philosophical account, Nussbaum characterizes compassion as the reaction to somebody else's suffering, which involves three basic thoughts. First, we consider the plight to be serious, caused by the deprivation of goods of primary importance. Secondly, the suffering is considered undeserved, not the sufferer's fault. Finally, as in any other emotion, there is the eudaimonistic judgment—we feel compassion for another person's deprivation when we care for her, i.e. when we include her in our idea of a good life (*eudaimonia*). This last thought may be aided by the judgment of similar possibilities. We are more prone to feel concern for the people with whom we have something in common (both abilities and limitations) so that we can imagine that a similar plight might befall ourselves as well.[10]

On the whole, when we respond with compassion, we acknowledge that a person who matters to us is vulnerable and has actually been hurt. This emotion combines the thought about neediness with the recognition of another's dignity—we feel it towards the people whom we perceive as *worthy of* concern. Therefore, compassion is one of the emotions compatible with the awareness of mutual interdependency, and so gives us an idea about the type of emotional attitudes that need to be cultivated for the sake of the stability of political liberalism.

Anthropodenial

In order to find out how these can be nurtured, I suggest that we analyze the obstacles which compassion, as the exemplary emotional response, has to overcome. There are certain emotions which can seriously thwart or limit compassion and are present already in infancy or early childhood. Of these, two seem particularly dangerous. First, there is the emotion of shame. Drawing largely on Andrew Morrison's work, Nussbaum observes that the primitive type of shame emerges when a child realizes her helplessness (which is simultaneous with the development of self-awareness). Shame records this sense of incompleteness and, more importantly, indicates the repudiation of such imperfection. In its primitive form it expresses frustration at one's inability to realize the unrealistic ideal of completeness (Nussbaum 2001, 208–9, 236–37; 2004, 183–86; 2013, 362–63). Another emotion of this type is disgust. It appears later than shame (at about the age of two or three) but, nonetheless, is especially pernicious (Nussbaum 2001, 201). Here Nussbaum refers most often to the research of Paul Rozin, who has provided an elaborate account of the cognitive content of this emotion. The conclusion of his studies is that disgust expresses the belief that certain things are contaminating and, therefore, should be shunned. And since among its basic objects are bodily fluids and products (or animals which resemble them, such as snails), Rozin concludes that what we in fact find disgusting is our animality and, more specifically, our mortality. Bodily fluids and waste remind us that we are made of decaying matter, bound to decompose. It is this ultimate type of vulnerability, Rozin (Rozin, Haidt, and McCauley 1999, 2000, 429–45) argues and Nussbaum (2001, 200–206; 2004, 86–98; 2013, 182–84) follows him in this, that we reject in the emotion of disgust.

Why are shame and disgust so dangerous to compassion? They both exemplify the attitude that the Dutch primatologist Frans de Waal described as "anthropodenial," i.e. human tendency to repress the awareness of their animality (Nussbaum 2013, 159, 172). This rejection does not target our animal nature in all its forms (we take delight in many features of our bodies, such as physical beauty, strength or agility) but is directed at the helplessness which inevitably goes with bodiliness (Nussbaum 2013, 172). This shunning of the unpleasant part of animality is the expression of a deeply entrenched human tendency to flee from vulnerability, which, in a different form, can also be observed in the narcissism characteristic of early infancy. At the beginning, infants perceive external objects, including other people, only in relation to their needs. They treat people around them as mere means to their goals, not as autonomous persons, and expect the world to be at their beck and call (Nussbaum 2013, 171). This narcissistic demand is undermined by the same anxieties that are expressed by the emotions of shame and disgust since it reflects the fear of vulnerability, which goes with the imperfect of control over the environment. On the whole, then, human beings have difficulties with accepting their weaknesses, which largely turn on their problematic relationship to animality—the fundamental source of imperfection.

Thus, shame and disgust, as symptoms of denying one's own bodiliness, and narcissism, as an attitude towards other people which reflects the sense of insecurity that goes with vulnerability, are two sides of the same coin. As such, they jointly work against compassion. For, as the eudaimonistic character of this emotion suggests, we respond with it to those people who are within the circle of our concern, this judgment being aided by acknowledging the similarity of their possibilities to ours. We are more likely to care and, thus, feel compassion for persons whom we perceive to be our fellows (Nussbaum 2001, 422). The aim of moral development, guided by the idea of equal human dignity, is to extend this sense of fellowship so that it comes as close as possible to embracing all of humanity.

However, shame and disgust, on the one hand, repudiate the very features of the human condition which compassion implicitly acknowledges (fragility, exposure to harm, etc.). So when we are moved by these emotions, we exclude animality from our idea of humanity. And on the other hand, narcissism prevents us from seeing other people as dignified subjects, narrowing the scope of our compassionate concern. Taken together, these two tendencies lead to stigmatization and projective disgust. In the first case, described extensively by Erving Goffman, certain individuals are made to feel ashamed of some of their features, such as bodily injuries or infirmities, which remind others of their own animal weaknesses. Projective disgust, in turn, attributes disgust-arousing qualities to vulnerable groups (women, African Americans, Jews) so that the majority may have the illusion of being less bodily than they are (Nussbaum 2001, 342–50; 2004, 107–15; 2013, 182–91, 359–64). On the whole, shame and disgust make us insensitive to the lot of certain people, who come to seem less human because of their animal imperfections. They bear the traces of early narcissism because they reflect the not-worked-through approach to our weaknesses, which blinds us to the dignity of other people (in these cases—members of certain groups). They are anthropodenying because they see animality as a good ground for denying somebody her full humanity. The result is that stigmatization and projective disgust seriously limit the scope of compassion. As Paul Bloom has put it, when we are reminded of our animality, we become much less responsive to other people's situation (Bloom 2005, 136).

Naturally, a longing for invulnerability is not the only factor to impede compassion. As Nussbaum often stresses, this valuable emotion can often work against one since, like most emotions, it tends to be particularistic, privileging the familiar over the strange.[11] It could also be objected that the link between early shame and disgust and their socially exclusive types may sometimes appear tenuous. For example, although it seems plausible that women were discriminated against (at least partly) because their physicality—at once attractive and repulsive—reminded men of their own bodies, it would be more difficult to explain the exclusion of Jews and African Americans from the larger community simply by citing the power of disgust. Rather, in these cases the disgust may have supplemented and supported prejudices which had arisen on other grounds. On the whole, it could be argued that Nussbaum's idea of stigma and projective disgust is too broad and covers quite distinct instances.

The general lesson from this excursion into psychology, however, is that humans' problematic relationship to their bodies is, even if not the sole, then one of the major impediments to moral development. There are, Nussbaum argues, dark and menacing forces lurking in the human psyche, which can cause and often do enhance social injustice.[12] Until we have come to accept our vulnerability, and hence bodiliness, we will be prone to look for scapegoats on whom to project our own weaknesses. This tendency either leads to exclusions—as in the case of stigmatizing people with disabilities—or entrenches existing prejudices.

Thus, this overview of psychological research has helped us understand the connection between one's relationship to one's own bodiliness and one's moral development. The self-deceptive rejection of vulnerability engenders anthropodenying emotions (shame and disgust) and narcissism, which together limit the content and scope of our understanding of human community. These tendencies therefore threaten politico-liberal values and need to be "kept at bay" (Nussbaum 2013, 3) for the sake of stability. This is, then, the descriptive part of the reasonable moral psychology. We need yet to define the methods of nurturing positive attitudes to bodiliness and the corresponding emotional responses.

Play against Insecurity

As I have already mentioned, this normative task has to be pursued with particular care lest respect for reasonable pluralism, which is embraced by political liberalism, be violated. A reasonable moral psychology—backed up by scientific research and, therefore, potentially shareable—is intended to provide an alternative to comprehensive accounts of civic education.

Based on the overview of moral development sketched above, the main challenge which we are facing now is the question of how to combat the human tendency to reject vulnerability, and most notably how to overcome anthropodenial. Here, again, Nussbaum finds D. W. Winnicott's works helpful. His most valuable insight, argues Nussbaum, consists in recognizing the importance of play in the maturation process. For Winnicott, play takes place in a "potential space," an intermediate realm between illusion and reality (Nussbaum 2010, 99). A toy is essentially symbolic—at first it represents a parent and brings comfort during her or his absence but later it becomes endowed with other meanings. Thus, when at play, the child manipulates and, at the same time, "creates" external objects by attributing senses to them (Winnicott 2005, 1–34, 51–70).

On the whole, play constitutes a realm of illusion which nonetheless nobody questions. The child is allowed to exercise control over it even though she in fact is dealing with autonomous elements of the external world. This has two important consequences. On the one hand, when the child explores her creativity, she experiences herself as an agent. Thus, she discovers that she is not entirely helpless and can, to some extent, influence the world around her. On the other hand, she learns the limits of her control by discovering that reality has some independent properties and cannot bend to her expectations completely. In this way, play serves as a safe zone, in which the child can experiment with her own possibilities and the external world in a relaxed manner (Nussbaum 2001, 207–209; 2010, 97–99; 2013, 177–81). Such creative exploration helps her adjust her aspirations to reality without sacrificing her individuality. Thus, ideally, a healthy human being will neither be unaware of her limitations nor totally submissive (Winnicott 1990, 39–54).

How is this account of play relevant to the problem of the rejection of vulnerability and, more specifically, anthropodenial, then? Well, we can clearly see that play enables the child to combat early narcissism. Having gained confidence in herself, she no longer requires the world to revolve around her and serve only her needs. This, in turn, has a crucial impact on her relationships with her parents or caretakers. At first, it is their role to slightly loosen the bond with the child so as to encourage her to explore her own agency. When she experiments with the limits of her control over reality, she begins to realize that, like other objects, her parents are independent entities. What distinguishes them from inanimate things, however, is that they are subjects just like herself. This truth is also arrived at with the help of play, which does not always take place in solitude (Nussbaum 2013, 179) and, apart from toys, often involves interaction with other people. Through play, the child learns to see other persons as autonomous sources of activity and not as mere means to her ends (Nussbaum 2013, 178–81; 2010, 99).

Thus play prepares the child to enter the state of mature interdependence, in which people recognize one another's autonomy and at the same time acknowledge that they rely on each other (just like people at play). The reason why play makes these initially unbearable facts acceptable is, Nussbaum suggests (Nussbaum 2001, 236–37; 2010, 99–100; 2013, 174), that it draws on the child's capacity for wonder. This is not Winnicott's original term to refer to the infant's delight in her creative impulse, though he expresses a similar idea (Nussbaum 2001, 189). According to Nussbaum (2001, 55), wonder is an important and special emotion since, as far as it is possible for an emotion, it is non-eudaimonistic. However odd this might sound at first, wonder can be interpreted as disinterested interest in the world. When we approach an object with this emotion, we take delight in it for its own sake, without referring to our prior scheme of goals. Such openness to the world, the outward movement toward its elements, Nussbaum argues, is just as basic an attitude as anxiety, the need to be held, etc. Apart from "scanning" them in the search for support, infants reach out to their surroundings with cheerful curiosity (Nussbaum 2001, 189–90). The potential space of play creates an environment in which they can safely indulge this natural interest in the world. They experiment with various objects and possibilities, knowing that the consequences of their activities, even if real, will not be grave. Their curiosity does not kill the cat (yet) but rather prompts infants to venture further and further.

Thus understood, wonder-infused play has a double role in human moral development. First, it encourages infants to see their humanity in a delightful manner. In the world of play, all human possibilities are approached with curiosity, as something to be explored and experimented with. And so, for example, infants can discover their bodies, treating them as fascinating and mysterious objects, and not just as sources of limitation. The lack of control which goes with interpersonal relationships likewise takes a different, delightful form in the world of play. Infants let themselves be surprised by other participants of play, enjoying the unpredictability of their behavior. By allowing for wonder, therefore, play enables them to befriend the human condition. Even its otherwise disturbing aspects, such as animality and dependency, appear as interesting and pleasurable. Thus, play helps us come to terms with our weaknesses and appreciate what may be valuable about them (Nussbaum 2001, 237; 2013, 178–79).

Secondly, even though wonder is not rooted in the preconception of one's flourishing, it can shape its understanding. For once we have found something *wonder*-ful, we start to care for it for its own sake. This is particularly important for the development of healthy interpersonal relationships. When infants and children approach their co-participants in play with wonder, they see them as autonomous sources of activity. Thus, they begin to realize that other people are not just the means to their own goals but have inner worth, i.e. dignity. This helps them exercise the capacity of imagination as, curious about those wonderful people around them, they try to envisage their points of view. And since their agency seems delightful and fascinating, through wonder children gradually come to care for other people. This broadens their circle of concern by helping them discover that there are autonomous goods (other people around) worthy of being included in their emerging ideas of flourishing (Nussbaum 2001, 55, 321–22).

In the long run, then, wonder-activating play can forestall the negative moral consequences of the experience of vulnerability. It encourages us to accept our animality and reveals to us the delightful aspect of interpersonal relationships with their uncontrollability and upredictability. Moreover, it teaches us that the autonomy of other people is not to be dreaded but has to be respected and cared for. In this way, wonder and play prepare us to embrace the idea of humanity in all its richness and width, acting against the tendencies that cause stigmatization and projective disgust, and facilitating compassion. Through play, we come to include animality and vulnerability in our understanding of humanity and are more likely to sympathize with the plight of others. We learn to extend our circle of concern solely on the basis of the recognition of their dignity. Plus, the role-taking that play involves helps us exercise the capability of imagination, making us more understanding of different perspectives. On the whole, then, wonder-infused play prepares us for inclusive compassion.

Art

What practical consequences are we to draw from these considerations, though? Surely we cannot be expected to successfully complete moral development already at the stage of childhood play. It is rather an ongoing process, which we can never complacently declare finished. Play activates the forms of understanding crucial to moral thinking. It also, Nussbaum argues (2013, 180–81), provides the model of interpersonal relationships since these, like play, should involve both interdependency and respect for the other's autonomy, mutual responsiveness, openness to surprises, etc. What is needed in order to cultivate these attitudes is not only play itself but also its extension—the world of art.

Winnicott saw the area of cultural creativity in general as the continuation of play in adult life. Art, religion and even scientific imagination all take place in what Winnicott called a potential space between the human mind and external reality. In these realms, we are allowed to exercise our creativity by transforming the world for aesthetic purposes, adding spiritual meanings to it or offering novel ways of thinking about natural phenomena (Nussbaum 2010, 101–103; 2013, 181–82; Winnicott 2005, 19, 128–39). The reason why I have singled out the arts from among these spheres of human creativity, however, is that the aesthetic experience seems to be most akin to Nussbaum's idea of wonder. As disinterested delight in an object, wonder certainly resembles and possibly is involved in the contemplation of beauty. The wonderful has the same quality of non-instrumentality that we often associate with the beautiful. Hence, on Nussbaum's account, wonder-infused play appears to be the prototype of the aesthetic experience, and the arts emerge as the extension of the world of children's play.[13]

In this way, Nussbaum's reasonable moral psychology enables us to "deduce" the moral significance of art. We come to recognize the dignity of another person with the help of wonder, this emotion being also involved in the experience of beauty, which suggests that the latter value may somehow support the acknowledgment of the former. This is not to say that dignity and beauty, or judgments of them, are identical. However, since they both are the objects of wonder, the perception of somebody's beauty can aid the perception of their dignity. Likewise, we are more willing to include in our understanding of dignity those aspects of humanity that we perceive as beautiful. Thus, if our bodies appear beautiful to us, we learn to see animality as being not contrary to dignity. On the whole, then, the practical consequence of the reasonable moral psychology sketched above is that the arts provide the means of cultivating a respectful approach to other people. And, given the morally problematic nature of our attitude to animality, this cultivation should in particular alert us to the beauty of the human body.

Appearance, Perception, Performance

These considerations provide a theoretical context in which I would like to interpret performative art and performance. I shall understand these terms in a very broad and non-specialized manner. Namely, I interpret performative art as any type of artistic activity which can be carried out in a particular moment and place, in the presence of the public, performance being the actual enactment of a work. Thus theater, concerts, dancing and even urban design all could classify as performative art. Before we move on to some examples of how they can be employed for the purposes of political stability, however, it needs yet to be explained why performative art stands out from the other types of artistic creativity. The reason for this, I suggest, has to do with the pair of concepts mentioned in the previous paragraph, i.e. perception and appearing.

The idea of perception plays an important role in Nussbaum's early ethical writings, where it figures as the Aristotelian alternative to "scientific" models of practical rationality such as Platonism, utilitarianism or Kantianism. These approaches are scientific in that they offer to guarantee ethical certainty by providing an infallible method of reasoning, defining a set of principles or determining one universal measure of value. Against this, Nussbaum argues that a less ambitious and at the same time more nuanced model of rationality is required to capture the specificity of human moral experience. This she finds in Aristotle's idea of perception (*aesthesis*) as the type of context-attuned responsiveness, capable of apprehending the richness of values involved (and sometimes conflicting) in a particular situation (Nussbaum 1990b, 54–105, 168–94). Arguably, such a conception of ethics could be considered as Nussbaum's own comprehensive doctrine regarding moral philosophy. This is not to say, however, that it could not be reconciled with her political liberalism as a part of the overlapping consensus. That is, even though it should not be treated as a binding account of practical rationality which ought to be used in the process of justifying political principles, it may be compatible with politico-liberal values and provide one of the possible ways of putting them into practice.

This, indeed, seems to be the case. First of all, perception strongly relies on emotions, which, along with imagination, are important means of interpreting the situation at hand (Nussbaum 1990b, 75–84, 180). So the model of perception could be backed up to some extent by the reasonable moral psychology. Secondly, with its sensitivity to the plurality of goods, perception seems particularly compatible with Nussbaum's capabilities approach (which, as I have argued, influences her understanding of politico-liberal values) (Nussbaum 1990b, 56–67, 97–101). And finally, the equivocal nature of the original term, *aisthesis*, captures well the specificity of Nussbaum's understanding of moral reasoning. For, on the one hand, aisthesis initially referred to sensual perception. In the context of ethical judgment, this points to the bodiliness of humans as moral beings. On the other hand, the modern meaning of aisthesis suggests an affinity between ethical judgment and aesthetic experience. Indeed, Nussbaum (1990b, 84) compares perception to an extraordinary capability of vision most convincingly delivered by great realist narratives (such as the novels of Henry James or Charles Dickens) or to theatrical improvisation (93–97). Such an overlap between the ethical and the aesthetic is, again, supported by the reasonable moral psychology. Thus, on the whole, the idea of perception seems to convey well the manner in which human animals reason ethically, this ability being related to their capacity for aesthetic judgment.

Among the "objects" of perception are other people, whom, as I have argued, we may come to perceive as inherently valuable and, *as such*, crucial to our flourishing. In this case, however, it seems that the notion of perception should be complemented by the concept of appearance. Naturally, in a basic sense of these terms, perception is always a response to the way in which things appear to the perceiver. What is special about perceiving another person, though, is that she can to some extent consciously project an image of herself. Therefore, it might be useful to introduce an Arendtian motif here and say, paraphrasing the author of *The Human Condition* (Arendt 1998, 199–207), that all humans have *the power to appear* by virtue of their being agents. Now, I do not intend to offer a possible supplement to Nussbaum's philosophy with Arendt's theory, as it would far exceed the framework of this paper. Arendt's lexicon, however, helps us to see the dimension which seems to be logically implied by Nussbaum's assumptions, even if she does not refer to it explicitly (possibly this is because she deals with the notion of perception in ethical, rather than political, writings). For example, we could say that in the emotion of wonder we perceive another person as inherently valuable by recognizing that she has the power to appear, i.e. to act autonomously in accordance with her own scheme of goals. Thus, perceiving and appearing are in a constant dialogue. An individual perceives other people with emotions which both reflect her own ideas of flourishing and respond to their appearances. Her expectations and their conscious self-projections interact, her perception of them being the result thereof.

It is this connection between perception and appearance that suggests the particular importance of performative art and performance. For, on the one hand, if the arts are the means of the moral cultivation of interpersonal attitudes and these depend on the process of perceiving-appearing, we need to turn to the artistic activities that also involve such interaction.

Performance, as defined above, meets this condition. Concerts, theatrical performances and dancing shows all comprise spaces in which performers appear to the perceiving audience and, no less importantly, to each other. This enables them not only to project specific images but also, even more crucially, to present themselves as capable of doing so. In other words, performances bring us the recognition that other people are not simply the objects of our perception but autonomous subjects endowed with agency. And this, it will be remembered, is the basic moral insight which underlies the state of mutual interdependency. Thus, performance seems to be the form of artistic activity most compatible with the dialectics of appearing and perceiving, which characterizes the development of mutual attitudes between persons.

On the other hand, performative art and performance add a particularly valuable dimension to this process. As I have said, performance happens in a specific time and place, between flesh and blood individuals. And, given that it always involves an element of bodily expression, it enables bodies to appear and be perceived in a beautiful and wonder-inspiring manner. Thus, performance is an event in which human beings take part as, among other things, animal creatures, their very animality being one of the means of the artistic activity. In this way, through performance, bodiliness can come to be included in our understanding of ourselves and one another as dignified, creative agents.

The interactive dimension and the exposition of the human body suggest the special role of performative art and performance in general. However, this observation is not only a conclusion drawn from, but also (hopefully) a development of, Nussbaum's project. For she herself does not privilege performance over other forms of art (which is, again, probably because she does not speak about appearance explicitly). Indeed, when considering the problem of political stability in her recent book, she mentions performative art along with literature, film, political speeches and even comics (Nussbaum 2013, 257–313, 346–75). All these types of art play an important role in the cultivation of politically desirable, and the prevention of dangerous, emotions. Just as there are many impediments to compassion (Arendt 1998, 199–206), so are there many ways of overcoming them. Still, if I am right to argue that, first, interpersonal relationships are shaped through the interaction of perceiving and appearing and, secondly, human vulnerability and in particular, animality, is one of the major challenges to moral development, performative art and performance seem to offer the most for the advancement of political stability. Unlike other forms of art mentioned, they are not mediated by individual imagination (of the narrative voice, film director, or political speaker), but instead provide a space in which real people can enter a dialogue of appearance and perception. In this way, they create sites for the politico-liberal value of equal human dignity to be cultivated.

Practical Implications

Nussbaum provides a couple of examples of how this can be achieved. I would like to conclude with a short overview of them, which, however, should by no means be considered exhaustive. My intention is rather to sketch an area of the possible implications of the considerations presented in this paper. On my interpretation, Nussbaum's philosophy offers a theoretical background which can be used for practical application in, among other fields, the realm of the arts. This, in turn, suggests that we need to secure the ongoing presence of the arts in public life.

I suggest that we begin with an example which also opens Nussbaum's argument in *Political Emotions*, i.e. Mozart's opera *The Marriage of Figaro*. In view of my interpretation, it is telling that Nussbaum has chosen this work as her point of departure since opera would classify as performative art in the meaning adopted in this paper. Hence, performance seems to be at the center of Nussbaum's project. An opera—a work to be enacted by singers and musicians on the stage, in the presence of the audience—becomes the paradigmatic example of the political significance of art. Obviously, it is not only because of its formal features that Nussbaum refers to *The Marriage of Figaro*. Mozart, however, combines the form and content in a fruitful way. Here Nussbaum mentions Cherubino, a young male character, whose manly yet delicate body becomes the vehicle for subverting the norms of invulnerability and impenetrability. Mozart's opera uses the bodily expression characteristic of this form of art to redefine our understanding of animality and, hence, humanity. This aspect significantly contributes to the overall egalitarian message of *The Marriage of Figaro* (Nussbaum 2013, 27–43).

When Nussbaum moves on to review the historical accounts of political emotions, she provides another example of the use of performative arts. As I have said, she rejects Comte's and Rousseau's projects as being at odds with reasonable pluralism. According to Nussbaum, however, a much more convincing model can be found in Rabindranath Tagore's theory and practice. Tagore was an Indian educator who at the beginning of the 20th century started a school in Santiniketan (later to become Visva Bharati University), which became a site of influential pedagogic innovations. Tagore's agenda was closer to political liberalism than Comte's because of its respect for pluralism. Tagore sought to educate open-minded citizens of an inclusive society, which quest he understood as involving the cultivation of proper emotions. Moreover, he saw the connection between the rejection of one's own bodiliness and the mistreatment of other people. Therefore, to use Nussbaum's terminology, he aimed at enhancing compassion and sympathetic understanding, on the one hand, and overcoming disgust, on the other. These goals he intended to achieve through a curriculum in which great emphasis was laid on the arts in general and performative arts in particular. Theatrical performances, dancing and singing were emphasized in Tagore's school. These activities required students to step into various roles and imagine the perspectives of their co-performers, thereby teaching them interaction and mutual attunement. They also inspired them to discover the beauty of their own and each other's bodies, encouraging a type of physical intimacy which worked against the exclusive tendencies of disgust (Nussbaum 2010, 103–6; 2013, 84–100). Thus, Tagore entrusted performative arts with the task of cultivating political emotions through the development of imaginative responsiveness and the befriending of bodiliness. Here, again, performance lies at the heart of the egalitarian socio-political project, as an important means of inculcating the value of equal human dignity.

The paradigmatic examples of the political relevance of performance, however, are probably Ancient Greek theatrical festivals. The fact that they had the status of public celebrations proves that they were seen as a crucial part of political life. Festivals offered, Nussbaum argues, two types of spectatorship—tragic and comic. In the first case, they familiarized the audience with human vulnerabilities, presenting them in a wonder- and compassion-inspiring manner (Nussbaum 2001, 350–53; 2013, 261–66). Comedies also dealt with difficult matters, such as death and bodily weakness, but approached them in a playful, light-hearted spirit (Nussbaum 2013, 272–75). This was yet another way of befriending the human condition, with both its glory and its precariousness. On the whole, then, theatrical festivals displayed human possibilities and taught proper emotional responses to them.[14] Bodiliness featured prominently in these performances, if only because they involved bodily expression. Often, however, human animality would become one of the subjects of a play (a tragic example being *Philoctetes* and a comic one *Lysistrata*, Nussbaum 2013, 262–64, 274–75), whereby, as in the case of *The Marriage of Figaro*, form and content would jointly work against the rejection of bodiliness.

Interestingly, when looking for contemporary counterparts of Greek theatrical festivals, Nussbaum provides many examples which involve public monuments or, more generally, the arts in public spaces. For it is not sculptures locked up in museums that she endows with political meaning but artworks located in public, open settings and therefore inviting much more inclusive participation and, possibly, interaction. And so Nussbaum (2013, 284–288) cites the Vietnam Veterans Memorial in Constitution Gardens in Washington as a site of a tragic festival. V-shaped and horizontal, this monument evokes a sense of vulnerability and vaginal imagery, especially when juxtaposed with the nearby phallic Washington Monument. Also, unlike the latter, it offers a much more individualized vision of the nation, having the names of the casualties carved in its surface (both the femininity and the non-unifying character may be traced back to the person of the designer, Maya Lin, a female Asian American artist). Finally, the monument is made of a highly reflective material, which allows visitors to see themselves and each other in its surface (Nussbaum 2013, 287). In this way the Memorial gives people a chance to connect to each other in grief, while at the same time enabling them to embrace vulnerability as part of the national history and, ultimately, humanity. It achieves this not the least because of its performative features—the visitors become the part of the monument when, reflected in its surface, they stroll along its walls. Thus the Memorial mediates in establishing a relationship between people and creating a sense of community (Nussbaum 2013, 287–88).

A comic counterpart to the Vietnam Veterans Memorial can be found in Chicago's Millennium Park. One of its main attractions, Anish Kapoor's Cloud Gate (or "The Bean") is also a reflective structure, which, however, comically distorts spectators' bodies. Thus, Nussbaum suggests, it invites visitors to discover the playfulness of their bodies and, even more importantly, to join with other people—often complete strangers—in an auto-ironic game of distorted reflections. Spectators are encouraged to reveal the awkwardness of their physicality to each other and respond with good humor to one another's funnily grotesque images. The Crown Fountain, another popular site in the Millennium Park, plays a similar role. The two glass brick towers, located in a granite pool, serve as screens on which the images of human faces are projected, spitting water every couple of minutes. This construction, again, invites people to act playfully, to shirk the embarrassment of getting wet. It also opposes the stigma which used to be associated with sharing swimming pools and drinking fountains (Nussbaum 2013, 299). In this way it encourages a form of physical intimacy, opposing the exclusionary workings of shame and disgust (Nussbaum 2013, 298–301).

These examples of contemporary tragic and comic festivals seem particularly inspiring in that they point to the aesthetic potential of the public space. It can function as a site of performance because it is, ultimately, the sphere in which people appear to each other. When filled with art, it has the ability to transform citizens' mutual perceptions. Pushed out of the galleries and museums and located in the public space, art becomes accessible on more egalitarian terms. Thanks to this, it can play an empowering role. For, if people present themselves to each other through the medium of art, they are perceived as beautiful and dignified, as creative subjects capable of projecting their own appearances.[15]

Conclusion

The aim of this paper was to analyze the recent development in Martha Nussbaum's philosophy, i.e. her reasonable moral psychology, so as to point to the political dimension of the experience of bodiliness and the relevance of performative arts for its reshaping. The larger philosophical questions of political liberalism and its stability allowed me to, first, place Nussbaum's project in the proper theoretical context and, second, capture the specificity of its content. Both the idea to turn to psychology for an account of human moral development, and the values which are meant to be acquired in this process, reflect politico-liberal assumptions with their focus on individual dignity and respect for pluralism.

Recognition of the problem of stability stems from the general project of political liberalism. As I have argued, however, Nussbaum's solution to this problem is influenced by her own variety of political liberalism, namely her capabilities approach. This Aristotle-inspired theory points to the centrality of bodiliness as an element of the human condition. It also helps Nussbaum appreciate the role of emotions in practical reasoning, emotions emerging as value judgments marked with the sense of neediness. These assumptions can be backed up by contemporary psychological research, which Nussbaum extensively cites. On the whole, the rejection of vulnerability, and therefore of animality (as one of its major sources), seems to be at the root of many forms of immoral behavior. Overcoming anthropodenial through the cultivation of proper emotions appears, thus, to be one of the main aims of moral development.

Here, again, Nussbaum combines psychological research with her philosophical intuitions (in this case, her account of wonder) to point to the role of the arts in the nurturing of desirable emotions. When combined with her earlier writings on perception, which, in turn, can be supplemented by the idea of appearance, this contention leads to the recognition of the special place of performative arts. As I have attempted to demonstrate, these artistic activities (in the broad sense adopted in the paper) have an important empowering dimension. They help us perceive each other as creative, dignified beings, at the same time uncovering the wonderfulness of our bodies.

Thus interpreted, Nussbaum's project can be assessed differently and from various perspectives. As a theoretical elaboration of political liberalism, it may not be as neutral as it purports to be. In many important respects, it is influenced by Nussbaum's own philosophical project (whose politico-liberal character could also be disputed),[16] which partially determines her choice of psychological evidence. Nonetheless, Nussbaum argues powerfully for the reevaluation of human bodiliness and its inclusion into the idea of dignity. Whether this assumption is already a part of the politico-liberal consensus or not, it certainly deserves to be considered by political liberals. And, aside from these theoretical intricacies, Nussbaum certainly offers a convincing defense of the political relevance of the arts. She points to their crucial role in the cultivation of respectful relationships within a pluralist democratic society. And this is a valuable argument for the ongoing presence of the arts in public life.

References

Arendt, Hannah. 1998. *The Human Condition*. Chicago, London: The University of Chicago Press.

Bloom, Paul. 2005. *Descartes' Baby: How the Science of Child Development Explains What Makes Us Human*. New York: Basic Books.

Crocker, David A., and Ingrid Robeyns. 2009. "Capability and Agency." In: *The Philosophy of Amartya Sen*. Edited by Christopher Morris, 60–90. New York: Cambridge University Press.

Crocker, David A. 2007. "Functioning and Capability: The Foundations of Sen's and Nussbaum's Development Ethic, Part 2." In: *Women, Culture and Development. A Study of Human Capabilities*. Edited by Martha Nussbaum, Jonathan Glover, 153–98. Oxford: Clarendon Press.

Nussbaum, Martha Craven. 1990a. *Liberalism and the Good*. Edited by R. B. Douglass et al. New York, London: Routledge.

—. 1990b. *Love's Knowledge: Essays on Philosophy and Literature*. New York, Oxford: Oxford University Press.

—. 1992. "Human Functioning and Social Justice." *Political Theory* 20 (2): 202–46.

—. 1995. *Poetic Justice: The Literary Imagination and Public Life*. Boston: Beacon Press.

—. 2000. *Women and Human Development: The Capabilities Approach*. New York: Cambridge University Press.

—. 2001. *Upheavals of Thought. The Intelligence of Emotions*. New York: Cambridge University Press.

—. 2003. "Rawls and Feminism." In: *The Cambridge Companion to Rawls*. Edited by Samuel Freeman, 488–520. New York: Cambridge University Press.

—. 2010. *Not for Profit: Why Democracy Needs the Humanities*. Princeton, Oxford: Princeton University Press.

—. 2007. *Frontiers of Justice. Disability, Nationality, Species Membership*. 1st paperback ed. Cambridge, Massachusetts, London, England: The Belknap Press of Harvard University Press.

—. 2008. *Human Dignity and Political Entitlements*. Accessed December 5, 2014. http://bit.ly/2kTKFRn.

—. 2009. *The Therapy of Desire: Theory and Practice in Hellenistic Ethics*. Paperback reissue. Princeton and Oxford: Princeton University Press.

—. 2011a. *Creating Capabilities: The Human Development Approach*. Cambridge, Massachusetts, London, England: The Belknap Press of Harvard University Press.

—. 2011b. "Rawls's *Political Liberalism*: A Reassessment." *Ratio Juris* 24 (1): 1–24.

—. 2013. *Political Emotions: Why Love Matters for Justice*. Cambridge, Massachusetts, London, England: The Belknap Press of Harvard University Press.

Okin, Susan Moller. 1989. "Reason and Feeling in Thinking about Justice." *Ethics* 99 (2): 229–49.

Oon, Shaun. 2010. "Culture and the Limits of Capability." In: *The Capability Approach on Social Order: Proceedings from the Unseld Lecture 2010*. Edited by Niels Weidtmann, Yanti Martina Hölzchen, and Bilal Hawa, 95–108. Berlin, Wien: LIT Verlag.

Rawls, John. 1993, 1996. *Political Liberalism*. New York: Columbia University Press.

Rozin, Paul, Jonathan Haidt, and Clark R. McCauley. 1999, 2000. "Disgust: the Body and Soul Emotion." In: *Handbook of Cognition and Emotion*. Edited by Tim Dalgleish, and Mick Power, 429–45. Chichester: John Wiley & Sons.

Sen, Amartya. 2001. *Development as Freedom*. Oxford, New York: Oxford University Press.

Winnicott, Donald W. 1990. *Home Is Where We Start From*. New York,
    London: W. W. Norton and Company.
—. 2005. *Playing and Reality*. London, New York: Routledge Classics.
Wrocław's Application for the Title of European Capital of Culture 2016.
    2011. *Spaces for Beauty Revisited*. Wrocław.

Notes

[1] The project has been funded by the National Science Centre (Poland), based on
the decision number DEC-2013/09/N/HS1/02864.

[2] As Nussbaum observes, Rawls offers two understandings of "reasonability." In a
more general sense, it refers to the readiness to offer and accept equal terms of
cooperation, and as such represents the moral attitude of respect for fellow citizens.
In a more specific meaning, used particularly with respect to comprehensive
doctrines, it concerns the formal requirements which such doctrines which must
meet if they are to classify as reasonable (these are: a certain degree of coherence
and consistency, practical applicability, relative stability and rootedness in a
specific tradition). The first sense is much laxer and, therefore, inclusive, which is
why Nussbaum prefers it (Nussbaum 2011b, 6–11, see also: Rawls 1993, 1996,
48–65). Throughout the paper I also use this broader interpretation of
reasonability.

[3] Following the convention adopted in the texts on the subject, I use the term
"capability approach" with reference to the paradigm based on the notion of "a
capability" in general. I reserve the term "capabilities approach" for Nussbaum's
variety of the paradigm. This is because Nussbaum insists on the need to define a
catalogue of priority capabilities.

[4] On Nussbaum's idea of dignity, see also Nussbaum 2008, especially "The
Aristotelian/Marxian Alternative" and "Dignity and Its Basis."

[5] For early, strongly Aristotelian explications of Nussbaum's account, see, for
example: Nussbaum 1992, 202–46; 1990a, 203–52. For recent Aristotelian
references see Nussbaum 2007, 159–68 and Nussbaum 2000, 70–77. I leave aside
the issue of whether, given the Aristotelian roots of Nussbaum's project, it can
indeed be considered as politico-liberal. Nussbaum's approach has evolved in this
respect, following the development of Rawls' philosophy. Whereas her first
writings on capabilities are explicitly Aristotelian, she later changed the status of
her project from the Aristotelian theory of the good into political liberalism,
without really changing its content. This has led some critics to doubt the non-
comprehensive character of Nussbaum's approach (Oon 2010, 95–108; Okin 1999,
115–31). For the purposes of this paper, however, I assume that it can be defended
as such and focus only on the influence of Nussbaum's particular (politico-liberal)
philosophy on her understanding of political liberalism in general.

[6] Nussbaum distinguished three types of capabilities: basic (inborn equipment,
such as the ability to learn a language), internal (developed states of an individual,
which, as far as she is concerned, enable her to perform certain functionings) and
combined capabilities (Nussbaum 2000, 83–84; 2011a, 20–21).

[7] The list includes the following items: life, bodily health, bodily integrity, senses, imagination and thought, emotions, practical reason, affiliation (this includes the ability to form relationships with other people and protection from discrimination), relation to other species, play, and control over one's political and material environment (Nussbaum 2000, 78–80; 2011a, 33–34).

[8] Nussbaum 2001, 19–88. On the whole, ancient philosophy differed from modernity in seeing emotions as cognitive attitudes and not as blind, totally a-rational forces. It was present already in Plato and, more importantly for our purposes, in Aristotle. The Stoics, however, were most radical since they were the first to *identify* emotions with judgments (Nussbaum 2009, 371–72).

[9] Winnicott (1990, 239–59) speaks about democracy as a form of government conditional on the state of emotional maturity and points to the role of the family in the provision of the latter.

[10] This points to another capability, which supplements emotions, namely the capability of imagination. It belongs to the central capabilities included in Nussbaum's list and, indeed, it plays a crucial role in our practical reasoning. Nussbaum understands imagination as the capacity for perspectival thinking, which enables us, first, to appreciate the richness of somebody's inner life, and, secondly, to step into their shoes and try to understand their point of view (Nussbaum, 1995, 36–39; 2001, 208–9, 236–37; 2013, 156–57). The example of compassion shows that emotions and imagination interact with each other: we are more likely to care for the people whose problems we can understand and, in turn, we try to understand those who matter for us. Therefore, the cultivation of compassion always involves the cultivation of imagination. As we will find out shortly, the reverse also obtains, i.e. limited imagination goes with exclusionary emotions.

[11] The particularistic nature of compassion reflects, in turn, the limitations of imagination. After all, imagination produces images and these are always specific and non-abstract. The mutual dependency between compassion and imagination results, thus, in our tendency to privilege the local over the general, which can also be expressed in such emotions as stigmatizing shame and projective disgust (since these target the less familiar envisaged as the less human). On the whole, we may stipulate that it is this connection between emotions and imagination that determines the inextricably particularistic character of the former, which, as Nussbaum argues *contra* Rawls, needs to be confronted if we are to arrive at a feasible account of political emotions (Nussbaum 2013, 156–57, 316–20). Thus, the limits of compassion cannot be explained only by external factors. Nor are shame and disgust the only emotions which work against compassion from without. In *Political Emotions* Nussbaum mentions also fear and envy, which, although not directly linked to anthropodenial, impede our sympathetic understanding. As a judgment about potential danger to one's own or one's group's well-being, fear can be narrowing when the idea of one's community is narrow. People excluded from the community are not protected by fear for their welfare and may even be seen as a threat. Envy, in turn, is a painful emotion which we experience when we (or our group) possess fewer crucially important goods

than somebody else (or another group). In envy, we perceive other people as rivals, not as fellow citizens in a common enterprise (Nussbaum 2013, 320–59). In these ways, envy and fear make us insensitive to the plight of other human beings. It is also worth noting that in *Political Emotions* Nussbaum mentions shame alongside fear and envy, as a compassion-impeding emotion which does not stem from narcissism and the rejection of animality. However, in keeping with the account sketched above, she later interprets shame in terms of the unwillingness to accept one's own imperfection. And in her earlier seminal book on emotions, *Upheavals of Thought*, she speaks of shame next to disgust, when dealing with early emotions and the development of the self. She also considers these two emotions in conjunction in *Hiding from the Humanity*, where she analyses their negative social consequences, which she links to their anthropodenying character. Therefore, shame does seem to express the specifically human problematic relationship to animality and in this respect appears to be closely related to disgust. I propose to consider it in this context and I find it difficult to explain Nussbaum's recent decision to situate it differently.

[12] Following Kant, Nussbaum calls this propensity to act immorally "radical evil." It is "radical" because it stems from certain tendencies which are deeply entrenched in human nature (our problematic relationship to animality is one such tendency, Nussbaum 2013, 3, 166–68).

[13] To this we can add a more general observation about the role of imagination in the cultivation of emotions. The arts strongly appeal to this capability, which therefore can be nurtured through the aesthetic experience.

[14] Today, we would probably object to many exclusions involved in the Greek understanding of who counts as "human." Most notably, this distinction was denied to barbarians and slaves. However, even if in its scope it was narrower than we would like it to be, in terms of the content, the idea of humanity promoted by Greek plays was rich, comprising not only rationality but also vulnerability and animality.

[15] Wrocław's successful application for the title of European Capital of Culture seems to draw on similar assumptions in its call for the opening up of spaces for beauty (Wrocław's Application 2011).

[16] See—endnote 5.

CHAPTER TWO

FROM SOMAESTHETICS
TO THE STYLISTICS OF EXISTENCE:
STYLES OF READING, WAYS OF LIVING

ALEX CIOROGAR

"Manners maketh man"—Gordon Matthew Thomas Sumner introduced this proverb in the lyrics of his famous 1988 song, *Englishman in New York*, the video showing his bohemian self, draped in an overcoat, wandering through the snowy streets of the metropolis. I chose to begin this article by invoking not, as one would expect, the works of a celebrated writer, but the image of a famous musician—Sting not Shelley—in order to engage with Richard Shusterman's longstanding defense of the popular arts. The other reason was to emphasize the important role that style plays in our lives, to the point of the *How* not only supporting, but also dominating over, and giving a new meaning to, the *What*.

Shusterman's reputation stands on his efforts to (re)adapt pragmatist philosophies to (more or less traditional) aesthetics while maintaining a certain emphasis on popular culture. Surpassing analytical philosophy, elaborating on Pierre Bourdieu's sociological ideas (Bourdieu made style a keyword in his sketch for auto-analysis), rejecting hermeneutical relativism, textual domination, and radical formalisms (such as deconstruction), while, at the same time, paradoxically adopting a pluralist logic of interpretation or comprehension (inspired by Wittgenstein's language games), and, finally, critically engaging with pragmatist accounts (Richard Rorty's most noticeably)—these are, in a nutshell, the building blocks of Shusterman's intellectual career (Puolakka 2010). In France, Shusterman has the reputation of a radical philosopher polemically interested in the theses of French and German theoreticians, a pragmatist with an unconventional taste for the popular arts, especially rap (Shusterman 2009), a hedonist used to pushing the limits. Nonetheless, relocating the human body at the center of a Pragmatist Aesthetics Philosophy is so far Shusterman's most radical and biggest achievement. He personally divided this multi/trans/ interdisciplinary research field into three main categories: analytic, pragmatic, and practical somaesthetics (Shusterman 1999, 304–7).

How does somaesthetics influence contemporary literary studies and, especially, stylistics? I would like to reflect upon those aspects of somaesthetics that apply to what we call style (be it corporeal or otherwise) by tracing the impact of his theories on literary studies, particularly on the works of an esteemed contemporary French researcher, Marielle Macé (2010, 2011).

The Pragmatic Turn

Style has been long discredited for being subjective or imprecise, but it is nowadays becoming a key notion of the humanities. It is being embedded in broader theoretical frameworks, as various fields have recently shown interest in the notions of body and style, suggesting a truly remarkable extension of their usual employment. In his *Introduction* to André Leroi-Gourhan's *Gesture and Speech*, Randall White, for instance, argues that over the past decades, there has been significant concern with the concept of style which, while "generally recognized as expressive of social identity, has been viewed in juxtaposition to function" (Leroi-Gourhan 1993, xviii).

Stylistics, it must be said, like the humanities in general,[1] are in desperate need of social justification. Contemporary politics also demands that artistic forms respond to something else, something more than just delivering subjective experiences to individuals. How do literary forms serve society? From the point of view of stylistics, they are responsible for organizing human lives through the forming and shaping of individuals, which is also to say that literature constructs collectiveness. Style no longer refers only to expressivity, but it also applies to action or different forms of practice. We have no longer to ask ourselves what style signifies, but what style can do (Jenny 2011). Without losing its former values, style became a describer of behaviors. Consequently, in order to grasp the complex dynamics of style one must also appreciate its corporeal anchorage. Without missing an ethical dimension, somaesthetics describes the stylistic dimension of human bodily existence, ranging from sensitive manifestations to physical culture.

There has been, one might say, an epistemological revolution (Egginton and Sandbothe 2004). We could call it the Pragmatic Revolution of Style. The New Philosophies of The Body represent a series of movements in modern sciences devoted to tying perception to action which began with

Maurice Merleau-Ponty's *Phenomenology of Perception* and Henri Bergson's philosophical ideas. Today, they also comprise the Cognitive Sciences and Affordance Theories. Although "The Decade of the Brain," as George H. W. Bush once called it, is now long gone, we can truly say, no doubt about it, that we are living in a new decade of the body. If the sciences have witnessed an enormously productive act of extrapolation of mechanistic naturalism from the body to the mind, as Daniel Dennett[2] has shown, philosophy, I believe, is now witnessing, thanks to Shusterman's somaesthetics, an equally fruitful extrapolation of a subjective ontological reasoning from the mind to the body.

Richard Shusterman's Somaesthetics

What's in a word? Somaesthetics quickly became one of hottest buzz-words in the humanities. Philosophers, literary critics, aestheticians, sociologists, and psychologists are equally interested in this all-encompassing field of study, because, in a sense, it expresses exactly what everyone's been seeking to express for a long time, something which everybody was aware of but no one dared to fully articulate. The good news is that the vastness of its application doesn't diminish its relevance, but actually increases the possibilities of interdisciplinary dialogue. Somaesthetics could actually become the common ground for the whole of human knowledge due to its indisputable empirical nature. Shusterman's attacks are aimed at replacing idealistic, essentialist, metaphysical points of view of classical aesthetic philosophies with the main claims of somaesthetics and, generally speaking, with the principles of pragmatist philosophies. In a way, we could assert that Shusterman is slowly but surely preparing a late secularization of the arts and aesthetics.

Shusterman believes that

> culture gives us the languages, values, social institutions, and artistic media through which we think and act and also express ourselves aesthetically, just as it gives us the forms of diet, exercise, and somatic styling that shape not only our bodily appearance and behavior but also the ways we experience our body. (2006, 3)

He therefore suggests that we should sustain a conscious reflection on and of the body while engaged in aesthetic contemplation. Shusterman defines art in Dewey's footsteps as an event or experience.[3] This is why he argues that some approaches to art are simply not made for interpretation, but rather for a Marxist-Frankfurt-School type of transformation. If we understand the soma as being the central human medium of experience, we have to acknowledge that the body plays a crucial role in the realms of cognition, ethics, aesthetics, and politics. Shusterman believes in self-expression, self-fashioning, and self-fulfillment because he views the body as "our tool of tools" (2006, 2).

Philosophy, he argues, before becoming an academic field, was a way of living, and, naturally, lifestyles involve one's body. Knowledge of self-improvement was as important as improving the surrounding environment of the self. However, the success of somaesthetics, I believe, like the success of every new philosophy (especially the North American ones), is largely related to Europe's wish and need for rethinking its own, already historicized 20th century philosophies and aesthetic traditions, ranging from Existentialism, Phenomenology, Marxism, Psychoanalysis, Post-Structuralism, and Hermeneutics, to Critical Theory, even though Shusterman fruitfully interacts with all of these. Let me offer some examples. As many studies have already shown, Shusterman praises Foucault for showing that selves are not fixed ontological entities, but socially constructed roles that can be refashioned through performance. He also credits Merleau-Ponty for showing that the body is our most important source of perception, meaning, and action. In his article "Le corps et les arts: la soma-esthétique" Shusterman introduces the body as the main agent in aesthetics, criticizing rationalist aesthetics in the line of Baumgarten, Kant, and Hegel by presenting means of perfecting our humanity and lives (Shusterman 2011a). Nonetheless, somaesthetics is inspired by Baumgarten because he envisioned aesthetics as a vast territory concerned with both perceptions and sensory-kinetic performances, but, at the same time, somaesthetics detaches itself radically from Baumgarten's view because it insists upon the exclusive belonging of the senses to the domain of the body and its perfectible perceptive powers. In other words, we can say that somaesthetics represents a fight against Descartes's famous split, a fight against Baumgarten's conceptualization of aesthetic theory, and, finally, a fight against Kant's and Hegel's idealistic perspectives.

When we think of the human body (Shusterman refers to a sentient perceiving body-mind entity; see 2008, 1, 48), we automatically associate it with experience, action, and images, as opposed to mind, thinking or language; but Shusterman basically rewrites aesthetics by placing the *Greek body*, "the soma" (a source of knowledge and an indicator of our limits), before or in front of perception. Shusterman understands the soma as, on the one hand, the source of every artistic action and, on the other hand, the receiving end of all art processes.

Somatic Styles

Shusterman argues for the existence, and importance, of a somatic style by employing analogies derived from literary examples (Shusterman 1997, 29 or Shusterman 1999, 299). Indeed, one cannot but admit the existence of an intimate relationship between the self as (re)presented in literature and style. Shusterman describes somatic styles by employing certain dichotomies or conceptual distinctions, such as voluntary and involuntary, conscious and unconscious, general or particular, evaluative and/or descriptive, and, finally, contextual or permanent (Shusterman 2011b, 147–95). Thus described, somatic styles can be understood as the worksheets of self-improvement. Of course, these somatic styles can be and are represented in literature. Consequently, they can be analyzed as being part of a kinetic style of a certain type of writing.

The kinetic style is defined as the connection between a body image and a corporeal scheme—it is that which produces the sense of being a subject, both to ourselves (as perception and thinking) and to others (as expression and communication). A literary work manifests a specific way of thinking about the body and this has an important impact on the formation of the narrative itself—plot, characters, backgrounds (Punday 2003). It creates an atmosphere because there is an intimate connection between narration and physical movements. Furthermore, the kinetic style of prose is composed by the ways in which the work chooses to communicate and make reference to body movements and perceptual simulations. The various styles of gestures bear witness to the vastness of human expression and its unpredictable character (Bolens 2008).

Somaesthetics, Shusterman (2000) declares, has nothing directly to do with literary criticism: disciplinary intersections are usually error cases of homonymy. He is more interested in what goes on *under interpretation*: he is an advocate of the benefits of direct comprehension and his work could be read as a plea for spontaneous action and non-verbal perception (Shusterman 2009), understood as a form of art itself. Shusterman emphatically claims that understanding can easily take place without interpretation. Somatic understanding, he goes on to argue, is a non-discursive type of knowledge which nonetheless can be related or improved by discursive practices. Finally, it is interesting to note that Shusterman asserts that there are non-interpretative discursive types of understanding literature.[4]

The Self, the Individual, Subjectivity

The humanities, as we know, deal with what it is to be a human being, a process in which style plays an important role. George Simondon (1992) defined the individual not as a source of, but as a simple moment in, the process of individuation. The individual is not a content, but a certain manner of assessing a certain content. In a sense, the individual could be viewed as a way of relating to one's self (Pachet 1993). In an interview for the journal *Parachute* Shusterman (2002) observes that

> self-fashioning is also evident in the fact that artists nowadays are often less interested in making objects or creating aesthetic experiences than in creating identities, particularly their own identity as an artist. They have to distinguish themselves; they need to make themselves almost like a commercial brand name. The prime artistic job is to create an artistic persona replete with a special style and image. The creation of this persona becomes the main oeuvre, the artist's self.

Consequently, self-fashioning is understood as a process of self-discovery and self-expression. Shusterman doesn't believe in a fixed, predetermined self that one can discover. He thinks about self-fashioning as "working creatively with talents, qualities, experiences and desire" (Shusterman 2002). The self, he suggests, is always a work in progress constructed on the basis of a series of habitual social practices. Self-representation involves auto-fictionalization and aesthetic self-fashioning. Besides the Augustinian element in the explanation of the self, Shusterman includes in his understanding of the self the leftist point of view of upon the individual. He also argues for the importance of the shaping of an individual and somatic style through the interaction with art (and in the course of reading, and writing, literature and philosophy):

> Part of the power of visual images and literary representations is that they give a substantive form to ideas and feelings that we're either not aware of or don't yet have. The practices of art, including the art of writing philosophy, are thus powerful tools for transforming the self. Art and writing can change who we are. Contemporary thought recognizes the self as a product of change and reconstruction. (Shusterman 2002)

Works of art offer resources for self-stylization. They open up this construction of the self because style enlarges our possibilities, it speaks to and captures our attention, our hearing, our every perception. While advocating towards a pluralistic logic of knowledge based on language-games, Shusterman confusingly draws our attention to the fallacies of liberal individualism (in other words, the fallacies of a certain ideological language-game). Indeed, his definition seems to be delivered in the form of a Ricoeurian understanding of the self via narration. Moreover, the self is apparently composed by a series of habits that can be described through certain ways of doing things: speaking, eating, breathing, walking, reading (Shusterman 1995).

Marielle Macé's Stylistics of Existence

Mostly known through her work on the theory of literary genres[5] and from her articles in *Le Monde des Livres,* Marielle Macé is one of the most important names in the young generation of French contemporary scholars. A graduate of the ENS, she authored a book about the French Literary Essay of the 20th century. She has also worked with prominent scholars including Antoine Compagnon, Jean-Marie Schaeffer, Laurent Jenny and Michel Murat. She currently works at the CNRS and teaches literature in Paris, New York and Chicago.

While in the last decade literary studies have witnessed a series of waves devoted to revalidating and justifying literature's presence in today's society, most of Macé's work is also oriented into rethinking literary objects from the perspective of vital and existential practices. Her latest book has gained recognition well beyond the limited sphere of specialists, speaking to a general reading public. Macé strives to develop the idea of an anthropology of style (Jousset 2008), expanding the notion of style to all individuals and their practices, be they mental, gestural, social, aesthetic or otherwise.

If one closely observes the history of the notion of style—which evolved at the same pace as that of subjectivity—one understands that style has represented successive and contradictory ways in which the individual is performed. By retracing the steps which led style into becoming a central concept in the understanding of the forms of life, Macé came to understand it as a transversal instrument which gradually opened her studies up to a point where it became an Anthropology of Practices or a Stylistics of Existence (a term she borrowed from Michel Foucault). In other words, Macé studies a major strand in the history of modern thought and literature, located at the intersection between aesthetic, social, and philosophical concepts. Simply stated, one's life cannot be torn apart from its form, its manners, its ways, its rhythms and gestures. While she is interested in the ways in which a literary form can act as a style of individuation, the novelty of her approach, as Laurent Jenny has shown, resides in recognizing forms of style as forces of attraction, mobilization, and orientation. If relocated at the center of our activities which appeal to the recognition and understanding of the stylistic character of human existence, literature, according to Macé, can sustain a political interrogation of the role of rhythms, forms and styles in our lives. There is no such thing as literature and life existing as separate entities. On the contrary, she argues that there are forms, images, and styles which circulate between human subjects and literary works. Styles apply to existence itself, to its inventiveness, its conventionalities. The power of stylization manifests itself in inventing artistic forms and aesthetic behaviors, physical postures, mental attitudes, sensibilities, ways of constructing the self, rituals, world visions, and techniques.

Styles of Individuation and the Practices of Reading

Marielle Macé also proposes a new approach to the process of reading: she redefines it as a negotiation between different styles of individuation. However, what is a style of individuation? A promise, as she puts it, of a new possibility of being. Like Shusterman, she also believes in the plurality of stylistic activities. For instance, a novel doesn't simply display various styles of being, but rather different ways of having a style. Style is usually understood as a performance of the self or as an existential engagement of the individual (Judith Butler saw style as the general category of performing the self). According to Macé, style is, as in Shusterman's view, not the equivalent of our human essence, nor part of a logic of distinction, but merely a mode of relation. Consequently, we come to the conclusion that we are not constructed or affected by style—it is our very nature.

Macé also reflects on the act of reading as an aesthetic behavior which, in her view, is a way of fashioning existence. She believes that the walls between subject and object do not, or should not, exist. Not unlike Shusterman, she also believes that style is never gained, but infinitely attainable. This process of reciprocal individuation describes the experience of literary reading. Admittedly, semiotic and narratological models view reading as an enclosed operation, separated from life, but reading is, Macé counter-argues, a part of a much larger stylistics of existence. Reading is one of those behaviors which, on a daily basis, offers an aspect, a flavor, and a style to our existence: being an aesthetic experience, reading does something to the ordinary forms of life. Reading is construed not as a task of decoding hidden messages, but as a certain conduct of a perceiving subject. Reading is not merely a pause in life, but a special performance of living life in a different way. Consequently, an individual is not only defined through his or her body, but also through the self-reflecting books he or she reads.

Living by Reading

We are at the beginning of a century which wants to reunite the mind with the body, reason with emotion, and imagination with intuition, a century in which the culture of the verb no longer dominates the culture of action. We have seen that both Macé and Shusterman believe in the possibility of modifying the self through aesthetic practices, although Shusterman understands it as an outward-oriented experience devoted mainly to actions related to artistic self-expression, thus stressing the important social dimension of constituting ourselves through stylistic mechanisms, while Macé strongly maintains the possibility and richness of change, viewing the process of individuation as an inwardly-directed process with means in and of itself. On the other hand, Shusterman believes that self-construction is habitual. Contrastingly, Macé emphasizes, as we have seen, the importance of breaking with our habits in the continuous quest of understanding and modeling ourselves.

What, then, constitutes the common ground of *somaesthetics* and *the stylistics of existence*? I've tried to show that Shusterman is basically looking for a way to (re)define the self through the development of conscious practices of the body (he focuses on what goes on under interpretation). Macé, in turn, focuses on the practice of reading. She also distances herself from the notion of artificiality or authenticity when defining the individual, mainly because she believes that stylistic properties are assumed by the individual when he or she is involved in the dynamics of forms. Significantly, she views reading not only as a subjective experience, but also as a subjectifying process. Disenchanting as it may seem, this means that reading doesn't simply reveal dormant identities; rather, it constantly challenges and reinvents them. No, reading is not a process of filling up gaps, but a continuous exchange between full, powerful forms.

Nonetheless, for both of them, the self is fundamentally a relational entity, engaged in significant aesthetic experiences. What did Foucault actually mean when he declared that man is dead? Obviously, he was acknowledging the changes and the future need to re-evaluate the human subject, both in practice and in theory. Through style, be it somatic or existential, Shusterman and Macé are doing just that—redefining, enriching our notion of the self. Isn't this what philosophy was all about? Wasn't literature?

References

Bolens, Guillemette. 2008. *Le style des gestes: corporéité et kinésie dans le récit littéraire* [The style of gestures: Embodiment and kinesis in literary narrative]. With a preface by Alain Berthoz. Lausanne: Éditions BHMS (Bibliothèque d'Histoire de la Médecine et de la Santé).

Dennett, Daniel. 2006. *Sweet Dreams. Philosophical Obstacles to a Science of Consciousness*. Massachusetts: The MIT Press.

Egginton, William, and Mike Sandbothe, eds. 2004. *The Pragmatic Turn in Philosophy: Contemporary Engagements between Analytic and Continental Thought*. New York: State University of New York Press.

Jay, Paul. 2014. *The Humanities "Crisis" and The Future of Literary Studies*. New York: Palgrave Macmillan.

Jenny, Laurent. 2011. *Le Style en acte. Vers une pragmatique du style* [Style in action: Towards a pragmatics of style]. Geneva: Métis Presses.

Jousset, Philippe. 2008. *Anthropologie du style* [The anthropology of style]. Bordeaux: Presses Universitaires.

Leroi-Gourhan, André. 1993. *Gesture and Speech*. Translated by Anna Bostock Berger and introduced by Randall White. Cambridge: MIT Press.

Macé, Marielle. 2004. *Le genre littéraire* [The literary genre]. Paris: Garnier-Flammarion.

—, ed. 2010. "Du Style!" [About style]. *Critique*, no. 752–53.

—. 2011. *Façons de lire, manières d'être* [Ways of reading, manners of being]. Paris: Gallimard, coll. "NRf Essais."

Małecki, Wojciech. 2011. "Things 'Too Amorphous to Talk About': Introductory Remarks on Pragmatism and Literature." *Pragmatism Today. The Journal of the Central-European Pragmatist Forum* 2 (2): 5–10.

Pachet, Pierre. 1993. *Un à Un. De l'individualisme en littérature—Michaux, Naipaul, Rushdie* [One by one: Individualism in literature—Michaux, Naipaul, Rushdie]. Paris: Seuil.

Punday, Daniel. 2003. *Narrative Bodies. Toward a Corporeal Narratology*. New York: Palgrave Macmillan.

Puolakka, Kalle. 2010. Review of *Embodying Pragmatism: Richard Shusterman's Philosophy and Literary Theory*, by Wojciech Małecki. *European Journal of Pragmatism and American Philosophy* 2 (2): 233–39.

Shusterman, Richard. 1990. "Beneath Interpretation: Against Hermeneutic Holism." *The Monist* 73 (2), *The Theory of Interpretation*: 181–204.

—. 1995. "Interview with Professor Shusterman." By Eva Maria Stadler and Thomas Trummer. *Austria* (August): 17–21.

—. 1997. "The End of Aesthetic Experience." *The Journal of Aesthetics and Art Criticism* 55 (1): 29–41.

—. 1999. "Somaesthetics: A Disciplinary Proposal." *The Journal of Aesthetics and Art Criticism* 57 (3): 299–313. Accessed October 3, 2015. http://bit.ly/2moPLJq.

—. 2000. "An Interview with Richard Shusterman." By Günter Leypoldt. *Quarterly of Language, Literature, and Culture* 48 (1): 57–71.

—. 2002. "Self-styling after the 'End of Art': An Interview with Richard Shusterman." By Chantal Pontbriand and Olivier Asselin. *Parachute: Contemporary Art Magazine* 105 (1). Accessed October 3, 2015. http://bit.ly/2jZEywl.

—. 2006. "Thinking Through the Body, Educating for the Humanities: A Plea for Somaesthetics." *Journal of Aesthetic Education* 40 (1): 1–21.

—. 2008. *Body Consciousness: A Philosophy of Mindfulness and Somaesthetics*. Cambridge: Cambridge University Press.

—. 2009. "Entretien avec Richard Shusterman: Interview with Richard Shusterman." By Bernard Andrieu. *Corps au travail*, no. 6: 5–10. Accessed October 3, 2015. http://bit.ly/2jZFwsn.

—. 2011a. "Le corps et les arts: Le besoin de soma-esthétique." [The Body and the Arts: The Need for Somaesthetics]. Translated by Brigitte Rollet. *Diogène*, no. 233–34: 9–29.

—. 2011b. "Somatic Style." *The Journal of Aesthetics and Art Criticism* 69 (2): 147–59. DOI: 10.1111/j.1540-6245.2011.01457.x.

Simondon, George. 1992. "The Genesis of the Individual." In *Zone 6: Incorporations*. Edited by Jonathan Crary, and Sanford Kwinter, 297–319. New York: Zone Books.

Notes

1 See, amongst many other contributions, Jay 2014.
2 We can say that the embodied cognition theory is the latest form of philosophical monism. See Dennett 2006.
3 See Shusterman 2002.
4 See Shusterman 1990, 1997.
5 See Macé 2004.

CHAPTER THREE

THERMO-PERFORMATICS: ENERGY AND PERFORMANCE STUDIES

KONRAD WOJNOWSKI

Among many notions used by performance studies scholars two in particular seem to occupy center stage, namely performativity and liminality. Although redeveloped on numerous occasions and in different contexts, they remain in a strong and steady relation to such areas of study as materiality of communication and processuality of cultural phenomena. As I would like to point out, both concepts can be more precisely defined and understood if supplemented by a definition of energy that would be formulated throughout from the perspective of performance studies. Building on some basic observations from thermodynamics, this essay is meant to provide such a definition and therefore make it possible to rethink communication and performance from a unified point of view. I will try to demonstrate that the understanding of energy provided by modern thermodynamics not only supports many intuitions inscribed in different definitions of performativity and liminality, but also opens up spaces for further elaborations. In the first part of my article I will briefly address the problem of the ambiguous references to energy in chosen theories of performativity and liminality. Then I will explain why the energy-related dimension of communication processes has not become a pivotal problem for humanities scholars. After making these introductory remarks I will proceed to my main argument. I intend to put forward a definition of energy and three related concepts: system, energetic distribution and context. Most of the ideas that I introduce will not be completely new for performance studies scholars. My intent is not to reinvent, but rather to refocus and re-contextualize, a few dispersed concepts within a hopefully coherent framework related to the notion of energy. This endeavor gains particular importance in light of the recent interdisciplinary interests of many theoreticians who aim at creating a non-essentialist ontology which could bind together many efforts scattered across a range of fields.

I am not confident that introducing hard sciences into the humanities will in any way instantly lead to promised lands of objectivity. Quite the contrary, in this article my sole purpose is only to borrow some tools from other scholars and elaborate on concepts which are frequently used, but can still appear ambiguous. In other words, I want to stress that my endeavor is not aimed at introducing scientific objectivity into the field of performance studies, but to offer definitions for concepts that are being widely used, although they have not been precisely explained. Therefore my goals are purely operational. Thermodynamics—the discipline to which I would like to refer—has always been just a way of looking at the physical world, at times incompatible with other perspectives. It has little ambition to explain reality in its totality; it works where it is applicable. While classical mechanics, an invention of the 17th century, focused mainly on trajectories and velocities—movements organized around a linear path and completely reversible time—thermodynamics, which was developed in the 19th century, searched for different properties: heat, temperature or entropy, introducing irreversibility to physics.

Performativity, Liminality, Energy

It is worthwhile considering how the concepts of performativity and liminality can be complemented by the notion of energy and why we should regard them as combined in the first place. The former term has been in use for a considerable time, and one of its roots may be traced back to J. L. Austin's theory of speech acts. Austin was particularly interested in the work that is done with the aid of language, which already implied some affinities between linguistics and physics, regardless of how remote these disciplines might be. His thought, deeply rooted in the tradition of analytic philosophy, neglects one of the basic premises of this tradition—the importance of truthfulness and falseness of a speech act. Instead, he underlines the importance of the dynamic, changeable context—institutional, cognitive or spatial. The idea of context, in the Austinian perspective, resembles another notion—that of a system, where the speech act is a way of doing work (performing). James Loxley convincingly shows Austin's materialistic interests in defining performativity when he draws an analogy between a speech act and a machine, both yielding uniform end-products in the course of predictable succession of procedures, which can be repeated, or rerun (2007, 91).

If Loxley's interpretation were to be followed, the definition of performativity would be reduced to the ability to do work with words. But Loxley's remark oversimplifies Austin's philosophy, tying it to mechanic discourses of the 18th and 19th centuries—speech acts were never conceived as cogs in a great machine. On the contrary, Austin could not have put more emphasis on their enormous impact and destabilizing potential for systems, as they could create new contexts and set new boundaries. In other words, the work done by language does not have to be understood in terms of mechanistic strictness and determinism. A declaration of war issued by a head of a state—seen from Austin's perspective—is possible thanks to the institutional hierarchies which enable him to issue the declaration, but it also produces new machines needed to execute orders, enable new speech acts and found new institutions. In other words, a speech act may release huge amounts of energy that have to be channeled and, irrespective of all previous preparation, it will require some adaptation to new circumstances. Words not only work for us, they build our world.

Performativity, at first a linguistic term, has undergone an evolutionary process and has begun to refer to an ability of any code—like gestures or social conventions—to perform and not only to mean. Nevertheless, the core of Austin's argument was preserved: any exchange of signs (*semiosis*) is able to produce material effects that exceed the dimension of referential meanings. For something to be called performative, it also has to be communicational—one cannot ask about how things are done (with words) without acknowledging that (for instance) a specific use of words happens in a communicational situation. Furthermore, this communication has to be conceived in its materiality—it is not an abstract process of exchanging ideal structures, but an exchange of energy that is governed by signs. This issue was worked out in detail by Erika Fischer-Lichte in her *Transformative Power of Performance* and by Jacques Derrida in *Signature Event Context*, but neither of these authors provides a clear definition of energy. Both of these problems—of energy and communication—are also addressed by many performance scholars who use the notion of liminality. Still, I will try to show that, when one tries to make use of liminality as a vantage point of any analysis, a different set of problems will appear and some doubt can arise concerning the possibility of treating the term "liminality" as a general category with ontological pretensions.

Liminality—unlike performativity—was not invented as a general term, although it is very often used as such. The term in its origins (the writings of Arnold van Gennep) referred to the middle phase of rituals in which participants no longer possessed their initial status, but the transformation—for example, from boy to man—was not yet complete.

Subjects of the ritual find themselves on the threshold between two states, in the so-called in-betweenness. Liminal events are not only objects of inquiry for performance studies; they also shape the discipline itself. As Richard Schechner states: "Performance studies is 'inter'—in between. It is intergeneric, interdisciplinary, intercultural—and therefore inherently unstable. … It is inherently 'in between' and therefore cannot be pinned down or located exactly" (1998, 360). The triumphant place of "liminality" as a focal point of performance studies was sealed by Jon McKenzie, who established this state as a dominant feature of contemporary western societies (2001, 49–53). In the case of both Schechner and McKenzie, liminality became an umbrella term that covers everything: from our culture to the discipline that studies it. But Arpa Szakolczai has convincingly shown in *Reflexive Historical Sociology* that this term, when applied in the field of social sciences, may well be more complicated from a political standpoint than it seems at first glance (2000, 207–218), thus demonstrating the limits of liminality as a general idea.

To sum up, liminality itself remains in between the historical and the universal—in between an abstract model and its historical implementation as a social norm or specific social procedure. It can of course be formulated in abstract terms as a particular way of circulating energy in a system, but in my opinion, it still remains too specific to provide foundations for any methodological approach. Similarly to performativity, it brings to the fore the problems of energy, communication and processuality, but unnecessarily narrows down the field of research: only one mode of energy circulation is at stake. Moreover, making use of the term liminality without previously defining what is meant by energy may cause numerous misunderstandings, and may in fact make it difficult to grasp its peculiarity. When liminality ceased referring exclusively to rituals, the term became unspecific. What happens when one is no longer speaking of simple rituals and liminality enters the dimension of governance and economics? What is liminality in theater performances, which rarely qualify as rituals? The questions point to one explanation: during the evolution of performance studies, which incorporated new fields of research, some of the discipline's basic terms became questionable, creating a situation that may call for a redesigning of the object of study. Before I elaborate in more detail on the concept of thermodynamic energy and the possibilities it opens up for performance studies, I would like to recount a peculiar story of the disappearance of energy from the horizon of cultural studies to justify my aims from a different perspective.

Culture and Energy—A Lost Path

Energy seems, at first sight, to be a crucial concept when analyzing communicational and media systems, simply because every medium is used for energy propagation and is propelled by it: from the muscle energy of people carrying stones to build pyramids to the nuclear-plant energy powering computer networks. However, the study of energy languished after Second World War and "energy" was replaced by another prominent notion, that of information. Norbert Wiener, the founding father of cybernetics, famously stated:

> If the seventeenth and early eighteenth centuries are the age of clocks, and the later eighteenth and the nineteenth centuries constitute the age of steam engines, the present time is the age of communication and control. (1989, 1)

However, it should be noted that Wiener's account of the relation between energy and information remained deeply ambivalent, as he sometimes stressed the intertwined character of both phenomena and sometimes drew a distinct line between them. That is why his works continued to be inspirational for some anthropologists (like Roy A. Rappaport) who were occasionally interested in energy exchange through rituals (Rappaport 2002, 37–64). This was not the case for cybernetics' unwanted child, informatics, which entirely neglected the importance of energy as a subject of interest. Computer and Artificial Intelligence (AI) studies became dominant in the mid-1950s, holding back cybernetics and any further developments in this field, which could have also been oriented toward energy-dependent processes. Andrew Pickering makes an interesting remark on this transition in the realm of academic interests. He claims that one reason why AI studies became so popular is that "the brain and mind," together, can be easily viewed "as the organ of knowledge, and AI thus conceived presents a straightforward problem of mimicking very familiar (especially to academics) mental performances" (2010, 62).

Eventually, scientific interest in energy outside the field of physics was abandoned, and, instead, new general trends developed; even paradigm shifts towards abstraction and idealization through mathematics took place. Thus cybernetics had nearly disappeared from universities across the world even before it had a chance to establish its basic fields of study, which is regrettable, for it was the only discipline that at its core wanted to marry hard sciences and the humanities. A new kind of Platonism came to power, one that searches for a common ground for human brains and microchips in the immaterial world of information and algorithms—the quest to replace grey matter with the non-matter of emulated brains has begun.

Paradoxically, it was easier to imagine analyzing culture from the perspective of thermodynamics in the 19th century than it is now. Auguste Comte's famous "social physics" is a great example of the approach, as are works of other less-known theoreticians like John Tyndall and Balfour Stewart, who wanted to use concepts from the newly emerging branch of physics as tools for creating final explanations of the nature of society and for criticizing growing social disorder from conservative standpoints (Myers 1985). For some early "social prophets," thermodynamics and Darwinism alike promised a new universal history and in a way were used for reinforcing the idea of a linear historical progression. After this short period of fascination with thermodynamics, the following attempts at applying it in the humanities failed to create even a small branch in any of the disciplines.[1]

Though, at this moment it is impossible even briefly to elaborate on the attempts to use the concepts of thermodynamics within the humanities— since they have been at most early drafts, proposals and intuitions, lacking coherence as a whole—it may be said without a doubt that a new field of study is slowly emerging and may hold great potential for the social sciences. Even if the inspiration for the humanities will not come from scattered sociologists, studies in complexity (i.e. Philip Ball) and new advances in brain theory (Karl Friston's theory of free energy) might introduce energy and thermodynamics into the humanities through the back door; and we should hope for this—there is much more room for interest in human cultural activity in theories concerned with energy than in those reflecting dreams about synthetic brains emulated on computers.

Despite these recent efforts, I would still conclude that energy was generally lost to the humanities for two main reasons. Firstly, there was the aforementioned decision by cybernetics, computer and media studies to follow their paths so as to make a clear distinction between energy and information. Studies of human communication excluded humanist scholars who would be potentially interested in the materiality of communication, allowing only trained mathematicians to enter through the doors of the new elite disciplines. Secondly, cultural theorists and critics reached out— or continued an inherited inclination—for theories focused on texts, symbols and representations; in other words, they took the path of semantics. To some extent, with the noteworthy exception of Jon McKenzie's book *Perform or Else*, even performance studies continuously referred to semantic theories, while trying to overcome their basic premises.[2] I do not claim that material aspects of culture or communication were completely excluded from the humanities, but rather that theories which revolved around the duality (and metaphysics) of sign and meaning gained prominence and were established as an absolute reference point (Barad 2003, 801). Materiality was seen from the perspective of the immaterial: information in hard sciences and accordingly meaning in humanities gained prominence at the cost of matter or energy. As Katherine Hayles points out in the context of the hard sciences, "this was a result of negotiations specific to the circumstances of the U.S. techno-scientific culture during and immediately following World War II," (1999, 50) and information gained prominence, because it was surrounded by an aura of techno-optimism and supported a myth of overcoming the limitations of nature with new discoveries and inventions. In the case of the humanities this was probably caused by the mid-twentieth-century hegemony of structuralism together with the metaphysical inclinations rooted in various European philosophical traditions.

"Thermo-performatics"—Basic Terms

At this point in my discussion, four notions will be defined—energy, system, context and energy distribution—forming a set of basic coordinates, which will support the understanding of energy as a potentially focal object of study for performance studies.

Energy: As far as thermodynamics is concerned, there is no simpler definition than that of energy—it is not explanatory, as the definition does not aim to give us insights into the truth about the universe or to draw a powerful ontological horizon. It simply states: energy is the ability to do work or cause change (Chaisson 2009, 3268), therefore it is to be understood within a specific system. This definition is only a beginning, because it still is not known who or what is doing the work, and how these changes are to be measured. Thus, I would like to elaborate on this simple concept (leaving the statistical mechanics aside).

What does such a definition have to offer for performance studies? First of all, it gives clarity. When we speak of the energetic dimension of, for example, a theatrical performance, anything may be meant: from symbolic surplus (energy as a remainder of symbolic communication) to an ethereal quality (the very material bond between living creatures). Such use of the term undoubtedly gives a lot of ground for creative speculation, but none for solid critique. For instance, most performances of so-called post-dramatic theater seem surprisingly conservative in terms of energy: actors are given space for movement and speech, whereas spectators sit in their chairs and are allowed only to rebel, walk out of the building or fall asleep (rebellion, which is actually only an attempt at changing energetic configuration, happens so rarely that it puts the whole institution to shame). To put it briefly, the energy of actors is used for establishing dynamic systems (communicating), while the energy of spectators is used (at best) for acute cognitive processes. Moreover, speaking about the energetic dimension of a given performance helps bridge the gap between two perspectives: embodied "subjective" experience which grounds an analysis, and an objective description which tries to fix a static model.

To take a different example, a university lecture is a similarly conventional and uneven performance: one individual is responsible for conducting communicational traffic, and the students' only possibilities are reception and transformation (without production). In both cases the situation is fixed not only because a set of rules forces the participants to obey, but even more because they are not in any way asked to creatively adapt. A lot of work is done by one side, far less by the other. Both situations funnily resemble a highly improbable situation of the arrangement of gas particles in a piston—all particles (and their kinetic energy) move to one side, leaving the other side empty. According to entropy law these particles will scatter inside the container to reach the state of highest probability (and disorder), so both aforementioned situations may be understood as efforts to overcome entropy through closure—interactions with the environment are made impossible in order to achieve equilibrium. Such an arrangement of energy potentials is possible in physics only when we construct a closed system which does not exchange matter or energy with the environment. Energy therefore can be researched only through actions and potentials— the only thing that matters is who does work and who is given a chance to do work (or to cause change). In both instances—during theater performances and lectures—I propose to understand energy in a strong relation to the physical actions in a given space. Someone is given room to act and someone remains stationary. It may seem an obvious observation, but to start from reflecting on infrastructural conditions in which an event takes place and how these conditions are maintained during the event, is to not take them for granted. Surprisingly, while studying cultural systems, we rarely follow this path. While remembering that thermodynamic systems in culture are always emergent (I will elaborate more on this topic later on), it should be distinctly noted that nothing can be said about energy without actually seeing the work done. In other words, distribution of energy within a system can only be observed when we pay attention to the actual work and infrastructures that enable it.

That is why the task proposed here is to recognize ways in which energy can be distributed and catalyzed—sometimes very still stage arrangements (e.g. actors not moving) may produce extreme tensions in the audience thanks to conventional procedures (e.g. suspense). Despite the complexity of such an analysis, which has to be well informed in matters of the performance's reception, one thing remains simple: energy is measured by what is or can potentially be done; the whole process avoids any metaphysical claims. One thing should also be noted at this point—such an analysis is impossible from a subjective perspective. Viewing performances as systems is only possible when we build an abstract model and make approximations, namely, single out entities and describe their changeable behavior and the relations in which they partake. It is crucial to note that this model cannot be static—systems emerge dynamically and lay down conditions for other systems. For instance, if we are to study a theatrical performance as an energetic system we should start by focusing on the dynamics of the preparatory phase and study the hierarchies in the group, the methods of work, and the surprising events that occurred before the actual performance took place. Only then, after we have delineated the initial, material conditions, can we see continuities and discontinuities in communication within the group and with the audience. To see the openness of the theater and its energetic potential we should look outside the auditorium for different spaces of possibility and never lose sight of the changes that a given system undergoes.[3]

To sum up, taking energy as the main focus of interest allows us to study the system's economics: how energy is set free, stored and processed during communication; only then can something be said about inequalities within the system. This kind of perspective demands a completely different starting point: the main assumption is that all semantic processes, ritualistic conventions, mimetic behaviors etc. serve one fundamental purpose—distribution of energy. A lecturer or a performer in the first instance establishes a system of energy distribution and subsequently sustains it through distribution of knowledge. Information, knowledge and symbols are not external to energy. On the contrary, energy is the condition of their existence, making possible any expression—every sign or bit of information is carved out in energy. It is not that energy is a necessary and troublesome addition to symbolic/informational processes (a structural approach) or manifests itself only in ruptures and disturbances (a post-structural approach that can be found in the philosophy of Jacques Derrida), but rather that every communication is inherently reliant on the exchange of energy. Hence, one will need to describe a system in order to speak of energy and one should be interested in symbolic exchanges only as propagators of energy-related processes. On both of these notions I will try to elaborate below.

System: When defining energy as the ability to do work or cause change, I said that it can be only applied within a specific system. To govern and measure energy in thermodynamics one has to construct a system, conceptual or physical—Carnot's engine is a great example of one. In 1824 Sadi Carnot invented a hypothetical machine which proved to be essential not for engineering, but rather for theoretical purposes, namely, dividing thermodynamic process into a series of states. Thermodynamics—before it codified all its laws—had to introduce devices that were both practical and theoretical: it needed simple systems to make basic assumptions about energy. To measure energy, observable work had to be done or changes made. One needed a model that was vivid and easy to imagine. The system was therefore both an ideal model and a real device: invention and abstraction.

Engines and other mechanical devices served of course as models for many researchers in the field of the humanities, who also spoke of social groups in terms of systems. For instance, Roy A. Rappaport, representing cultural materialism within anthropology, tried to establish a theory of culture concerned more with flows of energy and materials than with contents and values.[4] He spoke of rituals in terms of cybernetics devices—homeostats and transducers (2002, 61). For Rappaport rituals could be understood as machines, more complicated than Carnot's engine and manifesting behaviors that can be considered "living," but still, in his intentions, he remained mechanistic and reductionist. There are always distant perspectives which allow one to see machines that govern our cultural life, but, when you take a step closer, an abstract systems disperses into many unstable and more complicated microsystems—a high level (global) equilibrium is achievable only thanks to many (local) nonequilibrium processes. A university is a good example of a global machine—it works by steadily redistributing knowledge among thousands of students every year, whereas on a smaller scale local catastrophes occur frequently. Students discussing and revolting against transferred knowledge cause the system to adapt and develop new concepts. Seen globally, the university, highly hierarchical, institutionalized and interconnected through colossal networks and interfaces, is unable to evolve and change. However, on a smaller scale, when groups of people are at work, their quirks and instabilities allow the system to produce new concepts. The main problem with the mechanistic perspective is not its theoretical simplification (because modeling is always to some extent simplifying), but its philosophical consequences: the creative potential of unstable, nonlinear behaviors is valorized negatively or reduced to "bugs" or "mistakes." If we are searching for a more humanistic approach and want see the world not through the simplifying lenses of technology, we have to reach for more complex inspirations.

The question is how to define a system for performance studies and offer a diverse and practical toolbox to research energy processes. First of all, it may be helpful to introduce the very basic definition of a system as "sets of elements standing in interrelation among themselves and with environment" (Bertalanffy 1972, 417). But how can those elements be described and in what relation to each other do they stand? I would like to follow Manuel DeLanda's insights in *A New Philosophy of Society,* postulating a materialistic theory which avoids mechanistic, totalizing metaphors. If one wants performance studies to focus on energies, instabilities and openness, his theory offers very precise remarks on the ontology of open systems. DeLanda, one of the most important commentators on the work of Gilles Deleuze and a representative of the newly emerging field of speculative materialism, states that avoiding essences can be only achieved by defining each element through its relation to the exterior. No part within the system can be separated without becoming something completely different. Even extremely specified entities like human organs cannot be simply transplanted and expected to work somewhere else within a few seconds—they need time and stimulation to adapt to the new environment. Their abstract function alone will not suffice to form an essence, a thing sealed off "in itself." In this respect his theory not only differs from essentialist perspectives, but also from most functionalistic theories. Accordingly, we move Hamlet from performance A to performance B, although the spoken text does not differ. Moreover, Hamlets from one production are not the same from one day to the next, because in the meantime the system has evolved, catastrophes have happened, entropy has been at work: the actor has changed his lines, or has adopted a different attitude, and numerous other things could have affected his role.

DeLanda states that even if organs that make a larger whole are closely related, their interconnections (or the "relations" that bind them together) are not "necessary" in the logical sense. Instead, he describes these interrelations as "contingently obligatory." These links do not arise in the course of logical necessity, but in the course of evolution which they have undergone, as if, together, side by side, or, to use DeLanda's term, in the course of "coevolution" (2006, 12). Functions and relations are not essential structures, but realized possibilities, effects of long-lasting dynamic processes that never cease—every potential catastrophe will force an organism to adapt and alter the nature of a system. Correspondingly, the problem of essences will not arise when we analyze thermodynamic systems: they describe physical spaces according to physical parameters, such as temperature, heat, entropy etc.—and those are never given for a long period of time. The only way to preserve them is to make a snapshot that will show us an abstracted state. Thermodynamic spaces are never metricized—there is no concept of distance, only intensities, which are more temporal than spatial. It is of no importance if two systems are 5 or 10 cm away from each other—what counts is the amount of energy transferred from one to another. Or to put it differently, energy has no direction (vector). Every system is described by thermodynamic values and relations to its environment and not by its position in space. In other words, thermodynamic space has no norm (Byung 2004, 23). Boundary conditions (borders) are never fixed in space; they can be only potentially impermeable in closed and isolated systems, but in the case of cultural phenomena they never are. Academic lectures, mentioned earlier, are carefully organized to possess such borders, which allow for one-sided distribution of energy. But this kind of organization is always a utopia and fortunately so—if we could block the energetic investments of students or reduce their role to isolated and introvert recording, the university would lose all its purpose, as sound recorders would do the job of students incomparably better. What I want to describe is therefore a continuous and time-dependent movement of energy between system and surroundings, remembering that there are specified and various rules for such processes (there is no axiom, such as feedback, which would sufficiently describe all systems). For this one has to get rid of the mechanistic metaphor and turn towards other ways of thinking about systems—ones that do not take engines, computers or other machines as models for further conceptualization.

Almost any system that can be of interest for performance studies will be complex, nonlinear and often unstable. Almost any system that concerns human beings is complex, nonlinear and often unstable. Any system we call "cultural" is at the same time biological, unless we speak of empty libraries. Cultural systems are no assembly lines processing and storing books (cultural texts). Any kind of order observed in the work of a system emerges as a result of work of many entities capable of action (agencies). This set of simple assumptions is a mix of basic truths that lie at heart of complexity studies, a discipline strongly influenced by thermodynamics, and their possible extensions to the field of cultural studies. The aim of complexity studies is to describe systems that exist in nonequilibrium states—namely, those which are open and constantly changing—because of the constant movement (flux) of energy. When one compares this approach to the mechanistic metaphor of cybernetics, one can see that not only the subject of study changes—from simple devices to very complex and unpredictable systems—but also does the way of researching the given field of study, of grasping the material at hand. A ritual can be taken as a simple device or a complex system which involves many individuals and undergoes highly unstable changes. This complexity and instability does not mean that every system eventually turns out to be chaotic and unpredictable, but rather that every form of order is "emergent." Philip Ball writes that we can observe many examples of emergent collective behavior in nature. The most illustrative ones are the behavioral patterns observable in the movements of swarms of insects or flocks of birds. The term "emergence," Ball explains, refers in this context to the impossibility of predicting its system's evolution from the point of view of single element(s). That is to say, the order of the whole cannot be deduced from the laws of the particular. Hence, the study of emergence relies only on observation (or probabilistic simulations) of these unpredictable patterns of self-organization, which are not imposed by any centralized command unit (brain, leader), but emerge, as if, "instinctively" from within the system (2012, X).

Several questions emerge out of this synthetic description of the subject of complexity studies. Firstly, in what way does such approach differ from the mechanistic metaphor? Secondly, what are the roots of this approach and how can we name it? Thirdly, what does it offer for performance studies? I will attempt to answer them all in one brief description. Systems—seen from the perspective of complexity—emerge through negotiation between their elements and energy input. They do not follow linear logic, in which one element has its own specific and independent function of producing a fixed effect. Every entity (agent) is constructed in interaction (communication) with other entities. Patterns, orders and functions emerge as necessities among possibilities—islands of stability amid chaotic unpredictability. The most important characteristic of the mechanistic metaphor is that it works on the strength of determinism and causal relations between parts. In turn, complex systems operate on a world model which is characterized by randomness, irreversibility and spontaneously emerging relations. This radically different approach is rooted in the works of Ilya Prigogine, a Belgian physical chemist, who worked on such topics as dissipation, chaos theory, complex systems and second wave thermodynamics. For his work as a chemist and mathematician he was awarded the Nobel Prize, but he also—along with Isabelle Stengers—wrote more philosophically oriented texts on the meaning of his scientific findings for philosophy, in particular for new materialisms or the philosophy of science. His general observations were formulated in opposition to well established branches of science, which

even in the late 20th century were still marked by the deterministic
philosophies of the 18th century. His idea was to start from a point where
different sciences meet—namely chemistry, mathematics and physics—
and the notion of system served as a perfect vantage point. Inspired by
nonlinear thermodynamics, he offered a new mode of investigating
scientific problems which would take into account the unstable and chaotic
powers of nature. He argued that studies on chaos, nonlinearity and
indeterminism should move from the margins of science and start shaping
our ideas of nature, instead of functioning only as exceptions and oddities.
Leaving his most important notions aside, I would like to point out one
concept that is of the highest importance to the understanding of cultural
systems. Prigogine made the argument that while many deterministic
simplifications and idealizations of Newtonian mechanical physics may be
viable and useful, it is the paradigm of nonlinearity and complexity that
should provide the main reference point for the organic world. He
observes that, while infrequent in the inorganic universe, the "nonlinear
reactions"—whose results affect (in the course of "a feedback action")
their originating causes—are recurrent in the organic universe. This fact is
widely attested to by the research conducted in the realm of molecular
biology (Prigogine and Stengers 1984, 153).

    Nonlinear and nonequilibrium processes exist of course outside the
biological realm—weather is a great example of a chaotic phenomenon—
but sciences interested in chaotic behaviors still remain in the background,
far behind mechanistic approaches. But when it comes to organic and
living systems, nonequilibrium thermodynamics turns out to be the most
accurate tool for understanding them, as it allows systems to be
conceptualized in terms of emergent structures created through energetic
processes and overcoming entropy. Likewise, many theories associated
with performance studies manifest a similar approach to culture,
perceiving it in terms of emergence and irreversibility, although without
reflecting on the (material) background of these phenomena. From Victor
Turner, who indirectly makes use of thermodynamics by focusing on
states—instead of statuses and hierarchies—of social groups, and J. L.
Austin, who ponders the infelicity of speech acts, to Erika Fischer-Lichte,
who elaborates on reasons for instability in theatrical performances, the
question about the status of energy was hidden in the background.

    I would like to make an argument that seems strikingly banal, but is
nonetheless exceptionally uncommon: if we were to study energy in
culture, the latter should be understood organically; not in terms of a
simple metaphor (culture as organism), but rather through the lenses of
thermodynamics and studies of complex systems, which provide many

valuable insights into unstable, nonlinear behaviors. I want to suggest that performance studies should focus on culture's performance (not performances in culture), while acknowledging the biological aspect of culture: it is always a theory of human behaviors. Not human, all too human, but human in the sense of being part of the biosphere. In conclusion, to analyze energy in communication we need to define systems, but at the same time pay attention to non-linear behaviors, places of instability and every occurring transformation. According to Prigogine, openness and non-linearity constitute basic laws in the biological world, and we should bear this in mind if we want to emphasize culture's livingness (implying change and movement) at the cost of its humanistic "cultural-ness" (relying on heritage). In addition, thinking in terms of open systems helps us to overcome the unnecessary dualism of subjective and objective perspectives, because any analytic abstraction has to be grounded in empirical data and embodied observation, which spotlights nonlinear and rare occurrences. At the same time the system- and energy-oriented approach allows solid critique which outlines the material infrastructures, techniques and spaces of possibility which enable such unpredictable events to take place.

Distribution of energy: There are numerous or even innumerable ways of doing work/exchanging energy within a system: you can say a word (for example a short word like "no" and break someone's heart) or you can move a table. You can eat a burger or you can photosynthesize. Cultural systems which mostly involve human beings as operators are characterized by a particularity that is not shared by other systems, namely the use of complex languages. Austin's theory of speech acts can be considered the most important elaboration on this topic in the field of performance studies, as he was interested exactly in the topic of doing work by the means of language. In this part of my article I would like to briefly rework Austin's most important thesis about the performativity of language on the basis of the above-sketched thermodynamic theory of cultural systems and some remarks drawn from René Thom's biosemantics, which introduces the context of biological, discontinuous behaviors into the study of meaning. What interests me at this point is the question, which is also somehow very dear to performance studies scholars, of how energy can be propagated through language. Thus, I am interested in how it is possible for performance studies to speak of communication, without making distinctions between the semiotic and the performative or semiosis and aesthesis.

Many theories of language are based on a metaphysical division between the signifier (sign) and the signified (meaning). This division seems to provide an absolute vantage point for almost every theory of language—even pragmatics is interested in constructing meaning through context, and deconstruction eternally fights against metaphysics, its greatest supervillain. Whichever language theory we take, we will come across the notion of meaning as the most important distinctive characteristic of human language. This perspective is also present in Austin's theory, as at first he tended to single out performative speech acts from other uses of language and only later spoke of the performative aspect of language. Speaking of thermodynamic and biological systems in which human beings communicate requires that we take a completely different approach. One of the inherent characteristics of biological systems—not mentioned before—is their ability to communicate, that is, to negotiate and set energy values and patterns between parts. According to Prigogine and Stengers, dynamic systems which change patterns and introduce asymmetry have to communicate, that is to say that parts have to act as a whole. Communication is here understood not as an exchange of information, but of energy—a simple ability to interact. Hence, we have to reflect upon a difficult problem: how is it possible to exchange energy through language, and more importantly, how is it possible to change energy values of particular, dynamical systems? Of course, on the very basic level every production of symbols requires energy: the act of writing is a physical gesture in the same way that speech sounds are only possible thanks to the working of throat muscles; also hearing, reading and understanding rely on energy-exchange processes—electric impulses switching on and off in the cerebral cortex. Or to put it differently, a message is formatted energy that has the ability to make an impact on receptors: a sentence is a series of lightings. It does not mean that the message is meaningless or can be only measured quantitatively: these lightings leave marks—they engrave commands on plastic human brains. This simple standpoint—despite many differences—can be connected to Thom's statements about the expressive nature of language,[5] in which he claims that language is propelled by the necessity to cause significant changes in the environment (Thom 1985, 289). For him, there is no evolutionary rupture between the expressivity of animals and that of men, because language is not used for describing (doubling of reality on a plane of ideal forms), but for expansion in space and homeostatic regulation. Signs are constructed through irreversible processes: perceptual stimuli are imprinted on our brains as models that can be converted into signs. There is a materialistic continuity between object, icon and symbol. Only through this continuity is a reverse path possible—we can act upon the world through language. If the meaning of a sign were sealed off from reality (as representation), were completely arbitrary or even purely contextual depending on immaterial conventions, it would not be possible "to do things with words." Moreover, the nature of these signs is never given once and for all; they possess the quality of "pregnancy," inasmuch as they are always morphologically unstable. This means that in the process of communication (or thinking) they can adapt and "give birth" to new forms. Language, like other biological forms, is capable of evolving, and thus of overcoming communicational noise. Signs do not simply change meaning through time by substituting one for another, but rather undergo a discontinuous process of evolution—mostly based on smaller or bigger catastrophes (every sign can be seen as a break from continuity). Every sign can be understood as a way of changing energetic distributions within a dynamic system. Such an evolutionist perspective on language implies constant work of actualization and localization—meaning happens always within a system: it morphs, evolves and has the ability to cause change by interacting with the environment:

> we are led very quickly to make the distinction between the intrinsic meaning of the sign … and its spatiotemporal localization, which is the domain of spacetime, where the sign exerts its imperative effect (or sometimes "performative" according to the terminology of the Oxford School). (Thom 1985, 287)

In this passage Thom says something very similar to what Austin claims—every sign eventually ends up in a specific environment, a context, which will determine its potential, that is to say, give it material form. But what is interesting here is the fact that the "energetic charge" of a sign is always "small" compared to the systems involved (Bundgaard, Stjernfelt 2010, 50). Thom's theory opens language to the environment and lets it be understood as a kind of energetic operator, which makes possible acting (doing work) and changing non-linguistic reality, as there is no distinction between language and the world, only discontinuities. From this perspective we can say that every sign/sentence/message functions as order and even something that appears as alienated as description primarily has an imperative form. If we think of the first possible descriptions communicated by prehistoric hunters to the rest of the tribe after an unsuccessful hunt, these messages had to instruct and enable them to take more successful approaches. They were not intended to describe (refer to the past), but to change (point to the future). Such orders not only evoked cognitive reactions in the listeners, but also structured future endeavors, modified gestures and strategies, allowing energetic gains to be made (more animals hunted). Language in communication therefore can trigger and catalyze non-linguistic reactions that involve large—far larger in comparison to basic expenditure during the act of speech—amounts of energy.

Taking into consideration Austin's example of the performativity of marriage, the priest not only pronounces a couple "husband and wife," but also "fosters" the new relation through preaching: he explains at length what it means to be "husband and wife." In this sense a performative speech act gives birth to new forms within the social dimension that are responsible for energy distribution—in an old-fashioned, Catholic model it would mean designating the man as authority (distributer). Thus, we can understand semiosis as governing energy; semantics becomes a theory of change and not of meaning. Eve Kosofsky Sedgwick pointed towards such a possibility in her re-reading of Austin, which puts emphasis on the transformative impact of performative utterances, and similar arguments can be made on the basis of information theory.[6] Karen Barad's theory of "posthumanist performativity" also explores the physical impact of every (even purely descriptive) linguistic utterance. In conclusion I would like to explain this "energetic inequality" between a speech act and its consequences by introducing another term, that of context.

Context: Despite the popularity of the term, "context" remains an ill-defined concept. Although Austin speaks at length about the contextual nature of performatives, the notion itself remains undefined in his works. We may infer that sometimes context designates institutional surroundings that verify and validate every speech act (binding social norms), and sometimes connotes emotional states (moods), but its *modus operandi* is left unspecified. In the tradition of analytic philosophy (and contextual epistemology) there is also no distinct definition of this term, whereas cognitive psychology offers only a basic distinction between context and co-text, which designated two meanings of context that can be found in the dictionary. Co-text is described as the parts of a statement, in a spoken or written form, that come before or after the word or the passage in question. Their presence typically influences the meaning of the given passage or word. Context, in turn, is explained as referring to a happening (an event or a state): it comprises conditions (or circumstances) or actualities amidst which a particular event takes place.[7]

The problem with both definitions is that they are merely descriptive and not explanatory, as they do not attempt answering the question of how it is possible for signs to morph and change their function in different environments, even if the sender and receiver stay the same. How is it possible that objects on a theater stage can cast shadows on the meanings of words? I would like to offer an explanation of this phenomenon, relying on already-given definitions of systems and energy distribution.

The example of a head of state declaring war offers the most vivid image of materialist relations partaking in this particular speech act. To declare war the speech act has to be properly placed. It has to be expressed by a head of state in proper conditions. Firstly, a device needs to be created, possessing an enormous potential energy—a device capable of declaring war, a famous red button or a speech act in the form of a military order. Such a device requires a human being or an automatic program capable of triggering it. Then this device has to be connected to other devices (media) and energetic reservoirs. They allow for propagation of a message in space and time—triggering one device after another causes a chain reaction that releases huge amounts of stored energy. In the cinema such a device is mounted on a projector and is called a switch; in the theater it might be a lever that triggers the curtain. A president is not always capable of declaring war, as speech acts need sensitive receptors— not every word he says automatically attaches itself to bureaucratic machines and operates them. Language as a form of energetic distribution is therefore not dependent on subjects, but on places which provide a suitable infrastructure and energetic potential.[8] Hence, the president may declare war not because he is the head of state, but because he has access to a space where such action is possible. Accordingly, excitable speech— analyzed by Judith Butler (1997)—needs specific conditions to become a violent tool. Butler's analysis of the performativity of language is focused more on institutional possibilities of recycling signs for non-ordinary purposes, but the concept of excitability itself reveals language's quality of responsiveness to different stimuli, its openness and reactivity. Whatever is said and heard instantly becomes captured and reworked according to its potential energy and possible attachments; in short, it is defined by its place in an analyzed system. Potential energy can also be expressed in terms of pressure—the more elements are attached, the more pressure is exercised on a given point.[9] The word "context" stems from Latin *contextere* which means joining, interweaving—and, I would like to postulate, such operations are material (energetic) in their very core. These actions can be of course mediated in different ways through machines and institutional automata (in the example of declaring war) or they may remain on the level of purely biological interactions (a common dialogue) without any technological aid. But in both cases, and every time we have in mind human communication, they are not perfectly stable and impervious to catastrophes. Returning to DeLanda's theory of assemblages and Thom's biosemantics, we can conclude that the contextual positioning of every speech act is responsible for its inherent instability. It means that linguistic operators can never possess a stable, immaterial meaning and their function cannot be abstracted. Operators—speech acts—distribute and govern energy and at the same time are outcomes of already-triggered energy-related reactions. Computers can abstract their procedures;[10] humans cannot. Context can therefore be defined usefully for performance studies as material and energetic infrastructures and connections that enable and (only partly) determine the shape of communication.

Closing: Possible Perspectives

> For of all the known principles of Nature, thermodynamics has perhaps the most to say about the concept of change—yet change dictated by a combination of chance and necessity, of randomness and determinism. (Chaisson 2004)

This remark by Eric Chaisson formulates the basic interest of thermodynamics, as it points out to the possibility of a fruitful dialogue between two disciplines: physics and performance studies. In my discussion I attempted to show two things: where the defining of new concepts that draw inspiration from this dialogue could begin and in what ways this dialogue could turn out to be fruitful for performance studies.

But only one part of the story was told. The path I have outlined is not complete and should be read only as a form of introduction. Many concepts that are crucial for thermodynamics and could prove inspirational for performance studies were left aside, including the notions of entropy, irreversible time, dissipation and statistical reference frame, although I included them among my definitions. A more detailed elaboration of these topics could provide a better understanding of dynamic system behaviors, and in particular, stress the importance of catastrophes for their evolution; but this problem deserves an entire article of its own.

Thermo-performatics—which is a neologism, however awkward, and invented solely for the purposes of this text—as a materialist theory of communication helps to overcome a division that still shapes most approaches in cultural studies, namely that between nature and culture. This rupture quite often makes it impossible to find a connection between the humanities and hard sciences, which is a real loss for both sides. The humanities lose a very wide field of inspiration for new concepts and ways of looking at human behaviors; the hard sciences, in turn, sometimes forget about the human dimension of their endeavors, subordinating all their efforts to technological growth. At the beginning of my paper I stated that this text is about refocusing, but maybe reorientation would be a better word. I posit that some of the key concepts for the performance studies may be provided by taking the energy-related dimension of performances and communication as a point of departure, without the necessity of reaching for theories rooted in metaphysical concepts of meaning. Understanding performances from the perspective of energy may prove fruitful for researchers who are interested in the materiality of communication, especially those who try to analyze the inequalities and disproportions of energetic distribution. Thus, at the end I will repeat myself: to study energy is to observe what work is done (how we perform) and what can be done (where we perform).

References

Austin, John Langshaw. 1975. *How to Do Things with Words*. Cambridge: Harvard University Press.

Ball, Phillip. 2012. *Why Society is a Complex Matter? Meeting XXI Century Challenges with a New Kind of Science*. Berlin: Springer Verlag.

Barad, Karen. 2003. "Posthumanist Performativity: Toward an Understanding of How Matter Comes to Matter." *Signs: Journal of Women in Culture and Society* 28 (3): 801–31.

Bertalanffy, Ludwig von. 1972. "The History and Status of General System Theory." *The Academy of Management Journal* 15 (4): 407–26.

Bundgaard, Peer F., and Stjernfelt, Frederik. 2010. "René Thom's Semiotics and Its Sources." In *Semiosis and Catastrophes: René Thom's Semiotic Heritage*. Edited by Wolfgang Wildgen, and Per Aage Brandt, 43–77. New York: Peter Lang.

Butler, Judith. 1997. *Excitable Speech: A Politics of the Performative*. New York: Routledge.

Byung, Chan Eu. 2004. *Generalized Thermodynamics*. New York: Kluwer Academic Publishers.

Cantwell-Smith, Brian. 2010. *Age of Significance*. Accessed February 21, 2017. http://bit.ly/2kiooMY.

Carey, James. 2009. *Communication as Culture: Essays on Media and Society*. 2nd edition. New York: Routledge.

Chaisson, Eric. 2004. *Evolution, Energy, Ethics*. Invited paper for "Kognition og Paedagogik." Copenhagen. Accessed January 14, 2017. http://bit.ly/2jxAhSi.

—. 2009. "Exobiology and Complexity." In *Encyclopedia of Complexity and Systems Science*. Edited by Robert Myers, 3268. Berlin: Springer.

DeLanda, Manuel. 2006. *A New Philosophy of Society: Assemblage Theory and Social Complexity*. New York: Bloomsbury.
—. 2009. "Material Expressivity." Accessed January 14, 2017. http://bit.ly/2kWZIZA.
Derrida, Jacques. 1988. "Signature Event Context." Translated by Samuel Weber, Jeffrey Mehlman. In *Limited Inc*, 1–23. Evanston, IL: Northwestern University Press.
Dictionary.com. 2017. Accessed January 14, 2017. http://bit.ly/1wExOEP.
Fischer-Lichte, Erika. 2008. *The Transformative Power of Performance*. Translated by Saskya Iris Jain. New York: Routledge.
Hayles, Katherine. 1999. *How We Became Posthuman: Virtual Bodies in Cybernetics, Literature and Informatics*. Chicago: The University of Chicago Press.
Kosofsky Sedgwick, Eve. 1993. "Queer Performativity: Henry James's *The Art of the Novel*." *GLQ: A Journal of Lesbian & Gay Studies* 1 (1): 1–16. DOI: 10.1215/10642684-1-1-1.
Kossecki, Józef. 1971. *Cybernetyka kultury* [Cybernetics of culture]. Warszawa: PIW.
Loxley, James. 2007. *Performativity*. New York: Routledge.
McKenzie, Jon. 2001 *Perform or else*. New York: Routledge.
Myers, Greg. 1985. "Nineteenth-Century Popularizations of Thermodynamics and the Rhetoric of Social Prophecy." *Victorian Studies* 29 (1): 35–66 (Autumn).
Pickering, Andrew. 2010. *The Cybernetic Brain: Sketches of Another Future*. Chicago: The University of Chicago Press.
Prigogine, Ilya, and Isabelle Stengers. 1984. *Order out of Chaos*. Toronto: Bantam Books.
Rappaport, Roy A. 2002. "Ritual, Sanctity, and Cybernetics." In *American Anthropology, 1971–1995*. Edited by Regna Darnell, 37–64. Lincoln, NE: University of Nebraska Press.
Schechner, Richard. 1998. "What is Performance Studies Anyway?" In *The Ends of Performance*. Edited by Peggy Phelan, and Jill Lane, 357–62. New York: NYU Press.
Shannon, Claude E. 1948. "A Mathematical Theory of Communication." *Bell System Technical Journal* 27 (3): 379–423.
Szakolczai, Arpa. 2000. *Reflexive Historical Sociology*. New York: Routledge.
Thom, René. 1985. "From the Icon to the Symbol." In *Semiotics. An Introductory Anthology*. Edited by Robert E. Innis, 272–91. Bloomington, IN: Indiana University Press.

Turner, Victor. 2004. "Betwixt and Between: The Liminal Period in *Rites De Passage.*" In *Sacred Realms: Essays in Religion, Belief, and Society.* Edited by Richard L. Warms, James Garber, John McGee, 177–84. New York: Oxford University Press, USA.

Wiener, Norbert. 1989. *The Human Use of Human Beings: Cybernetics and Society.* London: Free Association Books.

Notes

[1] In 2007 a webpage http://www.eoht.info/ was launched to gather and systematize the attempts at applying thermodynamics, chemistry and physics to social sciences, but this is only a notable exception.

[2] A similar argument can be made for communication studies represented by such scholars as James Carey, who understands communication also in terms of "language and other symbolic forms" (19). Although inspired by the materialistic media theorist Harold Innis, Carey perceives communication as a deeply human affair and his theory of "communication as culture" necessarily relies on the concept of meaning, which does not lie within the spectrum of Innis's interests.

[3] Erika Fischer-Lichte (2008) in *The Transformative Power of Performance* also calls readers' attention to the unstable nature of every theater performance and the interrelations that take place in the auditorium, although she neglects other forms of openness. Theater, seen through the lenses of her theory, becomes open inside, but remains sealed off from the outside.

[4] Another interesting example is Kossecki's (1971) 'cybernetics of culture.'

[5] By 'expression' I do not understand here a production of meaningful signs, but rather something more plain and simple: creating significant patterns of energy that can be used for communication. This is close to the term "material expressivity," used frequently by Manuel DeLanda (2009). See http://bit.ly/2kSTHkE.

[6] Information, according to the definition given it by Claude Shannon (1948), is possible only through change and differentiation of message and has little to do with intersubjective meaning.

[7] Cf. http://dictionary.reference.com/browse/context?s=t.

[8] In line with this argument it would be to understand charisma as a skill and not as a feature.

[9] Impact factor is nothing but a mark showing how much energy (in different reservoirs) is attached to a text.

[10] However, a lot of effort has been made by Brian Cantwell-Smith (2010) to show that computation is also a material process that can never be fully abstracted.

CHAPTER FOUR

PRESENCE, ACTIVITY AND FADING IN *THE IGNORAMUS AND THE MADMAN*

SABINA MACIOSZEK[1]

In this essay I intend to analyze one of the early plays of Thomas Bernhard, *The Ignoramus and the Madman*, and the contemporary Polish opera of the same title, inspired by Bernhard's play and composed by Paweł Mykietyn. In my interpretation I will use the conjoined concepts of presence/being/duration, activity/action, and disappearance/fading. Analyzing the issues of (un)presence and (in)action of the characters of the play, I will refer to considerations of the issues of simultaneous materiality and ephemerality of voice that were introduced in *Opera, or the Undoing of Women* by Catherine Clément and in *A Voice and Nothing More* by Mladen Dolar. I will also use the notions and theories related to the concept of negative performativity discussed by Joanna Jopek, Bojana Kunst and Judith Halberstam.

Thomas Bernhard's play *The Ignoramus and the Madman* was published in 1972 and was first performed in the same year at the *Salzburger Festspiele*. This production ended in a scandal caused by the director's decision concerning the staging of the last parts of the text: the actors played their roles in complete darkness as all the lights, even the emergency lights, were turned off (Mittermayer 1995, 144).[2] The play was not performed at the Festival again. Despite the failure of the premiere, the play has subsequently been staged from time to time. The first act of the play takes place in a dressing room at the opera. There are two characters: the Doctor and the Father waiting for the staging of *The Magic Flute* by Wolfgang Amadeus Mozart and for the entrance of the main female character—the daughter, Queen of the Night—who is to perform an aria. The second act, in turn, takes place in a restaurant, "At the Three Hussars," where the characters of the play discuss, among other things, the past performance. In my interpretation, the final parts of the two acts seem to be the most important, especially the last verses of the play, which are a declaration of a complete exhaustion, proclaimed by the Queen of the Night. But "exhaustion" is related not only to her "artistic" and "mental" condition—I will try to define this term and analyze the ways it is manifested in Bernhard's play in further parts of this article.

The premiere of Paweł Mykietyn's opera, based on Bernhard's text and directed by Krzysztof Warlikowski, took place at The Grand Theatre–National Opera in Warsaw in 2001. In this article I'm focusing on selected aspects of this production because, to my knowledge, it is the only adaptation of *The Ignoramus and the Madman* for the operatic stage. Bernhard's text was a significant resource for Mykietyn's work; it was almost a ready libretto, and the content, adapted by Warlikowski, became the basis for composing the opera. Mykietyn's work is not only a form of embodiment of the play, but is also a story within a story about opera happening during opera, and it shows the process of exhaustion with regard to both the characters (and their activities) and the opera understood as a music genre.

In the context of Bernhard's play and its opera adaptation, the motto taken from Novalis' *Das Allgemeine Brouillon*—"Das Märchen ist ganz musikalisch," "The fairy tale is entirely musical" (Novalis 2007, 174)—is particularly significant. I'm interpreting these two terms, *Das Märchen* and *fairy tale,* as "fable," "fiction" and "invention." Novalis also wrote that

> a fairy tale is really a dream picture—devoid of all coherence—An ensemble of wondrous things and happenings—a musical fantasy for instance—the harmonious effects of an Aeolian harp—Nature herself. (2007, 171)

Most important for me is the term "an ensemble of wondrous things and happenings," denoting the power, the "prime mover" rooted in fairy tale. The musical element that is mentioned in the motto can be understood as the primary component of the level of language, which differs from the standard narrative structures related to the act of telling a story (Billen and Hassel 2005, 173). Narrativity (connected with literary genres such as the fairy tale) is here complemented by "musicality," which is, in a sense, pure occurrence and momentariness (an unadulterated event and an instant of time). Musicality also has its origin in the constant merging of the formation and duration of sounds with their obliteration, or the disappearance of what is heard. The very concept of *Das Märchen*, interpreted as fiction or speculation, adheres to the traditional understanding of the opera, which at the time of performance, suspends reality, and is a processual phenomenon developed through characters/performers' fading activities—

in other words, realized in the act of disappearance. Not until the process of naming of sequential parts and individual activities takes place, leading to their recognition, does talking about operatic fiction result in losing the element of music and the emergence of a fixed narrative.

The motto also suggests the soundable aspect of individual text phrases of the play—they approach, in Christian Klug's rendering (1991, 191), melodious speech. The verses of the characters function like symphonic phrases; each person has a different shade of color-tone, and in their reflections one can find—as in symphonies—leitmotifs, or multiple sets of fixed expressions and themes. Manfred Mittermayer (1995, 141), likewise, compared the texts by Bernhard to musical scores. Writing music into a score becomes the language of Bernhard's play, the symbol of denoting the "resounding" of the characters, the pace of their speech, but it also controls their appearances and disappearances. A minimal amount of punctuation expands the possibilities of interpretation done by the reader or the actor performing the text onstage.

The prose works of Bernhard include numerous references to music (understood very widely) and comments on the "musical cultural life" of Vienna. Additionally, the activities of some characters can be perceived as essentially amounting to the creation of (micro)treatises on various aspects of the art of music. For example, Konrad, the hero of *The Lime Works*, suffered from the inability to verbalize his study about hearing, which was contained in his mind (Bernhard 1986b). Rudolf in *Concrete*, for many years, tried to write a paper on Felix Mendelssohn-Bartholdy (Bernhard 1989a). Reger, the hero of *Old Masters*, complained that people have lost "the feel of music" and are characterized by a "sick consumerism of music" (Bernhard 1989b, 143). Similar statements can be found in *Woodcutters* (Bernhard 2011). In *The Cellar*, a part of *Gathering Evidence*, the narrator—spokesperson of the author—states his own opinions on Mozart and recalls his first heard, seen and performed opera, which was *The Magic Flute* (Bernhard 1986a).

Not only the motto but also the title of the drama is of importance here. The title figures of "ignoramus" and "madman" are the characters of the Father and the Doctor, which—according to academic writing about Bernhard's prose and plays—are complementary modes of existence (Mittermayer 1995, 144). These terms are emotional and behavioral typifications and presuppose some strategies of behavior which result in permanent enslavement. The character of the Father studies his own misfortune, stuck in a paranoid state of inability to move beyond dependence on everyone. His actions are controlled by progressive blindness and alcoholism. The Doctor, on the other hand, strongly depends on the mechanisms of generalization. He is stuck in the prison of his profession, which renders his statements full of ignorance and madness, especially in the case of very accurate descriptions of autopsies. Both characters aspire to an—actually unattainable—self-control and desire to exercise control over others. As a matter of fact, they are trapped in their helplessness, unable to live their lives (Mittermayer 1995, 136).

The Queen of the Night is suspended between these characters—she is the daughter of the Father, the prima donna. Her actions are central to my analysis. As stated by Bernhard Sorg, in the play the placement of the Queen, the perfect "creation of art," between the two destructive figures of the Ignoramus and the Madman leads to the inevitable exhaustion of everything (1977, 194). The last words of the Queen, "exhaustion / exhaustion and nothing more" (Bernhard 1974, 60), interrupt the play, leaving it in suspension and understatement.

Due to the fact that Bernhard's Queen of the Night owes its "name" to a character from one of the most famous operas, Mozart's *The Magic Flute*, I will make a distinction between these two figures in order to avoid specifying each time which of them I am referring to. Thus, in the case of the persona in Bernhard's play I will use the term Queen of the Night or the Queen; and when speaking of the heroine of Mozart's opera I will use the term *Königin der Nacht* or *Königin*. The role of the Queen of the Night contains elements that belong to the *Königin der Nacht*—an obvious one is the "name" and the performance, mentioned in the play, of two of the most famous opera arias in history, both from *The Magic Flute* (*O zittre nicht, mein lieber Sohn* and the renowned *Der Hölle Rache kocht in meinem Herzen*).

The Queen of the Night is described by the other characters in the first verses of the play, in the Doctor's statement addressed to the Father—indeed, the Queen becomes present because of his words. Her presence is, however, ephemeral and incomplete. The Doctor quotes single words and short comments from the press, reporting to the Father what kind of audience reactions his daughter has caused. She is defined not so much as a human being, as a woman, or even as an artist, but as a voice and "coloratura machine." And so this voice, according to what the Doctor reports to the Father, is "pure perfection" and "blamelessness," it is "technique" and "authenticity," and the upper tones are "phenomenal." The Doctor's enumerations, including a detailed report of the quantitative occurrence of the terms of praise in the newspapers—he counts how many times her voice is actually admired (Bernhard 1974, 29)—create an unequivocal image of the Queen of the Night: she is the perfect product of art, formed "at the right time / the right way" (Bernhard 1974, 31). Her voice, "the work of the incomparable Mr. Keldorfer" (Bernhard 1974, 31), is what defines her completely. As an artificial creation, the Queen of the Night is beyond the physiological states typical of living organisms; even sleep is beyond her—only her voice is the one sleeping. As the Doctor tells the Father: "when I think your daughter sleeps / I only mean / the most obvious thing / your daughter's voice sleeps / her voice / always only the voice my dear sir" (Bernhard 1974, 32). According to his further statements the Queen is a product of art, and "a product of art / becomes completely independent / it cannot / be with others / it applies especially to relatives"; significantly, "a person and a product are two separate things" (Bernhard 1974, 33). All this is stated several times in the play, including in the following words:

> It is primarily about the voice
> namely a quite specific voice
> which today is
> one of the most famous
> and let us remember, in fact, one of the most beautiful
> but it is not about a human being. (Bernhard 1974, 34)

Her voice, defined by comments from the press and the Doctor's arguments on art, is the essence of the Queen of the Night. It is an ideal focus; it draws attention to the Queen even before she appears in the play. That perspective, based on speaking about a voice as a self-sufficient phenomenon, is a consolidation of the patriarchal order, where men not only control women's lives, but also decide how to talk about them. But the issue of power and governance is not clear. In the initial fragments of the play the Doctor's statements are the only ones with causative power. He is the one speaking about the Queen, controlling the pace and topics of discussion (or rather his monologue), and he controls the opinions of the Father, who merely repeats his statements, like some kind of imperfect echo. Thus the Father's weakness is a result of the structure of the text itself (some of his statements just reiterate the last lines of the Doctor's monologues), but it is also related to his alcoholism, progressive blindness and—paradoxically—the success of his daughter. The Queen fulfills his dreams; her career plays a role of compensation of a kind, the Father confesses: "I had / a sad childhood / and my daughter always / has been spoiled" (Bernhard 1974, 45). Despite these signs of "weakness," it is he who controls her fate, even though the activity is hidden and negative—the Doctor says "performing in what we cannot stand ... / because we are forced to by different circumstances / for example, by one's own father / it's terrible" (Bernhard 1974, 48).

There occur repeatedly in the first act of *The Ignoramus and the Madman* passages in which the Queen's life is described as reduced to an "artistic chirping," "puppet theater"; she even observes that her "face / has to be quite artificial" (Bernhard 1974, 45). As I mentioned earlier, she is a product developed by her father, her teachers and the expectations of the audience. In this context, the question of ownership arises—is the Queen owned by everybody? Is her voice a "common good?" Undoubtedly the answers to these questions are affirmative, but these relations are not so simple. The Queen's inaction, her being subject to heteronomous standards and implementing what has been prepared for her by others, is on the other hand a part of an ongoing process of being the one in control, to whom everything is subordinated. The aspirations of the three main characters of the drama (the Queen, the Father and the Doctor) and the relationships between them and the others are marked by a common desire to take control. Construction of the complex relationships, based on exercising power over everyone and at the same time being enslaved, is depicted not only by actions and aspirations of the characters, but also by mutual communication. The effectiveness of actions depends on what was spoken and on the way it was done (Mittermayer 1995, 137). Being in mutually designated roles and continuously waiting for the occurrence of certain activities co-creates a system of interactions characterized by complementarity, establishing (building) and breaking (deconstructing) both themselves and others. According to Bernhard's play the world of opera is not so much the essence of artificiality but a metaphor of a pompous celebration of torpor (Sorg 1977, 193), with the "coloratura machine" placed in the center, destroying the schemata of imposed roles and the rules of functioning of herself and others.

The Queen, reduced to a voice and being a "machine for coloratura," becomes at the same time a being-as-a-voice, which has the power of a controlled immobilization, capturing and destroying the actions of others. The voice is formed in the concrete body and is physically received; however, its characteristic feature is that it has the ability to "separate" from the body and to function beside it. In the third chapter (*The "Physics" of the Voice*) of the book *A Voice and Nothing More* by Mladen Dolar, an interesting commentary on the voice that cannot be "seen," or that functions spontaneously beyond its source, can be found. The acousmatic voice, or sound, is the voice for which the source—or the body emitting it—cannot be easily identified. "It is a voice," Dolar says, "in search of a body, but even when it finds its body, it turns out that this doesn't quite work," because the voice does not remain attached to its apparent source (Dolar 2006, 61).

This is how in the first act the Queen's voice operates—it is separated from her (by the Doctor, the Father, press comments, the speaker in the dressing room, audience expectations), and gains the status of an artifact; it is an artificial creation that cannot be linked to the imperfect body. Disembodied—because reduced to the voice heard through the speaker—the "in-activity" of the Queen (or her performance of the aria) becomes the more and more perfect process of her transformation into the sole queen of her audiences' desires, into the woman that masters all that is audible. She is the only one that comes to play: the diva—*Die Königin der Nacht*. The Father and Doctor, and also potential drama readers and/or spectators of the play, are waiting keenly for her rendition of *O zittre nicht mein lieber Sohn* known as the first *Königin der Nacht* aria. It is important that the mere fact of the Queen's rendition of this piece, its concretization on stage, is mentioned only in captions, just like the immobilization of the Father and Doctor listening to her arias issuing from a speaker. When the Doctor and Father hear the aria from the speaker, they become motionless. Their lack of movement is at the same time the essence of duration. Bojana Kunst says:

> Duration becomes apparent when something does not work, stops or hardly moves. Perhaps the affective response is the consequence of the fact that it is the duration that shows that we ourselves are actually not moving, but are being moved, that our inner perception of time (the time of someone who freely and flexibly projects their own subjectivity) is, in fact, heavily, socially and economically conditioned. (2009)

So the stillness—caused by the Queen—of the Doctor and the Father could be interpreted as a sign of the Queen's power to control others' behavior, affects and activities.

The first act of Bernhard's play ends with the performance of the aria *O zittre nicht mein lieber Sohn*. On the one hand, the voice that is realizing this piece itself has an enslaving ability (it produces motionlessness); on the other, it sings about slavery. The story of enslavement can be interpreted from two perspectives—as it concerns the kidnapping of the *Königin der Nacht's* daughter (the *Königin* complains to Tamino that she witnessed the abduction of her daughter, and orders him to rescue her) and the same *Königin* professing that her fate is to suffer. In the context of the theory of Catherine Clément, proposed in her *Opera, or the Undoing of Women*, the enslavement of women is inextricably linked with the opera. What is more—due to opera's being granted a place in the highest level of Culture—it is masked by the banality of librettos and comments on the charm and artistry of particular works (Clément 1997, x); and it is socially permitted. This distinctive system of enslavement is created through a fixed framework comprising the specific content available in the libretto, the fixed duration of performances, institutional constraints, the conventionality of the genre and the mechanisms that control the rules of participation. The main purpose of the opera is to give pleasure. Voice functions as an autonomous entity that belongs to everyone watching, listening to and experiencing successive parts of the work. Clément often mentions, and comments on, the patriarchy that persists in the Opera—the diva, through which the arias are realized, is not regarded as a human being; as pointed out by Clément (1997, 30), she is treated as a human toy to be shown around to please the audience. Like the Queen of the Night in *The Ignoramus and the Madman*, she is also enslaved in the men's world: she functions as a product of the men's epistemic power and, therefore, as Clément indicates (1997, 11), she is seen as a living re-presentation of their expectations and desires. But in Bernhard's play, finally, she is the character that has control over other figures.

Considering this subordination and remembering the earlier attributions that define the Queen, especially the concept of voice, Bernhard's character should be compared with Mozart's. What is important here is that the coloratura passages of the *Königin's* parts constitute a specific language—a language that is beyond logic and sense, which frightens and attracts at the same time. What matters is not the meaning of the coded message, but the act of using the language, the moment of showing its affective possibilities (Clément 1997, 73). The *Königin's* part could be interpreted as some kind of madness which results from the fact that she exists in a world exclusively based on affects, situated opposite, and contrasted with, the men's world. Her touching voice (or the sound implementation of successive notes) makes audible the meaning-devoid sequences of sounds of which the aria actually consists (Clément 1997, 73). These syllables exist beyond the rational order of words; they carry no sense. The *Königin der Nacht* also remains in permanent rivalry with the luminous and sunny Sarastro, a representative of the male world. This is the model of existence in which the Queen operates. One of the Doctor's confessions directed to the Father deserves to be mentioned at this point:

> I sang once, twenty years ago
> amateurishly with a fairly nice bass …
> I sang arias of Sarastro and The Speaker of the Temple …
> And when you look around the homes of doctors
> you will find the entire collection of scores for piano
> from any possible operas. (Bernhard 1974, 38)

In a way the Doctor's world is permeated and controlled by fragments of operas, obtrusively returning popular arias, recognizable melodies. Recalling his former participation as a performer of passages from *The Magic Flute*, he automatically places himself in a contrasting position to the Queen.

Die Königin's arias from Mozart's opera took part in the social process of the "undoing of women" which redefined the position of opera artists— they were fulfilled in the roles of prima donnas, excellent embodiments of characters, each indicated by the representatives of the patriarchal world of characters in librettos. On the other hand, relentless action, frequently leading to the destruction of self and the surrounding world, was typical for heroines in opera. The "undoing" was actually a cover for the very active process of acting. Women in many operas operate through crying, by igniting revolutions, beseeching, murdering, poisoning (Clément 1997, 37). This is how the Queen of the Night functions: even the lack of her direct presence changes the reality in which the Father and the Doctor fit. Trails and shreds of her past actions bring about the Father's and Doctor's confusion, and things that she directly achieves lead to a complete change in the prevailing "men's order" and "play's rules." At the end of the second act of the play, after the Queen has decided to cancel performances in Copenhagen and Stockholm, the last words about exhaustion are spoken by the Queen. They are a response to the social, political and also artistic mechanisms controlling peoples' lives and imposing artificial social roles. Her (in)actions effectuate a new order, the order of exhaustion.

That is why I would like to refer to the concept of "negative performativity" as understood by Joanna Jopek. Arguing against passages in *Perform or Else* by Jon McKenzie, she states that in the case of some activities with "performative" status, "the point is not a powerful presence or a total absence: it is more about a gentle shift toward disappearance, renunciation, invalidation; ... the performed failure of presence/visibility/ productivity" (Jopek 2015, 31). The Queen's decision to stop being visible and audible on stage is a manifest denial of patriarchal knowledge-power and a renunciation of the enslaving mechanisms of both the prima donna and operatic works. To quote Jopek, the Queen enters "the fields of ignorance where we find an alternative information and ways of perceiving or feeling" (2015, 34). To quote Judith Halberstam,

> feminine success is always measured by male standards, and gender failure often means being relieved of the pressure to measure up to patriarchal ideals, not succeeding at womanhood can offer unexpected pleasures. (2001, 4)

The Queen intends to employ the ignorance and madness inherent in the Father and the Doctor and use these "qualities" as the key to creating a new "reality of negation," which is simply "exhaustion."

The Queen's words suppress the Father's and Doctor's indolence, while undermining their production of the next "portions" of insanity and ignorance. At dinner in the restaurant "At the Three Hussars," when the Queen declares that she has never, thus far, called off a concert (Bernhard 1974, 53), the Doctor responds by noting that to stop a habit—even if it is the habit of always being ready to perform—requires a resolve and determination (Bernhard 1974, 53). His observation seems to be one of the causes leading to the final, obliterating action of the Queen. By announcing exhaustion, the Queen also takes over (continues) and undermines (announces an end to) the madness and ignorance in which the Father and the Doctor are immersed. What is more, she does not do it in the madly-ignorant way, as imagined by the Doctor—"for example, in the middle of a Revenge Aria,"[3] by interrupting her performance "to stand / and do nothing / … and suddenly to show [her] tongue" (Bernhard 1974, 53)—but instead declares that she will break contracts and, like an ignorant madman, just announces her own death in allusions.

An intriguing issue related to the proclamation of exhaustion is the question of the significance of this manifestation—isn't it just a demonstration exposing the conventionality of things that have "ended"? The exhaustion proclaimed by the Queen could be interpreted as an act of opposition to operatic conventions, inscribed in the concept of *das Märchen* that I mentioned at the outset. According to the interpretation of Hal Foster in his book *The Return of the Real*, in the broad field of art every choice and its public "announcement" has the status of a performative act, allowing for the establishment of a new order and laws (1996, 20).

The process of embodiment on stage is related to the informal pact between performers and audience—each party for a certain time is involved in the construction of theater reality. The applause at the end of the show is for this reality. So if the Queen, being "just" a voice, decides to be absent from the next performances, she has decided on self-destruction. The duration/being of the Queen of the Night turns into nothingness—the Queen's gesture is a gesture demonstrating her own end, the exhaustion that was mentioned before. Mozart's *Königin* on the other hand prevails—in the libretto, in collective imagination and in the myth: it is those concrete incarnations, "perfect," "flawless" and "authentic," which were to take place in Stockholm and Copenhagen, that are annihilated. Looking from another perspective, the long duration of works of art such as opera is not created by narration and score, but by the singularity and uniqueness of individual performances, more and more recent incarnations happening on stage. So the Queen's gesture is also a kind of a perverse manifesto. The Queen—a "product" manufactured by others—ceases to exist by her own will, ceases to be an ideal "creation of art," but her words control the activities of the others. They bring chaos, which is fulfilled in the stage directions that end the play: "someone knocks over bottles and glasses on the table" (Bernhard 1974, 60).

In the works of Bernhard, characters are very often marked by an "identity of contradictions," which denotes existence at the last moment before non-existence (Bereza 1998, 450). That figure also defines the heroine of *The Ignoramus and the Madman*—the Queen exists in a permanent impossibility of existence, is situated between corporeality of her own voice (it is her own flesh and blood) and its disembodiment, her own voice functioning as a simulacrum of her. Her existence denotes being, in anticipation of a desperate act of self-destruction. Perhaps it is the formation of a new order, where an intervention is transformed into unique events. The Queen has no body, and does not speak her own language. What is left for her is (in)actions and interventions that could be transformed into events. But they become "negative events," non-events for those who are watching/listening/expecting the Queen. The "negative events" are associated with the inducing of motionlessness in other figures (Act One) and exhaustion involving other characters as well as the Queen (Act Two).

In the case of *The Ignoramus and the Madman* one can point out four ways in which the "negativity" is implemented, but only in three cases does the metaphor of "descent into disappearance" work—understood as active exposure to failure and deliberate negation of efficiency of actions. The first way was described above and is signified by the breaking of the contracts by the Queen, her refusal to be visible and audible. The second mode is related to the performance of arias which are understood as constant oscillations between appearance and disappearance, transforming the act of being into nothingness. Death is in fact an integral part of vocalization—before sound has enough time to appear, it immediately fades away and dissolves. In the case of singing, the voice is continuously in the process of "becoming," has affective power, is an event that endeavors for self-destruction and evaporates in the air (as noted by the Doctor, before the Queen enters the stage, "air" is the Queen's chosen word) (Bernhard 1974, 41). That's why singing could be a metaphor of undoing and decay. The third type of disappearance is the apparent passivity of the Father, for whom the world gradually vanishes because of his progressive blindness. His character functions thanks to a fixed set of actions, for example "sipping from a bottle," that recur like a musical refrain.

Another type of negation, which is different because it is co-created by words (narration) and not by action (occurrence), is the constant return of the Doctor to telling details of the autopsy. However, this is connected with (in)actions caused by the Queen. Zbigniew Mikołejko in his book *We władzy wisielca* (Under the rule of the hanged man) interprets Rembrandt van Rijn's *Anatomy Lesson of Dr. Nicolaes Tulp* from 1632 as an example of autopsy that does not seek to explore human existence or death, but is a demonstration of pride associated with exhibition of modern forms of power and gained knowledge (2012, 208). In such cases, the experience of an individual is gained through observation and naming, not—as in the case of the Queen in Bernhard's drama—by (in)actions, by the unplanned "begetting" of events. During the First Act the Father listens attentively to the Doctor's reports. Information concerning the interior of the dissected body is interspersed with the Doctor's comments on the voice and actions of the Queen and the current state of the art and the theater. In the Second Act the situation is similar, and comments such as "culture is a heap of dung" (Bernhard 1974, 55) and "the voice of your daughter / was of highest / excellence today" (55), or referring to the Queen, her "hectic excitement … / and related with it / hectic madness" (56), closely correspond to the story about the fragmentation of human flesh. The Doctor dissects a body using words and sentences, disassembling it and naming the individual parts. He uses professional medical terms interjected with Latin words. His activities are represented in the act of telling—his "professional" report is a presentation of power and knowledge, but he also captures the quintessence of bodily decay. The destructiveness of the Doctor's verbal expressions involves a combination of words that—by reducing the human body to the category of a labyrinth composed of smaller and larger pieces of meat, with sophistication and subtlety separated from each other—is in contrast to the "ideal" of the concept of voice and being "a creation of art." Disembodied, perfect and actively announcing her own exhaustion, the "coloratura machine" is a textual supplement to the organic, inefficient and subject to overview machinery of a corporeal-body. Heading the concept of supplement as understood by Jacques Derrida, the figure of the Queen could be interpreted not only as a being that functions as an "excess" for the "normal body," but also as a being that simply could complement the "normal body-emptiness" (which is caused by her vocal talent). She is a hybrid fullness, a connection of body machinery and artificial coloratura machine.

These concepts such as duration/being and exhaustion can be regarded as constituting the essence of Mykietyn's opera, which was composed in 2001 and directed by Krzysztof Warlikowski.[4] The performance in Warsaw could be taken as an embodied representation of the motionlessness of Bernhard's characters and their simultaneous verbal (over)activity.[5] Motionlessness is not so much physical immobilization, or the inability to perform movements, as much as it defines a potential of the behavior of the characters and their representation on stage by particular artists. Their actions are based on small and quite hectic movements linked with verbal/musical phrases which are specific for every figure.

In Mykietyn's work, being was emphasized by relevant repetitive musical phrases—the characters were assigned relatively constant and recognizable melodic-rhythmic motifs. The Queen's lines were the most vibrant and eclectic at the same time, the Doctor's lines recalled the recitation of psalms, and the parts sung by the Father seemed like nervous shuddering. Each of the characters of the opera not only spoke the words of the play, but was defined by a specific melodic-rhythmic process. That stressed the coexistence of the three characters and emphasized the conflict between them, which was carried out as a musically consonant, three-voiced whole.

The play, due to its inherent "musical element," was almost a ready-made libretto. Statements cited at the beginning of this article—by those scholars who, examining Bernhard's plays and prose, interpret his work as texts filled with vibrant fragments (Klug and Mittermayer, likening these texts to symphonies and musical scores)—confirm the rhythmic and temporal potential contained in his lines. The opera characters were defined by the performed words and phrases which formed a harmonious whole. Thus, the use of the text on the stage, that is, its concretized evocation (by a particular artist at a particular time) was a clear manifestation of its causative powers, the transition into the sphere of action and the realm of being able to change the prevailing order. In Mykietyn's composition, "speech" is a process carried out by means of speaking and singing—but it is not only the adequate juxtaposition of recitatives and arias, but the constant interpenetration of the operatic form, and what goes beyond it, which is its failure but at the same time a successful demonstration of Bernhardian exhaustion. This also applies to Mykietyn's opera, because exhaustion describes not only the characters in the play, but the whole reality of the stage on which they operate and act.

The task of the soloists performing individual parts was to collect and construct an opera out of this "exhausted" and "fragmented" play. The text of the play has been transferred to a new medium by the producers. However, the music that merged the words into a separate entity was slowly subjected to this "exhaustion"—the opera just gradually disappeared, became words. So this "novelty," that is, performing individual text phrases as parts that are sung, turned out to be a success only in the First Act; later it disappeared because of the disappearance of the opera form. Mykietyn's and Warlikowski's solution allowed them to show different types of actions performed by characters that were marked by failure, and those activities could be described as a "descent into disappearance." The exposition of these failures amounted to pinpointing some weak moments inherent in the opera (while, at the same time, proving their potential). In an interview, Warlikowski admitted that his directing strategies were a form of testing the degree of autonomy of the dramaturgy and narrative in the opera (2013, 40). To quote Łukasz Grabuś, dramaturgy is "shaping the aesthetic experience of the relationship between what is perceived and what eludes perceptual efforts" (2012, 31). In the case of Mykietyn's opera it is nothing but the realization of the Bernhardian endeavor to achieve a final exhaustion which would include everything, even the text itself and, thus, the score and libretto.

One form of pursuing a strategy of demonstrating the weakness, which is paradoxically also an asset of the opera, is related to the exposure of the opera fiction, and thus the production did not render all the opera's lines in Polish. Some phrases were spoken in the native language of the performers, in Ukrainian (Pasiecznik) and in English (Kenny). Those little phrases were a way creating a transition from the status of being a character to that of being a concrete performer, talking in the vernacular. It was a way of overcoming the operatic fiction. Another example was the appearance of the conductor onstage. Appearing as the Bandmaster in the libretto, Wojciech Michniewski spoke some lines (originally belonging to the Doctor in Bernhard's play) on "theatricality and musicality" (being a "dung heap") and on the vulgarity of the audience, and stated that "light is unhappiness." The universal nature of these phrases and the fact that they are spoken by the conductor, endow them with a heavy dose of (auto)irony, which concerned also the opera itself.

Mykietyn's work was characterized by instability of operatic form, coupled with the disappearance of operatic features demonstrated onstage. The opera demonstrated itself, appeared not so much as a whole but as a set of fragments having more or less "operatic" characteristics. One of the most interesting ways of showing the tensions between the opera and what is "non-operatic" was to be found in Mykietyn's work with the onstage actions of the Queen of the Night. The Bernhardian wait for the appearance of the diva, in Mykietyn's work, includes everyone—not only the characters onstage, but also the audience awaiting the performance of the spectacular aria. It is the audience who witness the stage's dissection into the part where the action happens and another where the "opera in the opera"—*The Magic Flute*—takes place. The space has been divided with a translucent cloth into two zones—at the front, closer to the audience, is a wardrobe (in the First Act) and the restaurant "At the Three Hussars" (in the Second Act), while at the back there is a "real" opera scene, where only the Queen has the right to enter. It is there that she performs the aria—Bernhard mentioned it in the stage directions—inducing the Doctor's and the Father's immobilization. In Mykietyn's work the excerpt from Mozart ends abruptly during its culmination, without regard to any melodic or harmonic principles and continuity of the text. The effects of this "severance" are different, but at the same time similar, for each act. So the immobilization of the two characters is transformed into an unsolvable suspension of the First Act, leading to the viewers' marching out for the intermission—this is Mykietyn's and Warlikowski's demonstration of the operatic form's exhaustion and a form of dialogue with commonplace outlines of musical phrase production. It is an unexpected beginning to the intermission and it leaves a feeling of dissatisfaction related to the spectators' expectation (or desire) to hear the complete, well-known aria. Another suspension takes place in the Second Act of Mykietyn's work, when the Queen, sitting by the table, stops singing the most recognizable melody from Mozart's opera—in this case it happens during one of the highest notes of the coloratura. At once the unrealized completion of this passage took place in the mental sphere, in the collective imagination of the audience—they didn't hear the whole aria, but they just had to remember its whole course.

Both cases of suspension of the arias can be considered as such moments which are situated between what is visible and what—as Grabuś describes it—"eludes perceptual efforts" (2012, 31). These moments of the opera provide a supplement to the performers'/characters' presence; they are a failure of the performers' productivity and constitute a form of embodied implementation of Bernhardian exhaustion. By ending the arias abruptly twice, Mykietyn and Warlikowski may also mean to represent the Doctor's desires mentioned in the play. His wishes the immediate and drastic "ending" of the performance by the Queen, discontinuation of the arias and ignoring everything and everyone. Performing the coloratura aria to the end would involve submission to the aesthetics of operatic excess;

ending it offers a feeling of deprivation and insatiety. The "full" presence of the aria is replaced by the "defective" real concretization, establishing a new order in which the masterpiece is ignored and the existence of the pristine prima donna is denied. Thanks to this the opera-viewers participate in a process of denudation, of "creative undoing," of operatic form.

Exhaustion of the musical themes that define the actions of the characters (and resulting from these actions) is implied not only in those arias, but also in the music composed by Mykietyn. In the First Act the Doctor's report of autopsy is a monotonous recitative with elements of recitation without accompaniment. The "Melody of autopsy," as representing the Doctor's character, is carried into the Second Act. And there it occurs as a recording of Kenny's voice form the First Act—but the recording isn't "complete" and "correct." It is broken by short pauses, by decelerations and by sounds that are out of tune. So it could be interpreted as a sign of the "de-composing" of the opera and the fading of onstage activities. It undergoes breakdowns and false notes changing the "right" tone and pace from the First Act. The recording not only suggests that the character is approaching exhaustion but also alludes to the specific feature of Mykietyn's composition: the oscillation between the appearance and disappearance of operatic forms.

In Mykietyn's work, as it is directed by Warlikowski, one can find moments perfectly depicting Bernhardian non-completion and exhaustion emerging from the overproduction of fixed sets of behaviors, the same imposed actions and unvarying social expectations. Transferring the text of a play to the medium of opera allowed for additional intensification of presences which are more or less invisible, which have passed into the realm of absence, in the sphere of suspended, unfinished, exhausted activities, and so which at the same time represent the potential for the occurrence of new events. The strategies employed by the creators allowed them to show the processes of musical, textual and theatrical embodying of tensions inherent in the structure of both works. Both in Bernhard's play and in Mykietyn's opera the actions that are accentuated deny what is considered to be effective and undermine the categories of wholeness and completeness. There is a new order proposed—the order of exhaustion.

References

Bereza, Henryk. 1998. "Oksymoroniczność" [The very essence of oxymoron]. In *Autobiografie* [*Autobiographies*], by Thomas Bernhard. Translated by Sława Lisiecka, 449–54. Kraków: Wydawnictwo Literackie.

Bernhard, Thomas. 1974. *Ignorant i szaleniec* [The ignoramus and the madman]. Translated by Grzegorz Sinko. *Dialog*, no. 5: 29–60.

—. 1986a. *Gathering Evidence: A Memoir*. Translated by David McLintock. New York: Knopf.

—. 1986b. *The Lime Works*. Translated by Sophie Wilkins. Chicago: University of Chicago Press.

—. 1989a. *Concrete*. Translated by David McLintock. London: Quartet.

—. 1989b. *Old Masters: A Comedy*. Translated by Ewald Osers. Chicago: University of Chicago Press.

—. 2011. *Woodcutters*. Translated by David McLintock. London: Faber and Faber.

Billen, Josef, and Friedhelm Hassel. 2005. *Undeutbare Welt: Sinnsuche und Entfremdungserfahrung in deutschen Naturgedichten von Andreas Gryphius bis Friedrich Nietzsche* [Meaningless world: The quest for sense and the experience of enstrangement in German nature poetry from Andreas Gryphius to Friedrich Nietzsche]. Würzburg: Königshausen & Neumann.

Clément, Catherine. 1997. *Opera, or the Undoing of Women*. Translated by Betsy Wing. London: I. B. Tauris.

Dolar, Mladen. 2006. *A Voice and Nothing More*. Edited by Slavoj Žižek. Cambridge: The MIT Press.

Foster, Hal. 1996. *The Return of the Real: The Avant-garde at the End of the Century*. Cambridge: The MIT Press.

Grabuś, Łukasz. 2012. *Formy śmiercionośne. Kilka strategii dramaturgicznych we współczesnej operze.* [Lethal forms: Some dramatic strategies in contemporary opera]. Kraków: Księgarnia Akademicka.

Halberstam, Judith. 2001. *The Queer Art of Failure*. Durham: Duke University Press.

Jopek, Joanna. 2015. "The Practice of Failure: Attempts at Negative Performativity." *Didaskalia. Theater Journal. English Issue*, no. 2: 28–36.

Klug, Christian. 1991. *Thomas Bernhards Theaterstücke*. Stuttgart: J. B. Metzler.

Kunst, Bojana. 2009. "How Time Can Dispossess: On Duration and Movement in Contemporary Performance." Accessed December 2, 2014. http://bit.ly/2kTS8ja.

Mikołejko, Zbigniew. 2012. *We władzy wisielca* [Under the rule of the hanged man]. Gdańsk: Słowo/Obraz Terytoria.

Mittermayer, Manfred. 1995. *Thomas Bernhard*. Stuttgart und Weimar: J. B. Metzler.

Novalis. 2007. *Notes for a Romantic Encyclopaedia: Das Allgemeine Brouillon*. Translated and edited by David W. Wood. New York: SUNY Press.

Sorg, Bernhard. 1977. *Thomas Bernhard*. München: C.H. Beck.

Warlikowski Krzysztof. 2013. "Muzyka, która wchodzi w kości. Rozmowa z Krzysztofem Warlikowskim" [A kind of music that goes to the bone: Interview with Krzysztof Warlikowski]. By Paweł Dobrowolski. *Notatnik Teatralny*, no. 72–73: 38–44.

Notes

[1] I would like to thank Michał Jutkiewicz for help with the translation of this essay.

[2] It is important that the theme of light and its absence is a problem repeatedly mentioned by the characters of the play. One of them, the Doctor, in one of the last lines of the play, says, "light / is unhappiness"; after this—according to the stage directions—"the stage is completely dark" (Bernhard 1974, 60). All the translations of quotations, unless stated differently, are Sabina Macioszek's. All translations of quotes from *The Ignoramus and the Madman* are based on the Polish translation of the play (Bernhard 1974).

[3] The "Revenge Aria," or *Der Hölle Rache kocht in meinem Herzen* (*Hell's vengeance boils in my heart*), is one of the most widely known passages of the opera *The Magic Flute*.

[4] The opera had its premiere on May 4th 2001. In this article I used a recording of *The Ignoramus and the Madman* from 5th of May 2001, that was lent to me by Biblioteka Muzyczna Teatru Wielkiego–Opery Narodowej (Musical Library of the Grand Theatre–National Opera) in Warsaw.

[5] The role of the Queen of the Night was performed by Olga Pasiecznik, Jerzy Artysz was the Father, and Jonathan Peter Kenny, the Doctor. The roles of the two other characters from Bernhard's play were performed by Stanisława Celińska (as Mrs. Vargo) and Jacek Laszczkowski (Waiter Winter). Another person on stage—in the role of the Bandmaster—was the conductor, Wojciech Michniewski. The author of scenography was Małgorzata Szczęśniak, and Stanisław Zięba was responsible for light directing.

CHAPTER FIVE

HOW TO WORK WITH THE BODY— THEORY AND PRACTICE: KAROL RADZISZEWSKI'S WORKS REGARDED IN THE CONTEXT OF MERLEAU-PONTY'S PHILOSOPHY

PAULINA TCHURZEWSKA

In contemporary Polish art, depictions of the body are frequently used in ways regarded as radical or even controversial. Recurrently, the body is associated with very expressive, even shocking actions, with the breaking of taboos or with transgressive, ecstatic exploration. On the other hand, there exists a philosophical tradition of exploring the problem of the body that is mostly epistemological and focused on perception issues. It is my aim to connect these two perspectives: to bring together the artistic and the philosophical explorations of the body. For that purpose I would like to regard Karol Radziszewski's exhibition *The Prince and Queens. Body as an Archive*—a work housed at the Centre of Contemporary Art in Toruń— in the light of Maurice Merleau-Ponty's philosophy of the body. In the official CSW publication, Radziszewski's *The Prince and Queens. Body as an Archive* is described as

> the fullest exhibition ever devoted to Karol Radziszewski's provocative work. ... The exhibition's title ironically states the three extremes of this project, based on the work of Jerzy Grotowski, Natalia LL, and the collective General Idea; different figures, chosen by the artist to investigate the concepts related to the body and identity, central themes in Radziszewski's oeuvre. ... *The Prince and Queens* brings together archival material related to Jerzy Grotowski, Natalia LL and the collective General Idea, to explore their creative potentialities: photographs, film, artifacts, and memorabilia, are displayed with new artworks especially conceived by

Radziszewski in order to underline characters and alternative stories
alongside the existing narratives. (Viola 2014, 3)

Merleau-Ponty states that when taking the body into consideration it is
easy to choose one of two opposite approaches: spiritual or materialistic.
The first is focused on a transgressive and internal experience of the body,
and the second is based on the opinion that the body is most of all a thing
of flesh. But it should be remembered that the human mind is embodied
and it is impossible to separate these two aspects of our physicality. The
mind and the body are dependent on each other. Radziszewski also uses, in
equal measure, the bodily and intellectual experience. They both are of the
same importance and they complement each other.

The exhibition in Toruń has several main figures: Jerzy Grotowski and
Ryszard Cieślak, Natalia LL and Ryszard Kisiel (and at some point Karol
Radziszewski). They have all worked with the body and explored different
aspects of its experience. Grotowski was more spiritual, Natalia LL
emphasized erotic and subconscious experience, and Kisiel and Radziszewski
have explored the male body. Their art has been interpreted from the angle
of various stereotypes: the work of Grotowski and Cieślak is considered as
being among the most important phenomena in the history of the theater;
the two men are associated with sublime explorations into the essence of
humanity. Natalia LL's art, frequently considered to be controversial,
expresses the concerns of feminism; it has also received considerable
attention from feminist criticism. Finally, Radziszewski himself, like
Ryszard Kisiel, is seen mostly through the prism of his homosexuality.

By searching for other contexts of the work done by the artists
portrayed in the exhibition, Radziszewski is trying to break down
stereotypes and show other sides to established knowledge. For example,
one of the more important parts of the exhibition is the movie *The Prince*.
The starting point for the film is Ryszard Cieślak's biography and artistic
work, his approach to the body and his specific relation with Jerzy
Grotowski. But it is not a documentary movie, as it doesn't try to
reproduce the facts. In some way it is a variation on Grotowski's artistic
achievements and also a presentation of the neglected or purposefully
omitted elements of his personal life. It is widely believed that Cieślak was
a great artist and his cooperation with Grotowski in the art community is
discussed in the terms of a myth, as if it had been something almost
sacred. Radziszewski had the courage to ask uncomfortable questions and
raise some surprising issues that had been never considered before. For
example, in the movie it is suggested that Grotowski could have been
homosexual. For Radziszewski it was a risky claim, because it could have
been construed as an attempt to reinterpret Grotowski's work as gay art.

However, Radziszewski's aim was not to shock by an overall reinterpretation—rather, it was to show another context of the Grotowski myth and say that there is no such thing as undisputed truth or unnecessary questions. The aura of mystery and indeterminacy, and the unresolved questions, in Radziszewski's film tie in with the conclusions of Merleau-Ponty who warns that the body's signals cannot be interpreted in a univocal, mechanistic way. Merleau-Ponty claims that the way the body works is not only limited to a simple "action-reaction" schema because this approach would be too mechanistic. All the impulses that the body receives and all the ways of stimulating it produce other, frequently unpredictable results. Moreover all gestures and actions carried out by a body have their own structure and meaning. It is possible to predict their strength at a certain point, but adding them together, it cannot be precisely defined how the environment would react. Despite the fact that they always have some influence on their milieu, this influence cannot be exactly foreseen.

The Prince is a really good example of this process. Grotowski and Cieślak were working with the deepest level of our human experience and existence. Although it was a very spiritual approach, they could not focus entirely on this realm. This is why Radziszewski shows all the different sides of the Grotowski myth and a great part of the history of the theater. He is trying to make us aware that we all have a much greater influence on our environment and sometimes we cannot even anticipate how our actions will be interpreted by other people. For example, in the Radziszewski exhibition there is what may be the most famous photo from *The Constant Prince*, which shows the naked Ryszard Cieślak. Posed on his knees with closed eyes and some kind of ecstatic expression on his face, he is presented with a naked torso and clearly visible muscles. It can be assumed that some could perceive this scene as erotic and find it erotically simulating. It is a beautiful male body so we cannot restrict it only to the domain of spiritual experience; and what is more, the actions of different bodies cannot be predicted when they interact with others. Furthermore, Teresa Nawrot, an actress employed by Grotowski, in the movie suggests that Grotowski could be fascinated by male bodies and this could be one reason why he preferred to work with men. On the one hand, we have this spiritual figure of a great director; but it is contrasted, on the other hand, with the image of a man employing in his art his sexual interests. However, these two ways of perception (spiritual and erotic) are not contradictory.

Merleau-Ponty is an opponent of dualism. He claims that it is not possible to separate a mechanical body from an immaterial mind because they are closely connected and have an influence on each other. In Merleau-Ponty's philosophy these two concepts, which are contrasted in dualism, are two sides of one somatic scheme. All somatic processes, connected to the same degree with the body and with the mind, are parts of a wider operating cycle and they do not work separately, but cooperate. The French philosopher points out that we have three orders of corporeality—physical, vital and human—and that they constitute three parts of one totality. First, the most primary level concerns the body as a mechanism, on the second level the body is an organism (living system), and the last level is about the human body with all its cultural meanings, ways of functioning in society and other aspects of human organization. Each of them has some characteristics and dominant features but the most important is that they cannot be considered separately. Together they create one structure and they overlap each other. It is impossible to reduce human behavior and its body to one of these orders.

This is also why Radziszewski wanted to show us some aspects of bodily perception which work together. We cannot limit our experience only to one type of these impulses. I have noted this opinion earlier with the example of the sexuality of the young male bodies in the movie *The Prince*. A continuation of this view is the performance *Rehearsal*, which could be seen during the opening of the exhibition. There were seven young men with athletic, attractive bodies doing physical exercises. Their bodily presence was very perceptible and for the viewers it might have been fascinating or embarrassing, or even both at the same time. It was also worthy of remark that women reacted to the male bodies in a little different way than did men. They were more comfortable with the view of a naked man, which can bespeak the existence of a strong taboo against the idea of a man being attractive to other men.

At the exhibition we had one more example, maybe even more emphatic, of different types of stimuli being experienced together. In one of the exhibition rooms we could see a big phrase on a white wall: "Natalia ist sex." This is one of Natalia LL's works, dating from 1974. The inscription is made from many small pictures, but when looked at from a distance it cannot be seen what they are showing. Viewers are forced to come closer and then, face to face with these pictures, they see that they are a naturalistic documentation of sexual intercourse. The reactions of viewers are various—some of them might be confused or ashamed while others might even feel offended or disgusted. Of course, they also can be completely neutral or comfortable with this type of presentation, but also it should be assumed that some people could feel sexual arousal or desire. Universally people are used to the fact that an art gallery is a place only singer, Lorca (1933) says, "Spanish genius, equal in power of fancy to Goya or Rafael el Gallo," escapes from perfection and makes the *duende* appear:

> *La Niña de Los Peines* had to tear apart her voice, because she knew experts were listening, who demanded not form but the marrow of form, pure music with a body lean enough to float on air. She had to rob herself of skill and safety: that is to say, banish her Muse, and be helpless, so her *duende* might come, and deign to struggle with her at close quarters. And how she sang! Her voice no longer at play, her voice a jet of blood, worthy of her pain and her sincerity, opened like a ten-fingered hand as in the feet, nailed there but storm-filled, of a Christ by Juan de Juni. (García Lorca 1933)

Thus, Federico García Lorca, who grew up in an environment suffused with the flamenco atmosphere, provides a theory of flamenco and the category of *duende* through his lectures and gives to it an excellent expression by means of *The Poem of the Deep Song*. Lorca wrote this work when he was only 23 years old. The rhythm of this poem is stylishly popular. The poem describes a number of old singers (cantaores) and it depicts fantastic wildlife, which constitutes a significant part of it. The Poem, as Arrebola claims, is "full of gipsies, candles, forges... and even has allusions to Zarathustra" (1986, 79, translation mine). Lorca, then, is the Andalusian poet who has brought into contemplation the flamenco and hands down a work which causes the *duende* inside us to explode, making us face somatically the painful events.[10]

A Dialogue between Somaesthetics and the Notion of *Duende*

Nowadays, flamenco has become popular all over the world and was declared one of the Masterpieces of the Oral and Intangible Heritage of Humanity by UNESCO in 2010. Nonetheless, in contrast to that recognition, only a few people have analyzed from the field of aesthetics the characteristics of flamenco, and particularly the notion of *duende*. It is due to the constrained concept of Fine Arts and traditional analytic philosophies that this particular way of performance has been undervalued and ignored within the Spanish context. Thus, I wish to examine more closely the aesthetic category of *duende* and flamenco through the new discipline of somaesthetics proposed by the American philosopher Richard Shusterman.

for sublime emotions, for artistic and metaphysical experiences. But all levels of our experience, metaphysical but also sexual, are parts of a bigger perceptive schema and they equally constitute our consciousness. There is no single proper place for some type of impulses and a different one more appropriate for others. We are constructed from different types of experience and in every moment during our perception of the world they are equally important and meaningful. It is the same as with these three orders of behavior in Merleau-Ponty's approach: it is impossible to reduce the human being to only one of them, so we should stop blocking "unwanted" emotions and impulses, and instead try to understand them and be more conscious of their role in this whole perceptive schema. All the signals from our body are information and we should know how to read and analyze them. The artist makes us more aware that our perception is constructed from many diverse elements which are also changeable and transitory.

It also should be remembered that the effects of our emotional states are not only the summary of the elements that provoke them. This is why Merleau-Ponty relies on Gestalt psychology. According to this approach, human perception is the result of complex interactions. To understand the way humans perceive, it should be comprehended that more important than the elements of cognitive processes is their organization. All our mental states create some structure and we cannot reduce it to its initial components. What is more, structures always have some influence on the environment. As Marek Drwięga argues,

> Behavior itself can be defined as structuralizing and shaping the environment and a given situation. Moreover, the concept of structure becomes central in analyzing behavior, thereby it has a crucial role for the issue of carnality. (2005, 168)[1]

Radziszewski wants to activate different levels of our bodily experience and show that they work together to create some progressive and original structure which influences our surroundings.

One of the most basic assumptions of the philosophy of the body is that the body is the foundation of all human experience. Perception does not exist without its instrument, the body, and every human being is subject to its limits. Radziszewski puts this idea into a social context in the next movie, *America is not ready for this*.

The inspiration for this movie was Natalia LL's travel scholarship to New York in 1977. During that time the Polish artist created one of her most famous pieces of art, called *Consumer Art* (*Sztuka konsumpcyjna*). This is a collage of photographs presenting young, beautiful women eating bananas or sausages in a very sensual and suggestive, erotic way. It was considered to be a provocative and controversial idea. When Natalia LL came to New York she wanted to show her work to a broader audience in one of the city galleries. She heard from the art dealer and collector Leo Castelli that "America is not ready for this." After 34 years Radziszewski is trying to find the right meaning for these words. He talked with artists and dealers who met Natalia LL in 1977. He concluded that America was not then too prudish for *Consumer Art* and that New York artists were doing a lot more controversial work then. This shows that memories of the same situation may vary greatly among different people, depending on their experience, knowledge, and origins. Radziszewski is also trying to find parallels and differences between Polish and American art at that time and compare them with his own artistic experiences. In effect it is research about two totally dissimilar worlds:

> On the one hand—the New York bohemian lifestyle, where the cult of the artist (the white, heterosexual celebrity) still prevailed. On the other—the perspective of a female artist from Europe, specifically from the Soviet Bloc, where people thought that the issue of women's emancipation has already been solved and normalised within the system. (MOCAK 2015)

It can be claimed that *America is not ready for this* is about necessity of spaciousness and temporality for our bodies and—as a consequence—the necessity of our perception. It is inevitable that a person will always put his or her own body and experience at the center of the world. For the philosophy of the body it seems quite obvious, but to locate this fact within social context, as Radziszewski did, makes for interesting trails of interpretation.

However, it should be noted that the body is a very imperfect tool for communication with the world. Our bodily existence accounts for our perception being limited through subjectivity and relativity. Moreover, the body often acts unconsciously or spontaneously. A person might not even know why his or her body was acting in some way, but still it has an influence on the environment and on others. The body may experience the world from the outside, but it never has the same, external experience of itself. The complicated and changeable structure of bodily experience, connected with the "egocentrism" of the body constitute an unpredictable and fragile construction. But this does not mean that our perception is untrustworthy; it is just necessary to know how to comprehend it. The body cannot be perceived like other objects in the external world; it is not a thing in the world but rather an instrument used to communicate with it.

Speaking of the difference between the body and external objects, it is worth mentioning that Natalia LL's works have a particular erotic energy. They show the joy of sex and bodily pleasure. She is not ashamed to speak about sexual experiences and their meaning for a person's life. She is concerned with sexuality as a way of expression. This also helps us to get into the fundamental layer of a personality and the metaphysical aspects of reality.

Natalia LL said:

Since the beginning, I have been interested in the profundity of erotic fulfilment, the inner quality of the experience, the very essence of eroticism, not in superficial aestheticism. ... For eroticism is on the one hand vitality, the joy of life, and elation, and on the other, fear and suffering. (Wierzchowska 2004, 411)

And further she says:

The spasm of erotic delight is a condition of transcendental suspense that permits us to cross the existential perspective. It is both an experience of oneself and death. Having come close to death, I think that the uniqueness of the individual, my own uniqueness, is the engine of every action. (Wierzchowska 2004, 414)

But it is also important that sexuality opens an individual up to other people. It makes an individual share the same type of experience—bodily experience—otherwise not accessible for an individual, isolated subject in the world. It also puts a person in a position to look for sensitivity in others. This type of affectivity is what makes one difference between a thing and the body (in fact the person). If desire is felt, it means that the body treats another body like itself, not like an object. The affective relation involves a different type of perception than objective observation. To feel love or desire means giving a meaning to another person. And what is important—it is not only a sexual meaning, but the distinction of a human being. This knowledge about the other person makes us open to him or her. The assumption that two bodies are at the same level and treat each other equally is the basis of communication.

Merleau-Ponty claims that when humans decide to show their bodies to someone else, they do it because they want to impress others or to incite admiration. On the other hand, however, they are always scared and ashamed to expose themselves to the regard of another person. It is as if the other, by looking, were arrogating the body which is so exposed. At the same time, however, the other runs the risk of being subjugated to the sight of the revealed body, of being conquered and dominated (Merleau-Ponty 2002, 193).

Merleau-Ponty assumes that shame is a primary feeling which we have in the encounter with other beings. An individual is scared for if he has (relation of possession) a body it could be reduced to an object. This is also why desire and love are so important—people are not loving or desiring simple objects, but objects that are animated by consciousness—it means a body as flesh, and furthermore, human beings. But shame and the fear of being treated like an object exist deep in our minds. In intersubjective relations the body, perceived as a medium through which our behaviors are manifested, is the first thing that we are faced with. At the first impression, other bodies are anonymous and objective. After a while, an individual can notice that each body has its own particular ways of expression which give it subjectivity. Then, it can be realized that all bodies could have the same shame and fear of being reduced to objects. This understanding is also a first step to making the body a subject.

I have already mentioned the performance *Rehearsal* with seven almost naked men in it. As I said, reactions were varied, but it is worth noting women's interest in these young men and especially in their attractive bodies. It is impossible to state clearly what they were thinking, but it could be assumed that women treated the young men as sexual objects. From the one perspective, it was perception against subjectivity, but from the other—the sexual aspect made this event less unambiguous and transformed it during this process. This objectifying could be broken up by the individual emotions and movements which was visible in the body of each model. There were five football players, one dancer and one actor—it was easy to discern what their professions were because of the characteristics of the exercises they performed (they were improvised). That type of peculiarity makes people more conscious that a body is not only an object or instrument but is the expression of a human being, presenting not only his or her identity but also information about his or her experience, history and social origin. It was also visible that the seven men in the performance were a little stressed, maybe even ashamed. They were exposed in the gallery, to public view, almost without clothes. The possibility of a fear of being objectified was decidedly increased. In those conditions it was also a test for viewers. They could realize that they perceive other bodies just like objects or they could notice subtle signs of subjectivity. This is also a proof that people express themselves by the body and this is what enables humans to communicate—because we all have this common platform.

In my opinion, Radziszewski shows us several ways of acquiring social knowledge and all of them are based on the body. By using the biography and art of Grotowski, Cieślak, and Natalia LL he presents how people build social beliefs and modes of acting, and how then they function in the society for years. There are some basic ways of getting information: from subconscious or spontaneous reactions of the body; from behaviors presenting the social context, origins, convictions and habits of an individual; from communication with other people; from ways of using the body as an instrument of self-expression. All of these levels say something about an individual's body and, in fact, about the person himself. Together, they create one compact but changeable structure which is the beginning of something much bigger—the social body. I want to refer this assumption to two of Merleau-Ponty's (2002) terms which will highlight both the entire and the most useful concept of this exhibition.

The first of these terms is the phenomenal body. I mentioned it while on the subject of three orders of corporeality. The phenomenal body is created by the living structure of all gestures and poses of a body. Taken together, they have their own immanent meaning and they influence the environment. This is the first important point that can be concluded: a person is something more than the elements of her behavior considered separately. The meaning lies in their connection and organization. And this meaning is never a constant and isolated state—it always works in the external world.

The second term is the body schema. The phenomenal body has an influence on the environment, but it is never a one-way relation. Perception is not a simple process of taking external facts, but requires also analysis and interpretation of this information. It could be imagined as a circle of action. First, the body takes data from the external world, then reads and adapts it to its needs and after that creates its own structure, based on the gestures and poses that are responses to the reality. Besides that, an individual never experiences the world only in an external way, but also in an internal one. All these processes, taken together, create a living structure which is in permanent contact with reality. At the simplest level, it could be compared to the mechanical working of the body:

By the body schema is meant at first a sort of summation of our bodily experience, which is able to provide a comment and meaning to current internal and external experiences. In that sense it is responsible for changing the position of the body and its parts, and with the movement of each of them, it makes possible a recognition of every local impulse in the totality of the body. It provides also the consciousness of this totality of movements that constitute each complex gesture. (Drwięga 2005, 185)

It could be claimed that awareness of the body is constructed from all possible impulses and information and it is always ready for use. People have some predefined structures of acting in order to be prepared for unexpected situations which require quick decisions. These structures are also needed to save energy and not waste it in repeatedly learning to solve anew the same simple task.

On the one hand, the body has these schemas of actions, of automatic reactions, but on the other hand, it can never be prepared for all possible types of situations. It should have a capacity for improvisation. The world is always dynamic and progressive—it is continually sending us new information. The structure of our experience and the body schema are being constantly brought up to date as they are constituted by continuously developing experiences. The body schema exists to give us some fundamental knowledge of our behavior but through the intentionality of the body an individual can experience the world in a dynamic process depending on the current situation. Furthermore, an individual can also create abstract ideas, clearly intellectual constructions, grounded in the imagination rather than in concrete impulses from reality. This allows us to build ideological structures such as religion, science and art.

According to Merleau-Ponty, human perception has three main dimensions: a stable and automatic body schema, complemented by the possibility of a dynamic interpretation of reality and the creation of abstract thinking. The proper functioning of these three fields is possible through a structure which Merleau-Ponty (2002) named "the intentional arc." It coordinates all perceptive, existential and intellectual processes so this is the most basic function of our perception and consciousness. It exists due to the fact that the human body is intentional, so again there is an argument indicating the essential role of the somatic experience. The intentional arc enables the functioning of moral, intellectual, psychical and physical levels; projects the concept of past, future and present; and makes possible the concomitance of all relations with the world in which man exists. As Drwięga states,

> Most simply speaking, it is the function which allows us to direct our orientation both into us and also beyond us (inside and outside us). This function also enables us take an attitude toward the encountered object, placing it in the actual and possible situations, which finally means that in a given behavior we need not rigidly stick to the actual scheme but we proceed to the most efficient one, and thereby in a free and creative way we modify the world around us. (2005, 201)

As I have already said, this dynamic, fluent structure is more like a circle, so movement is a very important quality of it. The body still perceives incoming impulses, it is still in movement. This means that our body is never finally constructed and constituted, but is always in progress—it is being updated all the time. At this point "acting" becomes a very important term. Within our environment we affect each other—we get knowledge through our actions and in that way we learn through constant development. The world, or reality, is the field for our actions. It is the space for our actions. These could be not only concrete, but also creative, abstract actions. Humans have the capacity to abstract and objectify the world. For this reason it is important to understand the way in which our perception and consciousness work. According to Merleau-Ponty consciousness is placed in the body and in some respect it is the body and its history itself.

It could be found that in Radziszewski's exhibition Merleau-Ponty's insights are moved into the social context. First, there are several artists dealing with the body, their own view of bodily experience and their own explorations of this subject. The second thing is that he takes the bodies of these artists and puts them in a double context: firstly, he wants to show the audience some historical background, and after that presents how this background is changing, how much it depends on other people's interpretation and the conditions that have existed at a particular time. But this is only the preparation for a different idea: that in some fashion the human body works like the social body. It could be claimed that if the body is the basis of human experience and interactions with others, it is also a basis of the functioning of the society. Because our knowledge is founded on the body, all social issues arise from the body too. Thus it could be understood how these two concepts work. What is important is that the bodily experience is based on intellectual recognition. These two types of experience are equal and neither of them is privileged. This is why Radziszewski begins with the pure concept of the body, but by mixing it with other ideas and contexts, he forces the audience to think about that and put it into some intellectual framework.

This tendency to combine different ideas and place them against other backgrounds is also very important when it is considered separately along with Merleau-Ponty's term of the body schema and concept of the intentional arc. Radziszewski asks how social knowledge is constructed. There is no a such thing as incontestable, unchanged truth independent of circumstances and interpretations. Radziszewski wants to encourage us to ask questions and undermine official points of view—not in order to make a revolution, but to be more conscious of the mechanisms that build our society. Of course, it is necessary to have predictable rules in the society, regulations, and the law. As in the body schema, it is just essential for an idea of society to have automatic ways of acting. But from a different perspective, the artist shows that sometimes people are too attached to the rules and believe only in one image of the world. They could not imagine that something (or even everything) could be drastically changed. This is why art should make us more conscious about the reality in which we live. The social body works like the intentional body: it is a dynamic, changeable structure, constantly perceiving new data and new contexts. People should be prepared to react spontaneously to new situations, to properly analyze incoming information. The society is a process; our knowledge is a process. But again, it is the same as with the body—functioning in society is not an action-reaction scheme. Impulses and backgrounds depend on each other, people's reactions have an influence on society and society answers them, too. It is also a circle. Human decisions and actions in social reality are interpreted and put into the form of some structure. Taken together, they could create new qualities. So living in society should not be considered only as a process of reaction to certain stimuli—it is also an intellectual viewpoint on these problems and an aware analysis of the social background. Summarizing, the society is a living structure, without a single, correct point of view. People should be aware how it works and they should be prepared to interpret constantly changing contexts and new information. If they were more conscious they could better function in society and they could be more useful for their community.

Could exhibitions like *The Prince and Queens. Body as an Archive* work effectively and have some social influence? I hope so. In my opinion it is already a success that an exhibition performing on many different levels was created in which a balance between artistic, social and philosophical elements is retained. The artist is not trying to force anyone to experience a specific reaction. He wants to make the audience more aware, giving them the possibility to analyze social reality and, at the same time, not saying what to do with it—this is a fair approach. It is also interesting and important how art can use the body to make people more open-minded.

References

Viola, Eugenio. 2014. *Karol Radziszewski: The Prince and Queens: Body as an Archive*. Translated by Aleksandra Jakubczak. Toruń: Centrum Sztuki Współczesnej "Znaki Czasu."

Drwięga, Marek. 2005. *Ciało człowieka: Studium z antropologii filozoficznej* [The human body: A study in philosophical anthropology]. Kraków: Księgarnia Akademicka.

MOCAK: Muzeum Sztuki Współczesnej w Krakowie. 2015. "Karol Radziszewski: America Is Not Ready for This." Accessed January 16, 2015. http://en.mocak.pl/america-is-not-ready-for-this.

Wierzchowska, Wiesława. 2004. "On Art Eroticism. Interview Given by Natalia LL to Wiesława Wierzchowska." Translated by Henryk Holzhausen. In *Natalia LL. Texty. Teksty Natalii LL. O twórczości Natalii LL* [Natalia LL: Texts. Texts of Natalia LL: On the creative works of Natalia LL]. Edited by Natalia LL. Translated by Marek Adamski et al., 411–13. Bielsko-Biała: Galeria Bielska BWA.

Merleau-Ponty, Maurice. 2002. *Phenomenology of Perception*. Translated by Colin Smith. London, New York: Routledge Classics.

Note

[1] My translation. All translations of quotations from Drwięga's book are mine.

CHAPTER SIX

THE MYSTERIOUS FORCE OF *DUENDE*: A DIALOGUE BETWEEN FEDERICO GARCÍA LORCA AND RICHARD SHUSTERMAN[1]

GLORIA LUQUE MOYA

In the year 1933, at the Friends of Art society in Buenos Aires, Federico García Lorca presented a paper about "a buried spirit of saddened Spain." In this presentation, Lorca takes the notion *duende* from Spanish folklore and flamenco and transforms it into an aesthetic category. In this way, Lorca exposes *duende* not as a question of skill, but of a style that's truly alive. That is, in contrast to intellectuals, Lorca describes it as a creative force or struggle in otherwise ordinary human lives. He asserts that we must arouse the *duende*, which lives in us, this mysterious force of immediate creation. We must abandon humdrum existence and let the indescribable *duende* perform.

The aim of this paper is to explore the aesthetic category of *duende* in Lorca's work. This is not an easy task because the *duende* cannot be considered merely as a category of art, but also as a key factor which plays a distinctive role in learning and in a corporeal form of training. The focus of these pages will be to emphasize this forgotten notion in relation to the discipline of somaesthetics by indicating the points at which this meliorative notion of Spanish experience, on the one hand, and the notion of bodily experience explored in somaesthetics, on the other hand, converge. Despite the fact that they have their distinctive features, I will try to show how the combination of these two proposals—Lorca's idea of *duende* and Shusterman's of somaesthetics—provides a perspective for creativity through the body and how it can suggest a way of leading a meaningful life.

I would like to begin by addressing the features of flamenco and the qualities of this term through some of Lorca's major poems and plays and through Spanish traditional songs. Also, I would like to establish a possible field of dialogue between the notion of *duende* in Lorca's work and the new branch of aesthetics founded by Richard Shusterman. Consequently, in this paper, I will attempt to indicate new possibilities, and new meanings, arising in performance studies due to this proposed interaction, whose starting point is life.

An Approach to the Notion of *Duende*

Federico García Lorca was the kind of person and artist who can be called a genius. He was a Spanish poet, playwright and theater director, who was not only keen on flamenco[2] but also tried on the brightest and darkest aspects of this kind of music, considered as a minor art. His poems, particularly *The Poem of the Deep Song*, were an evocation of the essence of flamenco and the notion of *duende*. He belonged to the Generation of '27, an influential group of artist and poets which arose in literary circles between 1923–1927 and worked with avant-garde forms of art.

Federico García Lorca[3] was born in 1898, in Fuente Vaqueros, a small town in Granada, in the south of Spain. He studied law, literature and composition; however he early felt a deeper affinity for the theater and music. He trained as a classical pianist and it was not until his piano teacher died that he published his first work. He travelled to America and Cuba and was a close friend of the composer Manuel de Falla and of the artists Luis Buñuel and Salvador Dalí, whom he met at the student residence in Madrid. He was executed by Nationalist forces during the Spanish Civil War.[4] This tragic end has no closure, because Lorca's remains have yet to be found.

Lorca's biography, as well as his work, was heartrending and marked by the claim of those human creative forces and somatic potential through which human beings, and particularly Andalusian, express the meaning of their lives.[5] The present paper was undertaken in hopes of fulfilling a purpose: to set forth the meaning and spirit of *duende*. However, this is a difficult task; as Arrebola (1986, 71) said, writing about García Lorca and flamenco implies a high risk because of the breadth of his approach. For that reason, I will start by dealing with flamenco and the presentation of *duende* that Lorca makes through his work.[6]

Early on, García Lorca together with his friend Manuel de Falla organized a *Contest of the Deep Song*, a celebration of the art of flamenco, which included music, song, and dance. This was held in Granada on June

13th and 14th, 1922, and its goals were to gain respect for the deep song as art, to protect this style from musical adulteration, to reward non-professional singers, and to show the influence that it had had not only in Spanish music but also in French and Russian. The contest was an attempt to connect the musical art of Andalusia with "universal" art, to transfer it from the local to the universal. Lorca promoted this event and spoke publicly in support of the Contest. The result of this promotion was a lecture which Lorca gave in Granada on February 19th 1922, entitled "Deep Song: Historical and Artistic Importance of Primitive Andalusian Song Called '*Cante Jondo*' 1922." This lecture,[7] which has an educative intention, reveals more about Lorca's and de Falla's own aesthetic principles. Lorca begins it by emphasizing how the festival intends to provide a new comprehension of this traditional music. For this purpose, he draws an essential distinction between the deep song and flamenco singing, based on antiquity, structure and spirit. The main difference between them is that the origin of the deep song must be sought in the primitive musical systems of India, "in the first manifestations of song," (Lorca 1922) while flamenco is a consequence of the first, established in the 18th century. Nevertheless, we should start by asking the question that Lorca (1922) formulates: What then is this deep song or *cante jondo*?

> The name *cante jondo* is given to a category of Andalusian song, of which the perfect and genuine prototype is the Gipsy *siguiriya*, from which derive other songs preserved by the people, such as *polos*, *martinetes*, *carceleras*, and *soleares*. Those called *malagueñas*, *granadinas*, *rondeñas*, *peteneras* etc., should be considered as merely offshoots of those mentioned, since they differ from them in their architecture as much as their rhythm. They are those grouped as flamenco song. (García Lorca 1922)

The deep song emerges from our environment and expresses the most profound gradations of grief and pain. This kind of music creates an unrepeatable atmosphere which is not only experienced as if coming from our body, but also performed through it. The music captures the rare complexity of the highest moments of human feelings and has with them a common resource, death. It is a song concentrated in terrible shadows, shadows that shoot their golden arrows to our heart, shaking our somatic awareness, despite that being the most proven part of life, the only truth that we have.

> Note the transcendence of *cante jondo*, gentlemen, and how right our people are in describing it as such. It is deep, truly deep, more so than any well, more so than all the seas that bathe the world, deeper than the present spirit that creates it or the voice that sings it, because it is well nigh

> infinite. It arises from remote peoples, traversing the graveyard of the
> years, and the fronds of parched winds. It comes from the first cry and the
> first kiss. (García Lorca 1922)

Our environment is not only biological and social, but also has an
aesthetic dimension. Aesthetic is an adjective for that process through
which people give meaning to their present, which is constantly changing.
Thus, living creatures are continuously suffering alterations, and it will be
during those heartrending struggles when the *duende* arises. The true
struggle is with the *duende*, because it leads us to see ourselves face to
face with death. The difficult endeavour is not simply a passive activity,
but a meaningful creative process similar to that of an artist.

The great artists of Southern Spain know that emotion is impossible
without the arrival of *duende* (García Lorca 1933). Lorca tells a story
about Pastora Pavón, known as *La Niña de los Peines*.[8] Once she was
singing in a little tavern in Cadiz, where there were people skilled in
flamenco.

> She played with her voice of shadows, with her voice of beaten tin, with
> her mossy voice, she tangled it in her hair, or soaked it in *manzanilla* or
> abandoned it to dark distant briars. But there was nothing there: it was
> useless. (García Lorca 1933)

The audience did not do anything, only remained silent. Then *La Niña
de los Peines* stood up, swallowed her drink and began to sing with a
scorched throat, without voice, but with *duende*:

> She managed to tear down the scaffolding of the song, but allow through a
> furious, burning *duende*, friend to those winds heavy with sand, that make
> listeners tear at their clothes with the same rhythm as the Negroes of the
> Antilles in their rite, huddled before the statue of Santa Bárbara. (García
> Lorca 1933)

The audience could not restrain themselves anymore and the emotion
of the *duende* erupted in their bodies. When the *duende* escapes, everyone
feels the effect. The deep song has its origins in that heartbreaking cry
which makes our whole bodies tremble; and, according to Lorca, it dates
back to the primitive musical systems of India. Flamenco, by contrast,
arises in the 18th century from the deep song.[9] Although this difference is
really important in Lorca, because the deep song has its origins in the most
heartrending emotions that human beings experience, throughout these
pages I use the terms deep song and flamenco interchangeably, for both
kinds of music. What is more, in *Theory and Play of Duende* Lorca uses
this term to name the fantastic flamenco singer *La Niña de los Peines*. This

To show how the category of *duende* is grounded in aesthetic tradition, I begin by defining somaesthetics and explaining why this category could be examined from the perspective provided by this new discipline. The purpose of this approach is not to show *duende* as a novelty, but to outline its aesthetic dimensions. I will consider the *duende* through the three dimensions of somaesthetics (analytic, pragmatic and practical) in order to outline its characteristics. For this, I will refer to some of Lorca's poems and traditional Spanish songs. Finally, I will conclude this section by raising an important issue: the significance of this mysterious force in every art as the impulse which awakens our somatic awareness and creative faculty. Nevertheless, it is necessary to emphasize that this approach does not pretend to set out some kind of detailed analysis or exhaustive study, but only to extend the existing research about the notion of *duende* by means of a dialogue with Shusterman's discipline, somaesthetics, in the hope that it will encourage mutual enrichment.

Richard Shusterman (2002, 267) defines somaesthetics as a philosophical discipline which focuses on the bodily experience as the object of study; it recognizes the role of the body in both perception and creation, the body being the locus of an individual aesthetic experience ("sensory-aesthetic appreciation," or *aisthesis*) and the medium and object of self-fashioning. As it is conceptualized by Shusterman, somaesthetics has several dimensions: analytical, critical and, significantly, meliorative. In this regard, the new discipline not only provides a perspective for aesthetic reflection about *duende* and the reason behind it, but also outlines the potential within the bodily dimension to improve our everyday interactions.[11] The concepts and ideas of somaesthetics can help us to demonstrate the qualities and particularities of this Andalusian way of dealing with bitter feelings, grief and sorrow.[12]

(1) Following Shusterman's proposal, the first of the fundamental dimensions of somaesthetics, the analytic, concerns itself with somatic perception and embodied practice; it also outlines how they both (corporeal perception and practices) shape the ways in which we make sense of reality (Shusterman 2002, 271). In relation to *flamenco* and the *duende*, this theoretical dimension introduces us to three different aspects: harmony, structure and melody. Flamenco uses a harmonic system described as the modern Phrygian mode.[13] Modifying this harmony, guitarists generate different chord shapes, which expand the repertoire of tonalities, creating new kinds or *palos* (such as *soleá*,[14] *bulerías*, *siguiriyas*, *alegrías*, *fandangos*, *malagueñas*, and so forth). Lorca explains how the musical scale of these songs is a direct consequence of what we

might call the oral scale, a scale founded in the immediate bodily dimension of human beings. In Lorca's (1922) words:

> Then the melodic phrase begins to unfold the mystery of tone, and withdraw the precious stone of a sob, a sonorous tear borne on the river of the voice. No Andalusian, hearing that cry, can resist a quiver of emotion, no regional song can compare in poetic grandeur, and it is seldom, very seldom, that the human spirit has created works of such nature.

The next particular feature is the melody. Flamenco's melody is characterized by intervals smaller than the semitone and a change from one note to another in smooth transitions. This effect is produced by the use of different timbres which singers make, and, in many cases, by the melodic improvisation which the artist spontaneously invents. Thus, the mystery of tone refers to the *duende*, that internal emotion which arises and creates the impression of sung prose, destroying all sense of rhythmic meter, though in reality its literary texts are assonant tercets and quatrains (García Lorca 1922). Referring to this, Lorca (1922) says:

> *Cante jondo* has been cultivated since time immemorial, and every illustrious traveller who has ventured to journey over our surprising and varied landscapes, has been affected by this profound psalmody which has traversed and defined our complex and unique Andalusia, from the peaks of the Sierra Nevada to the thirsty olive-groves of Córdoba, from the Sierra de Cazorla to the joyful mouth of the Guadalquivir.

The third characteristic is meter (*compás* in Spanish), which is commonly translated as rhythm, although meter has more connotations in Spanish folklore than in other Western styles of music. This is one of the main aspects of flamenco and is produced by the guitar techniques of strumming (*rasgueado*) and tapping the soundboard (*golpe*).[15]

The guitarist could be accompanied by hand clapping (*palmas*) or by hitting a table with the knuckles (*golpe*). This characteristic is really important because there is no flamenco without rhythm, and there are different types which vary in their layouts or use of accentuations. As I indicated before, Lorca explains how flamenco rhythm was born centuries ago, and compares flamenco rhythms with the rhythms of nature and the primitive song.

> Flamenco singing proceeds not by undulations but by leaps; its rhythm is as measured as that of our music, and was born centuries after Guido of Arezzo gave names to the notes.

Cante jondo is like the trilling of birds, the cry of the cockerel, and the natural music of woods and streams.

It is, then, the rarest specimen of primitive song, the oldest in Europe, bearing in its notes the naked shiver of emotion of the first oriental races. (García Lorca 1922)

According to Lorca, rhythm is rooted in the natural needs, constitution and activities of the organism. This way, he emphasizes our biological background and explains how human beings and other animals are pushed to self-expression by their personal and somatic needs. In this respect, Lorca's approach presents suggestive similarities with Deweyan aesthetics. In 1934 John Dewey laid the foundation of a Philosophy of Art which had its roots in the essential conditions of life, that is, the basic vital functions which human beings share with birds and beasts. Dewey asserted that at every moment living creatures are exposed to conflicts which arise in their surroundings, and at every moment they try to restore the harmony, to satisfy their needs.

Following Dewey's inspiration, Shusterman reconsiders this somatic naturalism from his own point of view. The discipline he has proposed focuses on the perceptive and creative dimension of the body, but also on the improving of the direction of our bodies through performance. Shusterman stresses that the ancient philosophical roots of this somaesthetic strategy go back to Socrates and ancient Greece, where the somatic training was part of the all-round education aimed at increasing one's knowledge and virtue (Shusterman 2002, 268). Besides, Shusterman (2002) shows how recognition of somatic training is an essential aspect of Asian practices of Hatha Yoga, Zen meditation and *Tàijíquán* (太极拳), in which the fine-tuning of the senses is essential for the gaining of a deeper understanding of the world.

(2) However, dealing with the meliorative function of bodily experience will be a task that pertains to the second dimension of somaesthetics, that is, pragmatic somaesthetics, whose goal is set as an improvement of the functioning of both the body and social ties, or of how we live through our bodies and in a society (Shusterman 2002, 272). Flamenco can be considered a pragmatic discipline, which has been employed to improve experience and use of the body (Shusterman 2002). This performance is not only a kind of music and dance, but a method of treating sadness and bitter feelings. The *toque*[16] of the guitar, the passionate voice of the singer and the emotional intensity of the dance express a unique emotion through the body. Flamenco arises from the awareness of somatic experience.

What is more, there is no distinction between its representational or experiential forms. Flamenco emphasizes the body's external appearance, just as it focuses on what Shusterman also emphasizes: the aesthetic quality of "inner" experience (Shusterman 2002, 272). When considering the inner experience, it is necessary to return to the notion of *duende*. When Lorca examines flamenco, he drops notions such as muse (from the German tradition) and angel (from the Italian tradition) and focuses on *duende* instead. However, when seeking the *duende*, there is neither map nor discipline. Each art has a distinct mode and form of *duende*, having their roots in that creative force or tensions which all human beings share and some philosophers put forward. The *duende* always implies change, new forms, the sweet smell of new meanings, energetic responses in which the body is the connecting thread.

Therefore, Lorca rejects the role that the Fine Arts have, thus far, performed and, through an apparently ordinary notion, recovers the creative aspect of our lives. We can ask: Where is that *duende*? But we only can find an answer through the manifestations that continuously occur in our lives and, however, go unnoticed:

> The *duende*… Where is the *duende*? Through the empty archway a wind of the spirit enters, blowing insistently over the heads of the dead, in search of new landscapes and unknown accents: a wind with the odour of a child's saliva, crushed grass, and medusa's veil, announcing the endless baptism of freshly created things. (García Lorca 1933)

 Human beings are shaken by this somatic force, which merges as an inner experience and displays its creative potentiality through the body. People are deeply affected by sadness and death, and the *duende* arises from these situations. When the muse sees death appearing she closes the door, and then bridges the gap. When the angel sees death appearing he flies in slow circles and, trembling, makes an elegy. However, as Lorca (1933) says,

> the *duende*, by contrast, won't appear if he can't see the possibility of death, if he doesn't know he can haunt death's house, if he's not certain to shake those branches we all carry, that do not bring, can never bring, consolation.

In every other country death is an ending, but, in Spain, this opens a new door. Many Spaniards live indoors till the day they die and are carried into the sun; and tales of death and its contemplation are familiar to Spaniards (García Lorca 1933). Lorca emphasizes this particular way of dealing with death and sadness and uses it in his works, such as *Blood*

Wedding. This work, written in 1932, focuses on the analysis of that tragic sense as arising from within an Andalusian landscape. The plot of this great drama is life and death—but only as regarded in an arcane and ancestral mode, which contains myths, legends and heartbreaking use of the body, which introduces the reader or spectator into a world of dark passions and death. In *Blood Wedding*, we can see how the *duende* rises from an unbearably sad situation as a way of facing it and gives it deep meaning by means of the somatic awareness developing in the interaction with the surroundings. Lorca (1933) quotes a traditional song to exemplify this:

> In the garden
> I shall die,
> in the rose-tree
> they will kill me,
> Mother I went
> to gather roses,
> looking for death
> within the garden.
> Mother I went
> cutting roses,
> looking for death
> within the rose-tree.
> In the garden
> I shall die.
> In the rose-tree
> they'll kill me.

This particular somatic method grows in Andalusian fields. Flamenco, as does Lorca's work, opens with an evocation of the landscape and the somatic involvement in that environment, which implies abandonment but also mindfulness. The land of these human expressions is a "dry land, quiet land of immense nights" (Loughran 1978, 63), and these nights provide that vital tension which needs to be given meaning. Lorca returns to dawn and sunset to draw that promise of renewal. That particular interaction between human beings and landscape implies a conscious somatic involvement in the cyclical death and rebirth of nature.[17]

In this way, the magic force of Lorca's works consists in their being filled with *duende*, gazing across the dark emotions of Spaniards and creating a *poiesis* which overwhelms the reader. The human struggle in devastating situations becomes expression and communication of a deep meaning which is rooted in the soma. The tragedy does not need to be explained or reasoned, the death is just simply a happening. We can see this aspect through *The Poem of the Deep Song*, like in "Memento"[18] or in the song of the mother of the embittered one in the "Epilogue," where Lorca faces, with different voices, the appointed day with death.[19]

(3) The third dimension of somaesthetics is called practical somaesthetics. This does not produce theories or pragmatic methods of somatic care, but is about practicing. This practical dimension we can easily show through flamenco performance. That is, we can theorize about characteristics of flamenco through analytic somaesthetics, we can explore the notion of *duende* by means of pragmatic methods, but we also need to participate in these aesthetic practicals. Traditionally, the *duende* has been identified in the different forms of flamenco expression: guitar, song and dance. However, for Lorca, the most impressive effects of *duende* appear in the bullring, "since it must struggle on the one hand with death, which can destroy it, and on the other with geometry, measure, the fundamental basis of the festival" (García Lorca 1933).

The bullfighter (*toreador*) must be brave to fight against bulls because if he shows cowardice he will lower himself to a ridiculous level by playing with his life. However, the bullfighter trains his body and concentration and displays the highest somatic awareness when he is bitten by the *duende*. He gives a masterful lesson and makes us forget that he is constantly throwing his heart at the horns (García Lorca 1933). In this sense, it is important to keep in mind that "the *duende* never repeats itself, any more than the waves of the sea do in a storm" (García Lorca 1933). The *duende* is that particular way of dealing with distraught moments, the force which merges in human beings and returns to aesthetic discourse the body and its dimensions which have been rejected.

For Lorca, each art, as is natural, has a distinct mode and form, although all of them share the roots from which they arise: the dark sounds and uncontrollable depth which disrupt our somatic harmony and threaten us. Lorca mentions different artists, singers and dancers who have developed the *duende* in their disciplines, but also thinkers whose thought was marked by the mysterious force of *duende*. His words about St. Theresa express this exceptionally well:

> Flamenca not for entangling an angry bull, and passing it magnificently three times, which she did: not because she thought herself pretty before Brother Juan de la Miseria: nor for slapping His Holiness's Nuncio: but because she was one of those few creatures whose *duende* (not angel, for the angel never attacks anyone) pierced her with an arrow and wanted to kill her for having stolen his ultimate secret, the subtle link that joins the five senses to what is core to the living flesh, the living cloud, the living ocean of love liberated from time. (García Lorca 1933)

Conclusion

By focusing on this dialogue between somaesthetics and the notion of *duende*—as structured with respect to the three main dimensions of this discipline and its representational and experiential modes—I have tried to explore and highlight the potential of this Spanish aesthetic category, which has been traditionally neglected. In hopes of fulfilling this purpose, firstly, it has been my intention to present the Spanish poet Federico García Lorca. This poet not only reflects about the notion of *duende*, but through his works helps us discover the *duende* which moves and affects Lorca's soma. Secondly, I have tried to set forth the meaning and spirit of the notion of *duende* by viewing it through the conceptual framework provided by somaesthetics. This approach emphasizes the aesthetic dimension of this internal creative force which merges with the heartbroken body. However, the subject of this paper resists being confined to the space of a few pages, and if we want to participate in and feel the *duende*, we need to attend a touching performance or to immerse ourselves in Lorca's verses, because:

> This mysterious force that everyone feels and no philosopher has explained is, in sum, the spirit of the earth, the same *duende* that scorched Nietzche's heart as he searched for its outer form on the Rialto Bridge and in Bizet's music, without finding it, and without seeing that the *duende* he pursued had leapt from the Greek mysteries to the dancers of Cadiz and the headless Dionysiac scream of Silverio's *siguiriya*. (García Lorca 1933)

References

Allen, Rupert C. 1972. *The Symbolic World of Federico García Lorca*. Albuquerque: University of New Mexico.

Arrebola, Alfredo. 1986. *El sentir flamenco en Bécquer, Villaespesa y Lorca* [The flamenco feeling in Bécquer, Villaespesa and Lorca]. Málaga: Universidad de Málaga editorial.

García Lorca, Federico. 1922. *Deep Song (Importancia histórica y artística del primitivo cante andaluz llamado 'Cante Jondo')*. Translated by Anthony S. Kline. Poetry in Translation Archive (2008). Accessed December 12, 2014. http://bit.ly/2ks5Jkj.

—. 1933. *Theory and Play of the Duende*. Translated by Anthony S. Kline. Poetry Translation Archive (2007). http://bit.ly/1A7V5vH. Accessed September 7, 2015.

Hewitt, Michael. 2013. *Musical Scales of the World*. UK: The Note Tree.

Loughran, David K., 1978. *Federico García Lorca. The Poetry of Limits.* London: Tamesis Books Limited.

Ossa de la Martinez, Marco Antonio. 2014. *Ángel, musa y duende: Federico García Lorca y la música* [Angel, muse and duende: Federico García Lorca and the music]. Madrid: Universidad de Castilla la Mancha.

Rabassó, Carlos A. 1998. *Granada, Nueva York, La Habana: Federico García Lorca entre el flamenco, el jazz y el afrocubanismo* [Granada, Nueva York, La Habana: Federico García Lorca between the flamenco, the jazz and the Afro-Cuban jazz]. Madrid: Ediciones Libertarias.

Shusterman, Richard. 2002. *Pragmatist Aesthetics: Living Beauty, Rethinking Art.* Lanham: Rowman & Littlefield Publishers.

—. 2012. *Thinking through the Body: Essays in Somaesthetics.* New York: Cambridge University Press.

Notes

[1] Quotations from Federico García Lorca's essays *Deep Song (Importancia histórica y artística del primitivo cante andaluz llamado 'Cante Jondo')* and *Theory and Play of the Duende* reprinted with permission from Poetry in Translation Archive (by A. S. Kline TRANSLATOR, Copyright © 2007–2008).

[2] Flamenco is a form of Spanish folk music and dance from the region of Andalusia, in the south of Spain. This kind of music includes singing (*cante*), guitar, dance and handclaps (*palmas*) and has three different styles, named *palos*. One of the most famous *palos* is the deep song (*cante jondo*), to which Lorca dedicates the *Poem of the Deep Song*.

[3] According to Spanish naming customs, García Lorca is sometimes referred to simply as "Lorca," his second surname.

[4] There is a significant controversy about the motives and details of Lorca's murder. Some academics have suggested that it could have had personal and non-political motives, such as his sexual orientation, but others have marked his liberal views as the reason for his murder.

[5] For a more complete view of influences in Lorca see Allen 1972.

[6] See also Ossa de la Martinez 2014.

[7] In 1921, Lorca had already started to write his *Poem of the Deep Song*, unpublished until 1931.

[8] It literally means The Girl of the Combs. The nickname comes from a stanza in tangos style, which she used to sing.

[9] For a broadened approach to the relationship between Lorca and music see Rabassó 1998.

[10] See e.g. Lorca's poem *Encounter* (translated by David K. Loughran, see Loughran 1978, 69).

[11] See Shusterman 2012.

[12] See e.g. *The Guitar*, a part of the second section of Lorca's *Poem of the Gypsy Siguiriya* (translated by David K. Loughran, see Loughran 1978, 57).

[13] The Phrygian mode is a diatonic scale, commonly known as modern natural minor musical mode. This differs in its second scale degree, because of its low semitone, and consists in root, minor second, minor third, perfect fourth, perfect fifth, minor sixth, minor seventh, and octave (Hewitt 2013).

[14] The *soleá* is one of the most basic forms or "palos" of Flamenco music, originating in Andalusia, whose name is an Andalusian way of saying loneliness (*soledad*).

[15] See e.g. *The Guitar*, a part of the second section of Lorca's *Poem of the Gypsy Siguiriya* (translated by David K. Loughran, see Loughran 1978, 56).

[16] The *toque* is the technique which flamenco guitarists use, playing the guitar between the sound hole and the bridge, thus producing a harsher sound quality.

[17] See e.g. Lorca's poem *Dawn* (translated by David K. Loughran, see Loughran 1978, 70).

[18] See *Memento* (translated by David K. Loughran, see Loughran 1978, 64).

[19] See *The Song of the Mother of the Embittered One* (translated by David K. Loughran, see Loughran 1978, 92).

PART II

LITERARY RECEPTION, CANON, AND HISTORY

CHAPTER SEVEN

PERFORMANCE OF NARRATIVE FICTION: LITERATURE FROM THE PERSPECTIVE OF THE PERFORMATIVE TURN, SOMAESTHETICS, AND THE THEORY OF INTERSUBJECTIVITY

JAROSŁAW WOŹNIAK

The main subject of my discussion will be anthropofiction. Arkadiusz Żychliński, a Polish literary theorist, uses this term to refer to narrations that enable an individual to understand what it really means to be a human being. I would like to situate the notion of (anthropo)fiction, and related issues, in three perspectives: performative turn, somaesthetics and the theory of intersubjectivity developed by Magdalena Rembowska-Płuciennik in her study *Poetyka intersubiektywności. Kognitywistyczna teoria narracji a proza XX wieku* (Poetics of intersubjectivity: Cognitive narratology and the 20th century prose). These three theoretical approaches, by overcoming the mind–body opposition, allow us, in my opinion, to enrich literary studies with a novel concept of literature and its reception and with the idea of performativity. Fiction, including literature, is, Żychliński argues, an expression of the human narrative disposition (2014, 70) and

> an institutionalized narrative, that is, a story located in a certain institutional frame. The Polish language emphasizes particularly that this story is imaginary and therefore unreal in a factual and referential sense. A story, however, if it is successful, is true in the sense of "the truth" which we could call existential truth (that is, a kind of insight into universal human bio-graphy). (71)[1]

For now, I will not comment on the statement that a "universal human bio-graphy" exists (which I highly doubt). What is more, Żychliński, by referring to, e.g., the literary scholar Brian Boyd and neuropsychologist

Donald O. Hebb, emphasizes that fiction is a space where reality is tested (simulated) and where human experience can be rethought. According to Żychliński, anthropofictions are stories which allow us to find a deeper answer to the question about the meaning of being human. The notion of anthropofiction and the concept of "universal human bio-graphy," that allegedly answers to the question of the fundamental mystery of humanity's essence, provoke, among others, the following questions: Where are we to find the feature common to all human beings? And what enables fictions to suggest an answer to this first question? Another important issue is the way in which fictions perform effectively, that is, win our approval of the presented truths. Of course, there are many possible answers, and I will not be able to address them all in this paper. However, the theoretical contexts applied in this paper strongly indicate solutions that stress the role of the somatic and experiential aspects of literature.

A reflection upon fictions/stories or, to be more precise, literature, has to include an analysis of the narration. This is highly problematic, since narrativism—the narrative turn—seems to be the opposite of the phenomenon known as the performative turn, which is one of the theoretical perspectives applied in my paper. Arkadiusz Żychliński argues that the interweaving of the world with narration/stories is a natural mode of human functioning in the world (Żychliński 2014, 73). As a consequence, the idea that the basic feature of human existence is its narrative, established in the relation between the language and the world, seems natural. However, as claimed by Ewa Domańska—a Polish scholar who works mainly in the field of the theory of historiography and posthumanities—the performative turn is a consequence of the devaluation of such currents as textualism and narrativism.[2] This perspective is opposite to those that concentrate on the language and textuality (Domańska 2007, 48). The performative turn assumes that *performance* is "a central aspect of the human condition and that it's a constitutive element of the community-building process" (Domańska 2007, 50), and its features are

> focusing on agency and changes caused in reality … and overcoming a textual metaphor of the world and the turn towards an understanding of the world as a multitude of performative actions and as a performance in which actors participate. (52)[3]

This view can be seen as the development of Milton Singer's notion "culture as performance," and also of Erving Goffman's research on social behavior. At this point I would like to devote some attention to the determinants and consequences of the performative turn as specified by

Ewa Domańska. I would also like to look at her concept of the hybridic strong subject.

Derived from performance studies, the metaphor of performance has quickly gained political significance in two dimensions, which is reflected in the distinction between the notions of performance and performativity. As Jon McKenzie points out, nowadays performance is defined as *liminal* process, and it is seen as something that transgresses social structures (McKenzie 2001, 8), which allows us to enact and undermine the institutionally imposed norms. And so, according to Domańska, the expansion of performance studies in the humanities involves the adaptation of the latter to the modern world, where it turns out that "the metaphor of the world as text does not have the power to explain the problems of the modern world" (Domańska 2007, 52). Domańska believes that the performative turn is also a kind of a revolt against reality (in opposition to textualism, which, according to her, implies only a contemplative attitude to reality). It affirms change and the active causative subject (performative subject) which acts in the world. This subject is called by Domańska "a strong subject," as opposed to the postmodern "weak" subject. The latter, she holds, is able only to maneuver and avoid the disciplinary power in the world of liquid modernity. As she claims, the performative turn has also a post-humanist side: agency is assigned to both human and non-human beings. A longer passage from Domańska's paper will be illuminating:

> The focus on the issues of performativity and agency allows us to go back to the discussion on the topics pertaining to the practice and performance (and generally with reality as such) … Thus, the performative turn can also be seen in terms of the "return of the strong subject." … The performative strong subject creates itself in happenings and events. This subject is no longer just a spectator, but rather an initiator and an agent. It is not a "lonely subject" (a romantic subject), but a subject which cooperates with others subjects and actors (with the human and non-human beings). (2007, 56)

In the context of this paper, Domańska's comments on the subject's agency and its essence seem to be very important. Significant also are her comments about the subject's performative (self)-creation in events and about its collaboration with others subjects. At this point it is worth looking at the type of essentialism that Domańska develops in her work. It is, to use the notion employed by the author herself, neo-esentialism—a position which does not claim to hold the truth about eternal and unchanging human nature and absolutist universalisms. Neo-essentialism assumes *some* essence, which is created situationally, in the dialogue. This kind of essence is relational, but, despite its processuality, it has, Domańska writes, the "potential to 'ground' the subjectivity" (Domańska 2012, 139). In my opinion, the most important idea—thanks to which it is possible to combine all three perspectives to which I am referring in this paper—is that of overcoming cultural determinism and taking into account both the biological aspect of subjectivity and the role of self-creation in the emergence of the subject. The entity is rooted both in culture and biology, and in itself (Domańska 2012, 139).

The adoption of this position has led Domańska to look critically at so-called *French Theory*. In particular, Michel Foucault's thought is up for review. Domańska claims that, although his work has contributed significantly to the elucidation of the mechanisms of knowledge-power systems, exposed the disciplinary assumptions of modern thinking, contested the repressive society and strengthened the criticism and suspicion of existing conventions, it has also created a vision of subjectivity "shaped by the relation to power and devoid of agency" (Domańska 2012, 148). So *French Theory* revealed the mechanisms of the oppressive system, but did not leave any hope that it might be escaped (Domańska 2012, 156). Therefore, there is the need for an approach which affirms the agency of the subject and overcomes "the discursive determinism"—in short, a performative approach. Indeed, Domańska asks: "Do we not find absurd the idea of the 'spiral of power,' where each liberation brings another (though different) phase of repression, solidified by recent victims?" (Domańska 2012, 160). The postulate of turning toward affirmative theory allows me to refer at this point to Richard Shusterman's somaesthetics.

Shusterman's project, including his pragmatist aesthetics and, its development, somaesthetics, assumes that individuals possess the ability of reflection and self-reflection. His philosophy might be contrasted with postmodernist pantextual concepts,[4] because it implies the possibility of emancipation, the liberation from the "spiral of power," by raising body consciousness and the affirmative approach to its role in the creation of meanings, understanding and interpretation. Shusterman is not the first thinker in the history of philosophy to emphasize the value of the body. His predecessors include Nietzsche, William James, John Dewey, Maurice Merleau-Ponty and—of course—Michel Foucault, not to mention ancient philosophers such as Socrates and Diogenes.[5] As Dorota Koczanowicz notes, in modernism the body was reappraised by being equalized with the mind, but in postmodernist currents its integral existence was called into question and the body has ceased to be "a place where the process of cognition may occur and become the result of the operation of the omnipotent social forces, anonymous and all-pervading power"

(Koczanowicz 2013, 128). Though I have a great admiration for Foucault's work (and I do not want to reject his philosophy), I also agree that, besides critical analysis, an affirmative project is needed.[6] Somaesthetics provides such an approach. At its center is a category of experience; and the main assumption is that by developing the capabilities of perception and by improving consciousness of the body an individual is able to perform better, not only physically, but also socially. These features of Shusterman's philosophy will be important in the later part of this paper, where I will discuss the category of intersubjectivity and the possibility of combining the three main perspectives discussed in this paper with literary studies. I do not intend to provide an overview of Shusterman's philosophy—firstly, a short paper is not the appropriate forum for this, and secondly, others have already done it (see for example: Małecki 2010). But I would like to draw attention to the elements of his work that allow us to look at literature from the perspective of performance studies and bodily experience and to combine them with literary studies.

It should be emphasized once again that Shusterman in his project of somaesthetics seeks to both complement and overcome the linguistic trends in philosophy that have led to the textualization of the human subject. As one might guess, this is the point where Shusterman's project meets the vision of the humanities proposed by Ewa Domańska. In contrast to the proponents of pantextualism, Shusterman insists on the recognition of the non-linguistic, or somatic, experience. However, the somatic experience cannot always be connected with non-discursive immediacy, because in many ways it is structured by the discursive environment and institutions in which our bodies perform. This is dictated also by some form of body memory associated with the social role of the individual (Koczanowicz 2013, 125). In somaesthetics it is thought that body consciousness and awareness of how the body is disciplined may lead to emancipation (Shusterman 2000b, 259–60).

A debate with other philosophers of the body is an interesting element in Shusterman's philosophy. Through disputing with them, he has constituted his own project. For example, while appreciating Maurice Merleau-Ponty's argument that the body is not only the center of all our perception but also the basis of our expressions and, hence, is fundamental for language and meaning,[7] Shusterman finds his criticism of conscious reflection upon the body unjustified. Shusterman's emphasis on the need to develop body consciousness—which might lead not only to the possibility of better functioning in the world, but also to a better understanding of oneself and other individuals—is significant for my argument, since, later in this paper, I will combine the category of body consciousness with the category of intersubjectivity and understanding. At this point, however, I wish to highlight the importance of intersubjectivity in Merleau-Ponty's philosophy and its connection to the fact of embodiment. Merleau-Ponty argues that the whole of human experience is rooted in corporeality. And in the experience of corporeality common to all humans—in intercorporeality—the source of intersubjectivity is located. As Monika Rembowka-Płuciennik, referring to Merleau-Ponty's theory, states, "all forms of human cognition, perception and being with others, all social practices involve the body. Thus, the primary level of intersubjectivity is the prerational, prelinguistic and prereflective level" (Rembowska-Płuciennik 2012, 100). For that reason Shusterman is right in his call for an increased awareness of the body. If, as Merleau-Ponty claims, and Shusterman seems to agree with this opinion, all social practices involve the body, then this means that the body—and not only the mind—is also involved in literature. And if this is so, the expounding of body awareness can also have a positive impact on the ability to understand art, including literature.

At this point, there emerges a relevant issue which I would like to briefly discuss before I move on to the next important question, which is the category of body-mind or the embodied mind. The issue I want to consider at once is the distinction between "understanding" and "interpretation" made by Shusterman. It is connected to his critique of hermeneutic universalism. Although hermeneutics has certainly contributed to the rejection of foundationalism, according to Shusterman, it can also lead to potentially dangerous consequences—namely, the notion of interpretation, if applied to all aspects of human life, will lose its validity. To avoid this, he proposes the introduction of the category of understanding, signifying an intelligent and meaningful relationship between an individual and the world. Understanding, in contrast to interpretation, is not always discursive. Shusterman does not agree with the view that understanding is limited to the interpretive and calls such thinking an interpretative mistake. As Wojciech Małecki has pointed out, this is a key moment in Shusterman's argumentation: while Shusterman understands interpretation as reflection, or an activity of conscious thought and reflection, he views understanding as an "intelligent behavior" which does not imply such activities (for instance, it takes place when someone understands a statement without thinking about it). However, Małecki rightly asks why the intuitive understanding of words cannot be considered interpretation. I would like to uphold this question: we cannot ignore the fact that that what is linguistic must be subjected to interpretation. But, it seems to me, the "understanding" in the sense that Shusterman proposes may relate to bodily states and sensations, and understanding happens because of the bodily intersubjectivity to which Merleau-Ponty points in his philosophy. However, Shusterman's arguments indicate that within hermeneutic universalism "interpretation" has become an all-encompassing category, and because of that it has lost all heuristic and critical value. Thus, the practical or functional distinction between understanding and interpretation is a needed alternative to the tendency of hermeneutic universalism to analyze human understanding of the world from the high theory perspective. At this point, I could go further and discuss Shusterman's dialogue with Dewey's philosophy, but I would like to postpone this moment and devote a few lines to the issue of the production of meaning in interpretation that emerges in Shusterman's work. In the term "producing the meaning" the author of *Body Consciousness* combines an active and reconstructive nature of the understanding of texts. The general goal of this understanding is not to reach a core of meaning, but to respond meaningfully to the text. For me it is a very important moment in Shusterman's philosophy, which has significantly influenced the view on the "anthropofictions" which I would like to propose. As claimed by Małecki, Shusterman's position might be summarized as "interpretive pluralism" in which "the meaning of the text is a 'correlate' of its use," and therefore may change. Moreover the understanding and interpretation cannot be absolutely complete (Małecki 2010, 99).

Finally, I can return to the discussion of somaesthetics, developed by Shusterman in his dialogue with Dewey's philosophy. The general conception of the body in somaesthetics, as Małecki explains, was mainly inspired by Dewey. Dewey dismantles—as Shusterman does after him—the body-mind duality. The Deweyan idea of the mind is pragmatic in that the mind is viewed as an "adaptive tool" that has undergone a gradual, evolutionary fine-tuning; it is a derivative of the evolution of the human neurological system. To Dewey, then, Małecki observes, the mind is not the opposite of the body. On the contrary, the two ideas are subsumed within the unifying concept of the soma through which we both live our sensory life and think (Małecki 2010, 149).

Here comes the Deweyan concept of body-mind, which, in the form of the idea of "an embodied mind" introduced by neurobiology, has found its application in cognitive narratology which strives to overcome computational approaches to the human mind. At this point some connection between somaesthetics and literary studies might be made. The concept of the embodied mind overcomes the dualistic mind—body opposition. Besides, this concept allows us to turn to the theory of intersubjectivity, as it was developed by Rembowska-Płuciennik, and to emphasize the social nature of the mind. The social character of human life and mind is also stressed by Shusterman, who reaffirms the Deweyan tradition. We all are material bodies dependent on our interactions with other material beings, including other humans (Shusterman 2008, 182).

The fact of embodiment, of possessing/being a soma, is a *sine qua non* for intersubjectivity. In Shusterman's philosophy the embodied subject somehow fills the gap between itself and the outside world with its corporeality. The thread that connects the subject to the world is, then, the bodily experience. At the same time, the embodiment of the subject makes it impossible for it to ever achieve a "universal perspective," and it is always restricted to its own point of view. The corporeality of the subject, its perspective, but also its connectedness to others through the experience of embodiment, will be important for the discussions of the category of intersubjectivity in literary communication and of the position of the reader in literary communication—the reader seen not as a textual function, but as the corporeal reader. This discussion will be conducted with reference to Rembowska-Płuciennik's cognitive narratology. All these notions of embodied subject and the corporeal basis of intersubjectivity allow me to include in this paper the performative perspective in its theatrical and sociological dimension.

Thus far, I have approached Shusterman's philosophy from the socio-political side of the performative turn, related to Domańska's concept of the strong subjectivity. Now I would like to return to performance studies, but this time to their theatrical and aesthetic dimension as seen through the lens of Shusterman's concept of "art as dramatization." This concept combines two meanings of the verb "to dramatize." In Shusterman's words,

> to dramatize means to "put something on stage" … This sense of "dramatize" highlights the fact that art is the putting of something into a frame, a particular context that sets the work apart from the ordinary stream of life and thus marks it as art. (2002, 233)

Literature constitutes similar "frames" also, but when we think about certain existential truths contained in anthropofictions, it is clear that the attention is focused rather on the experience. In the experiential meaning of art's dramatization, as Shusterman observes,

> art distinguishes itself from ordinary reality not by its fictional frame of action but by its grater vividness of experience and action, through which art is opposed not to the concept of *life* but rather to that which is lifeless and humdrum. (2002, 234)

Further he refers to the etymological roots of the concept of drama, which

> derives from the Greek word "drama" (δραμα) whose primary meaning is a real deed or action rather than a formal framing or staged performance. This suggests that drama's power derives, partly at least, not from the framing stage but from the stirring energy of intense action itself; for action is not only a necessity of life but a feature that invigorates it. (Shusterman 2002, 234)

Similar reflections characterize Anna Krajewska's attempts to transplant the achievements of dramatics and theater studies into the discourse of literary studies (Krajewska 2009). The "dramatic theory of literature," the inclusion of literary studies in the performative turn, implies talking about literature in terms of action, interaction and affect. But there is a significant problem—namely, a conflict between performance studies (performance) and literary studies (text).

The conflict between performance studies and the theoretical currents that are focused on text and narration was not caused by the difference between seeing reality, art and social life as a performance and seeing them as a text (although, within the performative turn, performance studies strove to describe human existence in terms of performance [see McKenzie 2001]). It had existed earlier in the field of drama studies and was associated with those researchers who represented a performative approach and opposed the textual approach to drama taken by the New Criticism. It was a kind of a conflict between performance studies and literary studies. As W. B. Worthen argues, the approach to drama in the second half of the 20th century was dominated by two critical models: New Criticism and performance studies. The first of these proposed a very restrictive model of reading and interpretation. New Criticism established a decontextualized way of interpretation, in which a poem was seen as a pure "verbal artefact." On the other hand, performance studies, described by Worthen as an "antidiscipline"[8] (Worthen 2010), have combined the achievements of anthropologists, sociologists, literary critics and theorists of communication. In his book *Drama. Between Poetry and Performance* Worthen tries to undermine the opposition between literary studies, which inherit a lot from the New Criticism, and performance studies. While the former trend creates a closed form, the latter tries to open it. But Worthen is determined to prove that writing need not be seen as being opposed to performance. Undoubtedly, Worthen is referring to one specific genre, i.e., drama, but there emerges the question whether the category of performance may be extended to literature as a whole. Difficulties in finding out how to read a drama stem from the need to situate the reading between literature as such and its implementation onstage. The adoption of the tools provided by performance studies, the turn toward the notion of performance in literary studies, and thinking about the acts of reading and writing in terms of performance and experience extend the same dilemmas to the whole of literature. There is obviously a need to focus not only on the text, but also on the situation of reading itself and on the interactions between the reader and other actors in literary communication and, finally, on how literature affects the reader, or what literature "does to the readers." The reader must be seen not as a function written into text, but rather as a real, embodied subject. That is why literary studies should not turn away from such new disciplines as somaesthetics.

Since the 1980s performance studies have opposed the "literary" approach in drama studies, considering such a method a limitation on the insubordinate nature of performance. Since antiquity, at the very core of drama studies there has been a dialectical tension between writing and performing (Worthen 2010, 36). However, I do not reckon that the narrative and performative approaches are necessarily opposed to each other, including in literary studies, in which important questions concern the affective power of literature, its performing at different levels, e.g. in social or literary systems. Recently, Dorota Wojda, recalling Richard Bauman's studies on performance, has pointed out that verbal art is increasingly recognized as a performance in the sense of artistic activity and artistic event: a situation of performance which includes the performer, the artistic form, the public and artistic frame (Wojda 2014, 149). Anna Krajewska's project of a dramatic theory of literature (strongly rooted in theater studies and deconstruction) is heading in a similar direction. The notions of agency, performativity and performance are applied both to the act of writing (which recalls the famous Derrida essay *Che cos'è la poesia?*) and the act of reading. In her book Krajewska argues that "writing is like a theatrical performance; it is a permanent playing of the scene, entering into dialogues with partners" (Krajewska 2009, 9). And the act of reading she describes by using a metaphor: "With the image of the liquid borders of performative identity of the writer and the text itself corresponds a dramatic process of interpretation, associated with the position of the reader as an actor who plays the text" (Krajewska 2009, 11). She highlights the difference between playing and acting out to illustrate the important role of the reader in the process of sense-making.

Now I will return to the notion of intersubjectivity, which I would like to incorporate into the reflections on the performative power of anthropofiction. The concept of intersubjectivity is already firmly rooted in philosophical discourse and the social sciences. Unfortunately, the scope of this paper does not allow me to include considerations about the career of this notion in the philosophies of such different thinkers as Husserl, Heidegger, Lévinas and Gadamer. However it is worth noting that for the Polish philosopher Paweł Dybel the category of intersubjectivity assumes that:

> Firstly, everything that occurs between people occurs between them as separate "subjects" capable of reflection and auto-reflection; subjects that—containing in themselves a base of all references to the others—are included in advance in a common sphere of communication that has an *a priori* transcendental character. Secondly, it is assumed that the interpersonal, understood analogically to "the intersubjective," constitutes a comprehensive phenomenon of an essentially homogeneous nature, in which the subjective separateness and individuality of particular individuals is completely blurred to become a universal totality which encompasses them all. (2012, 17)

Dybel is convinced that the category of intersubjectivity has its roots in the tradition of Cartesianism and was preserved in German idealism and British empiricism and, in the 20th century, in analytic philosophy and pragmatism, Husserl's phenomenology and the neo-Marxist Frankfurt School.

The concept of the subject emerging from the experience of participation is important for an understanding of human existence from the perspective of the performative turn. Only in experiencing a certain community and acting on some common field can the subject be constituted. This is not inconsistent either with Domańska's concepts of the strong subject and neoessentialism or with notion of intersubjectivity. The emergence of the subject through his/her opening to the Other, to playing the drama with the Other, does not, in my opinion, rule out the subject's being rooted in ground common to other individuals as well. Reaching out to the Other, creating the subject in experience, does not rule out the common ground of existence. It seems that such combination works in the concept of the strong subject. And a common base might be found in corporeal experience—as Merleau-Ponty found it. Of course, the category of intersubjectivity dependent on bodily experience, and unlimited by any doubts, may lead to dangerous ethical consequences, including taking at face value (or naively simplifying) commandments such as "do unto others as you would have them do unto you." However, by being aware of the immeasurable multitude of bodily experiences—even aside from differences arising from age, sex and gender—one can avoid the danger of totalization.

An interesting problematization of the notion of intersubjectivity can be found in the philosophy of Emmanuel Lévinas in *Totality and Infinity* (Lévinas 1979, 53). Lévinas's assumption that one cannot look at oneself from the outside, through the experience of other person, or to understand the other by referring to one's own experience makes it impossible to speak of intersubjectivity in the way Rembowska-Płuciennik does. It also undermines the sense of the notion of anthropofictions, because one cannot talk about "universal bio-graphies" without assuming that there is some common ground for many different subjects. However, studies on the embodied mind seem to somehow oppose this philosophical perspective (which, for sure, illuminates a number of significant ethical issues concerning the relationship between the I and the Other). Yet the assumption of some common ground does not exclude the necessity of "leaning toward" the Other.

Indeed, in Rembowska-Płuciennik's book the notion of intersubjectivity seems to rely on a common base for communication between individuals. It refers to the common experiences which result from a human individual being an embodied mind, whose capacity for intersubjectively looking at others and for empathy is an evolutionary ability.

As explained by Paweł Dybel,

> intersubjectivity is commonly understood as a total inversion of the relation I—Other. This means that by using this notion it is implicitly assumed that the self-referring of I, which is formed in relation to the Other, is accompanied by the analogic self-reference of the Other as I to itself. Thus, when speaking of intersubjectivity, an absolute symmetry in the relation I—Other is assumed. (2012, 27)

It seems, however, that the assumption of the absolutely symmetrical relationship is not necessary. The Other, playing on the same stage, is not just a mirror reflection. The ability to relate the experience of another individual to oneself and the capacity for conscious self-observation are the basis of the change and creation of "the subject in the process." However, for a change and development to take place, the symmetrical relation is not enough; a shift is necessary. Therefore, the intersubjectivity understood as being dependent on shared experience and common ground, and Lévinas's "asymmetric" intersubjectivity, complement each other and it is this that enables one to talk about the strong subject in the way that Ewa Domańska does.

If one accepts the performative perspective, one cannot reject the possibility of interpersonal communication—a communication in which each individual is granting the other that everyone owns a "unique perspective of the world" (Judycki 2012, 88). Referring this to literature, it is clear that fictional narrations about fictional characters show the reading subject "a unique perspective of the world" of another, similar to that of the reader, but still uniquely individual. Although literary characters are schematic language constructs, the research indicates that in the reception of literature the reader applies to them the same techniques of understanding, as when dealing with real people. Therefore, the experiential and affective dimension of reading cannot be ignored.

The notion of the common sphere where different subjects meet and perceive the external world, a world which is not permanently and completely separated from the human individual, allows us to think about the cognitive dimension of fictions. When adopting the perspective of Domańska's neoessentialism, and the Deweyan concept of body-mind, borrowed by somaesthetics, one must agree with the statement that narrative fiction is not only biologically rooted, but also "reflects the socio-cultural specificity of human nature" (Rembowska-Płuciennik 2012, 11). It is the expression of the human capacity for multiperspective thinking, and as such it is both the result and the cause of the ability to adopt an intersubjective point of view. Rooted in corporeality and the socio-cultural sphere, intersubjectivity is also a prerequisite for the existence and performativity of these fictional narrations which Żychliński called anthropofictions. Only the assumption of the existence of the level where interpersonal communication may occur gives us reason to talk about the "universal bio-graphies" and "existential truths" that can be expressed in anthropofictions. I believe that the combination of perspectives of the performative turn, in both its theatrical and socio-political dimesions, somaesthetics and intersubjectivity—the major component of cognitive narratology—inspired by the philosophy of Merleau-Ponty, may help us answer the question whether, and, if so, to what extent, talking about anthropofictions is justified, and how these fictional stories perform in the real world.

The three perspectives from which I would like to look at literature are linked by the assumption that the subject, in this case the reading subject, needs to be freed from the restrictions of textualism, strengthened and appreciated, so the reader is no longer perceived as only a textual function, but becomes again a concrete, embodied subject. Cognitive narratology also sees the reader as responsible for producing the sense. This role of the reader is endorsed by Rembowska-Płuciennik. From the perspective of cognitive narratology the reader is defined in the out-of-text categories as a real existing being, equipped with physical and mental characteristics specific to his own species (i.e. embodied mind) (Rembowska-Płuciennik 2012, 88).

Breaking the informational model of the human mind and the resultant abandonment of the dualistic opposition of the body and mind are crucial. Here, the links with somaesthetics, which argues that it is a mistake to think of human subjectivity as pure information, or pure mind, are obvious. This conjunction, however, does not lead to a simple reduction to mere biologism. As in somaesthetics, in cognitive narratology, too, it is emphasized that the embodied mind is embedded in the cultural environment and is never free from its influences. Thus, fiction is a product associated with the "social dimension of consciousness"; it is a story about the experience of the other as "a separate, but similarly embodied subject" (Rembowska-Płuciennik 2012, 20, 21). Richard Rorty was convinced that literature, fictional narration, is a great spiritual exercise. He thought that literature is an important way of establishing relations with other subjects and of acquiring knowledge about others' perspectives on the overview of reality. In his conception, literature is a true "redemption from egotism," which allows the reader to see the diversity of human life and the contingency of our own moral vocabularies (Rorty 2010). It is worth noting that Rorty's position corresponds in some way to Żychliński's comments on anthropofictions, except that Rorty emphasizes the contingency of our vocabularies, not the universal bio-graphies. However, both authors emphasize the importance of fictional narrations in the process of cognition and communication, which is also significant when approaching literature from the perspective of the theory of intersubjectivity.

An important consequence of accepting the hypothesis of the embodied mind—and of the application of the theory of intersubjectivity—is the view of the act of reading as experiential and somatic. As such it is described by Rembowska-Płuciennik:

> Reading fictional narrations satisfies the specific emotional and cognitive needs of a man and a woman. The experiential nature of literary reception is achieved by the silent intimacy of reading, by the psychosomatic resonance with the literary characters and events, often with the sense of "being absorbed by the fiction." That dimension of reading is for many readers a unique and intense experience, which may be compared to the experience of virtual reality or acting in the interactive environment of interface. (2012, 14)

Narration is deeply rooted in human experience, which is reflected—according to a narratologist, Monika Fludernik—in fictional characters. They are not just a construction made of signs, but are endowed with prototypically human features: the fictional representations of human consciousness, of the "personal center of cognition, perception and emotions" (Rembowska-Płuciennik 2012, 82). Literary characters, treated as psychosomatic beings familiar to the readers, become the participants of the communication or the reader's performance enacted on the intersubjective stage. As a consequence, fictional narrations about fictional characters evoke various psychosomatic and emotional states in the reader—the reader, who is considered to be the sense-producing center of the text, introduces the sense into the text by (referring to) his/her own experience and, at the same time, perceives the experience of the literary characters as an experience grounded on the base which he/she shares with those characters. As Rembowska-Płuciennik argues, to associate the narrative events with the category of an agent, the reader uses the same explaining mechanisms which he/she uses when dealing with real people. So there occurs some kind of a transfer between the reader of the text and the characters, who meet on the same level. This allows the reader to understand (an understanding which may be conceived along Shusterman's lines) the states and feelings of the characters, which, based on the psychosomatic experiences of the reader, are projected onto the characters who perform in the fiction—on the "prototypical human beings." This fact enables us to treat fictional narrations as anthropofictions. This may also help to explain the performative power of literature, and the fact that literature, through its influence on the reader (an embodied mind), is able to influence extratextual reality.

In his work *Emotion as Meaning. The Literary Case for How We Imagine*, Keith Opdhal proposes that the basis for the emotional involvement in fictional events—and thus for the affective work of fictions as well—is the process of identification of the reader with the characters, which is grounded in the experience of corporeality. Such an approach might be supported by Shusterman's somaesthetics and his reflections on the aesthetic experience, which he expressed in his famous "example of a cyborg" (Shusterman 2000a, 31), where he also underlined the importance of aesthetic experience in the process of understanding art. The conviction about the importance of the affective power of fiction for the understanding and interpretation of the text is supported by cognitive narratology, with its references to neuroscience, and by performance studies. The simple fact that in reality we all perform as somatic units is what makes us able to perceive emotions and states of narrative characters as typically human. It also enables us to empathize, or co-feel, with them. Characters are seen not only as constructs made of the signs of language, but also as anthropomorphic beings to whom—according to Rembowska-Płuciennik—

"the reader applies the same procedures of understanding as are used to form a mental picture of an actual human being" (Rembowska-Płuciennik 2012, 91). The turn towards the real, the embodied reader of a literary work, implies paying attention to the affective aspects of understanding and interpretation.

Although William James believed that each individual's consciousness exists in absolute isolation (James 1983, 221) from others, many of his ideas support the present research on the human mind which tends to reject a computational model of the mind. As he argued in *Essays in Radical Empiricism*, the body "is the storm centre" around which our experiences are organised. The body is the center of perception and action. Richard Shusterman notes that James's ideas correspond with the newer theories of neuroscientists such as Antonio Damasio. Shusterman notes that one of Damasio's key ideas is that our ability to solve intellectual problem—our capacity for reasoning and conceptualizing—is related to our unceasing perception of bodily senses. Further, Shusterman emphasizes that inspirations for such theories may be found in the philosophy of James (Shusterman 2008, 143). At present, it is becoming impossible to ignore the somatic and affective dimension of the reception of fiction, which has a considerable influence on the process of understanding. The aesthetic experience, whose importance Shusterman emphasizes, is also situated within the scope of this reception of art. In *Performing Live* Shusterman writes that the interpretation of artworks which focuses only on signs and contexts is incomplete without the affective dimension of understanding (Shusterman 2000a, 31).

To understand an artwork, as Shusterman suggests, emotions are necessary, and they are rooted in the body. And since the corporeal being-in-the-world is something that all human subjects share, and that enables us to talk about intersubjectivity, it seems quite clear that the understanding of the body and its processes can improve not only the ability to understand another person's psychosomatic condition, but also the ability to understand fictional narrations about other subjects. The pragmatic goal of somaesthetics is to improve the understanding of human existence through the development of the awareness of its corporeal dimension. If the reader of fictional narrations sees literary characters also in the terms in which he/she sees a real person, it can be assumed that by adopting their perspectives and familiarizing him/herself with their psychosomatic feelings, (s)he is able to improve his/her own understanding of his/her own somatic experiences. But also by having a better understanding of one's own somatic dimension, one may be able to understand better the fictional narrations, which are based on the intersubjective capacity of the human mind. Shusterman would probably agree with the view of Mark Johnson, who states (Johnson 2007) that cognition is not just some internal process performed by the mind, but rather a form of an embodied action. Cognition is located in the interactions between an organism and the environment; it is not locked in some supposedly private sphere of thought. Language and abstract thinking are socially and culturally situated activities. Johnson stresses not only the inseparability of the body and mind, but also the social and cultural aspects that affect the development of the subject and understanding. Also the theories of intersubjectivity, somaesthetics and performance studies emphasize the fact that human consciousness is focused on being in the environment of other human units, in which a significant role is played by socio-cultural mediation (Rembowska-Płuciennik 2012, 100). This seems to be a common feature of many currents which seek to overcome the dualistic opposition of body and mind. Dewey, whose philosophy has been a major inspiration for Shusterman's somaesthetics, saw this issue similarly. For him the biological approach to mental life essentially implies the social nature of the mind. Today, such a belief is confirmed by the discovery of the existence of mirror neurons, thanks to which, when we observe the action of another person, the same group of neurons in our brain is activated as would be active if we were performing the action ourselves. According to Rembowska-Płuciennik,

> this embodied simulation could be a kind of a bridge between … perception and imagination, between mental imagery and sensual reaction to it—and these issues can easily be connected to the experiential dimension of reading. (2012, 102)

Referring to the theme of simulation, it is worth recalling that Arkadiusz Żychliński talks about some kind of "reality testing" in fictional narrations, which may be called "simulation." What is more, as Żychliński argues, referring to Brian Boyd (2009), storytelling sharpens our ability to recognize social phenomena by provoking us to rethink human experience. It should be noted that the understanding of interpersonal relationships and of human experience, offered by fictions, is *not just* the derivate of the functions of language. In the words of Rembowska-Płuciennik,

> the argument that access to someone else's mind is only a conventional matter of language used for its description does not stand up to empirical research—human simulating behaviours appear in the first months of life and are far ahead of the understanding and learning of speech. (2012, 113)

It follows that, because we are all embodied subjects, we can adopt an intersubjective view of others, including fictional characters. However, this approach leads to serious consequences. Since the category of intersubjectivity, as Rembowska-Płuciennik emphasizes, is a category which demands the presence of subjects, its use in the context of literature implies "the empowerment of the participants of the literary communication: the author, fictional beings (narrator and characters), and the reader" (2012, 109). Of course, when we talk about literary characters we cannot put one form of reception before another, because only together do they constitute the specificity of the reception of a literary character.

A theoretical approach in which literature and the process of literary reception are viewed only in terms of functions and structures fails to explain the performative power of literature. Only the recognition of the embodiment of the reader and the bodily aspects of reading (including the phenomenon of intersubjectivity resulting from the embodiment of subjects) can account for the performative potential of literary works. When the reader is not perceived as a function of a text, one can start talking about the experiential nature of reading and its somatic reception, which aspects are not irrelevant to the meaning of the text, nor to aesthetics, moral evaluation and interpretation. "Interpretation," Rembowska-Płuciennik states, "is in fact rooted in the personal consciousness of one's own body and its internal states, emotions and sensual experiences. ... The understanding of the language (including literary language) is always activated in embodied experience" (2012, 317, 318). All this leads to the conclusion that both somaesthetics and performance studies could and should be applied in literary studies and studies on literary reception and production. The view that the narration is the core element which roots human subject in the world does not go against the theories which claim that it is performance that plays this role. Both perspectives are connected by a recognition of the need to embody the narrating and performing subjects, and moreover both are connected with the act of communication.

There is one more issue to consider. When Arkadiusz Żychliński writes about anthropofictions, he argues that they are fictions about which it could be said that they express some universal existential truths, some universal human bio-graphies. That statement seems to me quite dangerous. It makes me ask about the nature of these "existential truths" that are common to all human beings. Hence, I would like to devote the last lines of this paper to the notion of "truth" that anthropofictions are supposed to contain. I cannot accept the idea of there existing some universal truths. It will be instructive to consider Constantine Cavafy's famous poem *Ithaca*. This poem is often seen as "universal," a poem which, thanks to the references to ancient tradition, expresses some universal experience of man. This quality, however, quickly turns out to be illusory when the poem is read by someone from outside the European cultural circle, or simply a person who has never heard about Ithaca, *The Odyssey* and Homer. There are plainly too many factors which influence individuals to seriously talk about universal truths and bio-graphies. The only truth which, in my opinion, may be regarded as "universal" and common to all people, is the bodily existence of human beings.[9] However, and this may be obvious, this truth is not enough to fill countless volumes which contain fictional stories, which try to communicate something important about human existence. So what is the "truth" of anthropofictions? If I may say so, it is a "performative truth," which is created and creating. Of course, this approach to fictions makes them look like ideological constructs (and I do not think that it is an incorrect conclusion), but if someone wants to use the concepts of "truth" and "anthropofiction," he/she probably cannot avoid such implications. In this case, instead of defining what the truth of fictions is, the emphasis should be rather put on their goal. And if it is similar to the pragmatic goal of somaesthetics, which is to help individuals in understanding and performing better in their (socio-cultural) environment, then the fiction may be called an "anthropofiction." However, this—perhaps too optimistic—assertion should be complemented by the recognition of the performative, in the sense that Judith Butler has given to this word, power of anthropofictions.

References

Bauman, Richard. 1975. "Verbal Arts as Performance." *American Anthropologist*, no. 2: 290–311.

Boyd, Brian. 2009. *On the Origin of Stories. Evolution, Cognition, and Fiction*. Cambridge: Belknap Press.

Burzyńska, Anna. 2013. *Dekonstrukcja, polityka i performatyka* [Deconstruction, politics, and performatics]. Kraków: Universitas.

Domańska, Ewa. 2007. " 'Zwrot performatywny' we współczesnej humanistyce" [The "performative turn" in contemporary humanities]. *Teksty Drugie*, no. 5: 48–61.

—. 2012. *Historia egzystencjalna. Krytyczne studium narratywizmu i humanistyki zaangażowanej* [Existential history. A critical approach to narrativism and emancipatory humanities]. Warszawa: PWN.

Dybel, Paweł. 2012. "Kłopot z 'intersubiektywnością' " [The problem of 'intersubjectivity']. In: *Intersubiektywność* [Intersubjectivity]. Edited by Piotr Makowski, 17–28. Kraków: Universitas.

James, William. 1983. *The Principles of Psychology*. Cambridge, MA: Harvard University Press.

Johnson, Mark. 2007. *The Meaning of the Body. Aesthetics of Human Understanding*. Chicago: University of Chicago Press.

Judycki, Stanisław. 2012. "Tajemnica komunikacji pomiędzy osobami" [The mystery of interpersonal communication]. In: *Intersubiektywność* [Intersubjectivity]. Edited by Piotr Makowski, 87–112. Kraków: Universitas.

Koczanowicz, Dorota. 2013. "Ciało jako wehikuł krytyki społecznej w perspektywie somaestetyki Richarda Shustermana" [The body as a means of social criticism in the perspective of Richard Shusterman's somaesthetics]. In *Powrót modernizmu?* [The return of modernism?]. Edited by Teresa Pękala, 127–42. Lublin: Wydawnictwo UMCS.

Krajewska, Anna. 2009. *Dramatyczna teoria literatury. Zarys problematyki* [A dramatic theory of literature: Outline of problems]. Poznań: Wydawnictwo Naukowe UAM.

Lévinas, Emmanuel. 1979. *Totality and Infinity: An Essay on Exteriority*. Translated by Alphonso Lingis. London: Martinus Nijhoff Publishers.

Małecki, Wojciech. 2010. *Embodying Pragmatism. Richard Shusterman's Philosophy and Literary Theory*. Frankfurt am Main: Peter Lang Publishing.

McKenzie, Jon. 2001. *Perform or Else… From Discipline to Performance*. London: Routledge.

Merleau-Ponty, Maurice. 2002. *Phenomenology of Perception*. Translated by Colin Smith. London: Routledge.

Rembowska-Płuciennik, Magdalena. 2012. *Poetyka intersubiektywności. Kognitywistyczna teoria narracji a proza XX wieku* [Poetics of intersubjectivity: Cognitive narratology and the 20th century prose]. Toruń: Wydawnictwo Naukowe UMK.

Rorty, Richard. 2010. "Redemption from Egotism. James and Proust as Spiritual Exercises." In: *The Rorty Reader*. Edited by Christopher J. Voparil, and Richard J. Bernstein, 389–406. Oxford: Wiley-Blackwell.

Shusterman, Richard. 1999. "Somaesthetics: A Disciplinary Proposal." *The Journal of Aesthetics and Art Criticism* 57 (3): 299–313.

—. 2000a. *Performing Live: Aesthetics Alternatives for the Ends of Art*. London: Cornell University Press.

—. 2000b. *Pragmatist Aesthetics: Living Beauty, Rethinking Art*. Oxford: Rowman & Littlefield Publishers.

—. 2002. *Surface and Depth: Dialectics of Criticism and Culture*. London: Cornell University Press.

—. 2008. *Body Consciousness: A Philosophy of Mindfulness and Somaesthetics*. New York: Cambridge University Press.

Wojda, Dorota. 2014. " 'Zdanie złożone z kilku podań.' Poezja – futbol – performans" ["Zdanie złożone z kilku podań": Poetry—football—performance]. *Teksty Drugie*, no. 3: 243–67.

Worthen, William B. 2010. *Drama: Between Poetry and Performance*. Chichester: Wiley-Blackwell.

Żychliński, Arkadiusz. 2014. "Laboratorium antropofikcji. Prolegomena" [Laboratory of anthropofiction: Prolegomena]. *Teksty Drugie*, no. 1: 67–83.

Notes

[1] Unless otherwise noted, all translations are my own.

[2] See Domańska 2007. The defense of deconstruction was presented by Anna Burzyńska in her book *Dekonstrukcja, polityka i performatyka* where, referring to Ewa Domańska's thesis, she writes: "it is hard to deny that Ewa Domańska is right in her characterization of the main features of this current, but it is hard to agree with her main thesis, according to which the performative turn moved away from everything that she globally (and unfortunately inaccurately) called *postmodernism*" (Burzyńska 2013, 267).

[3] It must be emphasized that Żychliński's project, which describes philology as "a laboratory of anthropofiction," is not aimed at the contemplation of the world, but rather its understanding and analysis aimed at introducing change. Philology is a practice of giving meaning—it might be said that philology is part of the performative discourse, which Anna Krajewska characterizes as "the act of producing the truth" (Krajewska 2009, 35).

[4] Writing generally and imprecisely about postmodern concepts, I make a mental shortcut similar to that applied by Ewa Domańska in her works. Such a shortcut may be—rightly—criticized (Burzyńska 2013), but the limited space of this paper does not allow me to provide a complete and satisfactorily nuanced account of the issue.

[5] See Shusterman 1999.

[6] At this point I should, of course, also mention Foucault's project of caring for the self, which was developed in the last two volumes of *History of Sexuality*.

[7] See Shusterman 2008, 49.

[8] Such notion corresponds with Ewa Domańska's understanding of the performative turn.

[9] Of course, there is a troublesome issue that may put such an approach in question: namely, the belief in the linguistic, discursive mediation of reality. And although one can effectively argue for this point of view, it should be noted that

this approach excludes all individuals who for some reason have never started to use a language. It also ignores prediscursive bodily experiences.

CHAPTER EIGHT

KINETOSIS IN DON DELILLO'S
THE BODY ARTIST:
TRACING THE SOMATIC EXPERIENCES
OF THE READER[1]

LILLA FARMASI

One of the reasons why popular art is popular is that it relies on its power
to stir feeling and emotions. Some genres, such as the tearjerker,
characteristically try to cause a calculated effect on the reader, while
others are less of a sensational experience to read. However, all art has
powerful, if not properly recognized, somatic potential and can elicit
bodily reactions in their audience. This is so, because all experience, as
Merleau-Ponty has asserted, is embodied experience, and the very act of
meaning-making is anchored in our physicality. It follows that aesthetic
experiences carry patterns which are based on our embodied nature. I will
attempt to trace these in literary fiction by contrasting textual phenomena
with bodily experience. I assume that there is a strong relationship
between the structure and the effect of literary texts, and that the
experience of having/living/being a body plays a crucial role in it. In this
paper I aim at tracing the possible somatic experiences of the reader of
literary fiction, and defining their role and significance in the process of
reading. Norman Holland explains, leaning on neuropsychology, that
when we are immersed in a story, "prior, memory based knowledge [is]
outweighed by … one's current involvement in the narrative" (Holland
2009, 65). I assume that in this situation, which Holland likens to a
"trance," and Marie-Laure Ryan (2012) calls "immersion," peculiar
narrative and representational techniques can result in bodily experience.

In the course of my discussion I will apply an interdisciplinary
approach, incorporating narratology and cognitive theory. Researchers of
cognitive theory have been interested in what is called "embodied

cognition," that is, research programs that examine the interrelatedness of the functions of the mind and the body, to put it very simply. Their theories, models and research results can be highly fruitful for literary theory. I understand reading as an interaction between the reader and the text, and I plan to focus on representations of space and the characters' experience of it, as well as spatial metaphors in plot patterns, which may have an effect on the reader's body. I am particularly interested in the representation, (the protagonist's) perception and (the reader's) interpretation of space and movement in Don DeLillo's novel *The Body Artist* (2001).

My interest in this paper focuses on spatiality. I hypothesize that spatial metaphors, which are abundant in all languages, have a crucial role in constructing plots and influencing the reader's experience. In my view, besides serving as the skeletons of plots, as Hilary Dannenberg argues, they enter into a dynamic relationship with the cognitive activity of the reader, and the two mutually influence each other. Based on this relationship I will construct a reading model which includes the text as well as the mind and the body of its reader as active participators in the reading process. Through examining DeLillo's novel, *The Body Artist*, I will elaborate on the working of this model: in particular, I will trace the spatial imagery that possibly motivates certain plot patterns, as well as the reading experience of the interpreter of the novel.

Embodied Cognition Theory

My investigation requires an interdisciplinary approach. Embodied cognition theory is needed for understanding the reader's bodily experience while the phenomena that I will examine are most easily grasped with the help of narrative theory.

To view human embodiment as a significant component of reading experience, cognition has to be understood as a dynamic and changeable process, in which the mind is inseparable from the physical body and its environment, and in which the three components mutually influence each other. Many aspects of this approach are still heavily contested, and "sometimes the nature of the dependence of cognition on the body is quite unexpected, and suggests new ways of conceptualizing and exploring the mechanics of cognitive processing" (Wilson, Foglia 2011). In the following paragraphs I will outline the views of this approach, known as embodied cognitive theory.

The traditional understanding, relying on the distinction between the human mind and body, and on the view of the mind as being superior to the body, has been observable in Western philosophy since ancient times (Gibbs 2005, 3). Opposing this discourse, theorists such as Francisco J. Varela, George Lakoff, Mark Johnson, and Raymond Gibbs agree that conceptualization, even in its most abstract forms, is very often constructed through our bodies. Gibbs points out that, while the workings of the brain are sometimes envisioned like those of a computer, it is a mistake to reduce the mind to the brain. Likewise, it is an error to reduce the body to either a provider of the raw sensory input to the somatosensory cortex (a tendency in neuroscience) or, to have it doubly reduced: to a mental image and, subsequently, to the computational functions of neurons, or to information processing (a tendency in psychology). In both cases, the body is effectively—and erroneously—reduced to the brain (Gibbs, 5–6). Cognition, however, is inconceivable without embodied action, as it is explained in Varela, Thompson and Rosch's book *The Embodied Mind* (1993), where the term "enactivism" is introduced. The enactivist approach represents the pragmatic turn in cognitive science; it presupposes that the agent is not only embedded in a body and an environment but, importantly, that he or she is in constant interaction with his or her environment (Menary 2006, 2). Apparently this approach rejects Cartesian dualism. However, as Varela insists, even if the debates over the question of the body and mind have acquired a considerable depth (which Varela attributes to the development of cognitivism), they still revolve around the problem which is basically Cartesian: the question of "how two seemingly distinct things are related. (Whether these things are substances, properties, or merely levels of description rarely makes a difference to the basic structure of the discussion)" (Varela et al. 1993, 30).

Varela's point is crucial because it asserts that the body-mind relationship is not to be constructed but to be explored. Alva Noë states in *Action in Perception* (2004) that perception, action and thought have to be understood as inseparable, for these are three very similar and interconnected processes. Noë claims that, when we apply abstract mental structures in cognition, we are aided by our experience of embeddedness in the world, and also by our embodied abilities to explore the material reality of which we are a part (Noë 2004, 24). Like Gibbs, Noë also refuses the idea of modeling perception as something that takes place only inside the brain, for it "directly involves not only the brain but also the animate body and the world" (30).

Conceptual linguists and philosophers, notably George Lakoff, Mark Johnson, Mark Turner, Gilles Fauconnier, and Zoltán Kövecses have developed the theory of image schema and conceptual metaphors, which can provide an account for one of the basic sense-making patterns in linguistic, and consequently other, cognitive categories. Metaphor, as Johnson states in *The Body in the Mind* (1987), is "one of the chief cognitive structures by which we are able to have coherent, ordered experiences" (Johnson 1987, xv). "Schemata are typically thought of as general knowledge structures, ranging from conceptual networks to scripted activities to narrative structures and even to theoretical frameworks" (Johnson 1987, 19). They are not necessarily "abstract conceptual and propositional event structures" but also "embodied patterns of meaningfully organized experience (such as structures of bodily movements and perceptual interactions)" (19). It is important to emphasize that these cognitive patterns precede symbolic concepts, and that we use them unconsciously (Hampe 2005, 1). In the course of "explor[ing] the experiential embodied nature of human rationality" (Johnson 1987, 100). Johnson explains that "we are dealing with preconceptual levels at which structure emerges in our experience via metaphorical extensions of image schemata" (Johnson 1987, 85). The level of the image schemata, therefore, has a lot to do with bodily experiences, and it proves to be the organizer, the engine, of conceptual metaphors in language.

Due to these metaphors we are able to comprehend certain ideas in terms of others: for instance we understand quantity in terms of directionality when we say "prices rise," or we can conclude that in our conceptual structures "difficulties are impediments to motion" which we see when we say "He got over his divorce" (Kövecses 1998, 66). We know that prices do not actually move in any direction, and that the concept of divorce has little to do with spatiality, yet that is the way we conceptualize them: in terms of being and living (in) a body. In *Philosophy in the Flesh*, Johnson and Lakoff conclude that what they call metaphorical reasoning comes from using sensorimotor experience to create and express abstract concepts (Lakoff, Johnson 1999, 496).

But conceptual metaphors are not ends in and of themselves. While they still generate debates among linguists and psychologists, they are regarded as significant tools for understanding the human cognitive system. Although the theory of image schema and conceptual metaphors is usually examined on the level of words, phrases or sentences, it is assumed that the larger, higher, macro levels of a text might also have the same underlying, organizing system. Hence, plot patterns might get constructed in the same unconscious manner as cognitive metaphors. In the course of a close reading of DeLillo's *The Body Artist* I will attempt to explore the nature of this constructing process and see how it relates to the body of the reader.

Cognition and Embodiment in Literary Theory

Literary theory, which often and fruitfully applies the models, methods and findings of various disciplines, has significantly benefited from the work of cognitive theorists (Szabó 2012, 115). The most fruitful branch of cognitive literary theory is probably cognitive narratology. Research on narratives, in turn, is an important component of the exploration of the human cognitive system, since a considerable part of it is "narratively organized" (David Herman, quoted in Szabó 2012, 9).

Understanding reading as an interaction between the text and (the psyche of) the reader is not an entirely new idea; reader-response criticism and reception theory had proposed it as early as the 1960s. Nevertheless, the examination of literary texts with the help of psychology, neurology, or cognitive linguistics only became an acknowledged approach in the 1990s, and cognitive literary theory, similarly to the majority of disciplines within cognitive science, is still a far from homogeneous trend. However, one of its major propositions is that the structure of literary texts necessarily depends on the architecture of the human mind, and one of its main concerns is to discover the cognitive structures that take part in the processing of narrative texts. At this point cognitive literary theory agrees with the poststructuralist theory of the production of meaning. Opposing earlier theories, cognitive literary theory and poststructuralist theory claim that meaning is constructed in the mind of the reader. One of the main concerns of these considerations, which is also my main interest in this paper, is to suggest the rules that govern the production of meaning and the experience of the reader.

Cognitive literary theory and cognitive narratology have provoked significant new research questions about the reading process and the reading experience, which are important procedures of cognition. Systematic explanation is still needed for the relationship between the structure and the effect of literary texts (Szabó 2012, 115). The assumption that a text can be regarded as a set of stimuli, and the human psyche as an organism that responds to the stimuli (Horváth, Szabó 2013, 140), can be made more complex by the views of embodied cognition theory, as it also entails the consideration of the physical body as a component in the act of meaning-making, and the examination of the possible somatic effects that a text can have on its reader. With the help of image schema theory and narratology, in the following section I will outline the working of a reading model, which incorporates (the experience of) the human body as an active participator in the processing of narratives.

Space in Narrative Theory

According to Hilary Dannenberg, the bodily experience of space is an underestimated but crucial factor in literary works. As she begins her explanation,

> the bodily experience of negotiating and perceiving space underlies many sense-making operations, including the comprehension of time. The negotiation of space is one of the first orientational steps in life any human being must undertake; this knowledge is used to make sense of or metaphorically "map" other experiences. (Dannenberg 2008, 65)

Space and time—the experiential dimensions which cannot be wholly separated—have lately become important objects of narrative theory. The two are intertwined and presuppose each other, and, as Teresa Bridgeman observes, they are to be understood as essential constituents of the "fabric" of narratives as they fundamentally influence our understanding of fictive worlds (Bridgeman 2007, 52–53).

Space in narrative theory had been traditionally regarded as an intranarrative component: the spatial characteristics of the narrative world where the story is set. However, researches in cognitive science have brought about important new aspects of the discussion of space and narratives. Spatial imagery has inspired the work of Hilary Dannenberg, who studies the theories of image schema as skeletons of plot patterns; for instance, she considers the metaphors of "path" or "container" in terms of plot line or the setting of the story. Dannenberg has examined "the ability of narrative texts to re-create the schemata of real-world orientation learned and performed by the human mind/body in its cognitive interaction with space" (2008, 75). Dannenberg also claims that spatial schemata have a vital role in the reader's immersion in the text (2008, 65). Peter Brooks detects dynamics and movement in narratives in his study, *Reading for the Plot: Design and Intention in Narrative* (1984), when he claims that the reading of a plot brings about a "narrative desire" that drives us onward towards the ending of the story. Drawing on these ideas, I assume that, besides being the skeleton of narratives, image schemata can function as more active components of the narrative principle, and maintain a dynamic relationship with(in) the text.

I imagine a reading model that also includes a drive, but this drive is motivated by the complex relationship between the text, the mind and the body of the reader, which results in a loop-effect in the process and the experience of reading. Thus, to recapitulate, three entities are involved: the text, the reader's body and mind. If we accept that texts can be structurally based on certain bodily experiences (be it a movement along a path, as Dannenberg explains, or the experience of kinetosis, as I will suggest), and therefore can emerge similarly to conceptual metaphors, from a preconceptual, nonpropositional dimension, we can assume that during the processing of the text, the bodily experience, which was the original, image schemata level model of the text, can re-emerge and (re-)create another bodily experience which, again, influences the text. In the course of reading we produce somatic reactions, which influence the meaning of the text: readers rewrite it, and thereby bring forth the loop-effect. *The Body Artist* is a good example for presenting this driving force behind narrative plots, since it is impossible, even in retrospect, to put it together as an unchanging, linear, coherent story: descriptions begin, and as they are being processed one way, they are questioned and disproved; this keeps up the loop-effect of meaning-making and somatic experiences. Eventually the process creates a circle of constant attempts to build up the story, where the text, the reader's mind and his or her body influence each other. The literary work therefore is not only written on the paper and in the mind, but in the body as well, rendering literature a multimedial art form.

In the remainder of this paper I will analyze Don DeLillo's novel *The Body Artist* to trace the bodily experience of space and movement on which the spatial imagery of the novel is based and to further elaborate the model I have outlined. Firstly, I will examine the topographical level of the novel's narrative world, and the protagonist's experience of space and movement. However, I am also interested in the overall design of the narrative, some patterns of which are probably not the product of the author's plan of the text. These are observable on the level of the very verbalization, or textualization, of the story. I will elaborate on how image schemata might be projected into the plot patterns of DeLillo's novel, and provide an example for the functioning of my reading model.

The research of Marco Caracciolo is very close to what I am doing. In his study entitled "Tell-Tale Rhythms: Embodiment and Narrative Discourse," he also explores plot and the distinctive techniques of narrative composition both in literary fiction and in film. He seeks to explain how

> bodily feelings can emerge in response to narrative discourse, especially when there is a 'spill over' effect from the representation and thematization of the body to readers' and spectators' bodily experience. (Caracciolo 2014, 68)

I agree with him that there are numerous discourse-level phenomena which appear disembodied and abstract, while, in fact, they are closely connected to embodiment and can have an effect on the body of the reader. I assume that his views also fit the reading model I have outlined.

Summary of the Novel

The Body Artist is a rather enigmatic work, open to various interpretations. It is different from the earlier novels of DeLillo in the extremely narrow scope of the fictive world it employs; it focuses on one character, and the story unfolds in a very limited space. The novel is of "deliberately glacial pace," and it refuses "to offer the easy pleasures of narrative" (Bonca 2002, 58–68). It is rather difficult to explain what *The Body Artist* is about by referring to its plot points. Actions are few and far between, the dialogues are confusing and disjointed, and most of the events are seemingly unrelated. When it comes to interpreting the novel, there is very little to safely hold on to on the surface and due to that, it easily comes across as flat; yet the topic of the novel requires such tension and commotion.

The first chapter describes the breakfast routine of a married couple— Rey Robles, a film director, and Lauren Hartke, the eponymous performance artist—who have recently moved into a big, old, lonely house. The scene is set out in great detail. In a slow-motion manner Lauren and Rey are described as preparing food, eating, and having a sleepy, scattered conversation, partly about a strange noise they have both heard in the house. One senses the atmosphere of a half-awake early morning: at first reading the scene seems rather ordinary. The first chapter is followed by the obituary of Rey, who commits suicide on the same morning, when he leaves the house after breakfast. For the rest of the novel we follow the grieving Lauren, who decides to stay alone in the house until she recovers from the trauma of losing her husband.

During her mourning weeks Lauren isolates herself from the rest of the world; she rarely leaves the house and does not meet anyone. One day the strange noise that has haunted the story from the beginning returns, now embodied, in the form of a strange, nameless man of indefinable age, appearance or character. Lauren finds him in one of the rooms upstairs, and names him Mr. Tuttle. The two of them spend their days together, mostly sitting and carrying out meandering conversations, in which, as Lauren notices, Tuttle echoes fragments of dialogues she had had with her husband. As we follow her around the house and read the conversations she has with Tuttle, her psyche turns out to be just as unstable as her body and her voice(s). After a while, Mr. Tuttle disappears just as simply as he had appeared at the beginning. The novel has an open ending. In the last scene Lauren walks to the window and throws it open (DeLillo 2002, 124).

Altogether, it is impossible to get a firm grasp on *The Body Artist*. Its narrator and its protagonist are not much less obscure and volatile, both physically and psychically, than the ghostly Mr. Tuttle, and most of the events, actions and conversations in the novel remain incoherent. In fact, most of the reviews and studies written on *The Body Artist* contradict each other in their interpretation of basic events and actions. For instance, at certain points in the story Michiko Kakutani (2001) sees sexual encounters but I, along with the majority of the critics, do not; and there is a bathing scene where one cannot even surely tell whether or not Lauren is talking, when she names Tuttle's body parts without using words (DeLillo 2002, 68).

Narrative and the Bodily Experience of Space and Movement

The Body Artist traces the protagonist's digestion of a psychological trauma and it has a peculiar, seemingly unsystematic, fragmented quality. This quality can be traced back to the notion that both the story and the plot of the novel reflect the protagonist's traumatized consciousness, where perceptions of time and space become discontinuous. I suggest that there is an underlying, structuring principle beneath the unusual representations, and I will attempt to find its relationship with human embodiment. Following the enactivist approach of embodied cognition theory and cognitive linguistics, I assume that, as a part of the reading model I have outlined, image schemata might be involved in readers' understanding of plot structure.

I assume that somatic reactions that are elicited by literary fiction are understandable when one proposes that both the text and the bodily experience are structured by the same dynamics, not unlike image schemata. To trace these dynamics, firstly I will examine the representation of narrative space and the protagonist's experience of it, structures and patterns of the plot, and finally the possible underlying level, which, like the level of image schemata in language, is strongly tied to the conditions of human embodiment.

There are very few and short descriptions of space in the novel, and therefore one generally has to rely on hints of how the protagonist and the narrator relate to it. The first thing to observe is that the narrator and the protagonist represent one perspective. The novel is usually understood as being narrated by an invisible third person, but this idea is untenable when one observes that everything that is narrated in the third person is measured against the opinions and perceptions of Lauren. Occasionally, when reporting the thoughts of Lauren, the narration omits quotation marks or any mark that would separate the thought from the narrating consciousness. Some statements simply blend into the narrative telling.[2] In my opinion, the narrator shares the conditions and limits of Lauren's perceptions, which, in Merleau-Ponty's theory of bodily perception, implies that they have to share the same body (DeLillo 2002, 69); therefore Lauren's consciousness has to be behind the narrative voice. Due to this practice of internal focalization, the perspective is broken and presented through more or less detached channels, since Lauren's traumatized consciousness is rather fragmented. The narrative space is constructed by the perspective of this consciousness.

The thematization of space is simple to observe. The traumatized woman, whose consciousness becomes disconnected from reality, stays alone, isolated from the rest of the world. Lauren stays in the house almost throughout the whole story, sits around with Tuttle, and practices her performance in her workout room. The restricted space of the house represents her isolation and her being withdrawn from the world. Moreover, when she finds out that Tuttle imitates the voice of her late husband she is shocked on top of her traumatized condition, and she resorts to occupying an even more limited space: she gets in her car and sits there long enough to lose the track of time (DeLillo 2002, 52).

Still, while *The Body Artist* is dominated by the inertia of the main character, and is carried out in an isolated place, it places a premium on movement and the sensing of space and movement. The protagonist has the habit of sinking into her reveries, which she usually does unconsciously. Several of her reveries are depicted in the story, but the fact that these are not actual actions is not clear until they are interrupted or until they end. It is often unclear whether Lauren is daydreaming or not, and whether she really moves or not: the reader imagines her moving and then he or she is presented with the fact that Lauren was probably sitting or standing in one place all along. In the breakfast scene she reads a newspaper, which inspires her to temporarily, and mentally, move out of her actual surroundings, but the reader cannot be sure which conceptual frame to relate to at a given moment. Within the space of a short paragraph DeLillo pictures her sitting at her breakfast table, reading the newspaper, relishing her tea—her attention shifting between her little repast and the information recorded in the paper, hovering between now and then—and then, suddenly, he juxtaposes this description with an apparently unrelated line referring to "Rey," and concludes it with the sentence related to her pondering a conversation with a figure from the newspaper.[3] The last two sentences of the "breakfast" passage belong to two different conceptual frames. Similar situations occur on page 69 and 70. On page 70, she goes into town, and later it turns out to be a daydreaming period, which, in retrospect, makes it questionable whether or not, on page 69, she really has wandered quite a distance.

Her experiences of space and movement, and the peculiar focalization that creates the representations of these experiences, suggest that it is not possible for her to negotiate her perceptions about the (movements in) narrative space. Lauren, once she has apparently lost the ability to perceive time, space and her body in a linear way, starts to practice her performance, which could eventually help her cope with her traumatized condition. Her practices largely consist of simple movements, like checking the time on her watch, which she repeats countless times, and holding different positions for extended times. By fiddling with time,[4] she necessarily problematizes the representation and perception of space, too. Lauren actually has difficulties with sensing space when we witness her nearly collapsing one time. She does not tumble, or feel sick, but she is sliding down as if she did not know how to keep upright,[5] as if she were losing the ability to control her movements and keep her balance.

Considering the limited and partial perceptive processes, as well as Lauren's reveries and actual experiences, it becomes rather difficult to register and understand space and bodily movement in the novel, even on the simple, topographical level. While the house Lauren is renting is a clear category of space, narrative space on the whole is often incompletely constructed and undecided: the representations do not add up to a consistent sense of space.

The fragmentary, confusing depiction of the narrative world is the dominant technique of representation and narrative composition in the novel, and I assume it becomes a metaphor for the bodily experience of kinetosis, through which the (somatic) reading experience is also constructed. As I have explained, the narrator and the protagonist often hesitate, take back what they have stated, and, as the above explanation shows, these representations make the perception of narrative space problematic: the (bodily) experience of space and movement in the novel is created through incompatible, false, or partial perceptions of space. The uncertainty of the entire reading experience boils down to uncertainty about—metaphoric and actual—movement: the reader never knows whether there is movement or not, whether the actions in the plot really take place or not. Due to the nature of the text there are also two incompatible levels of meaning in the story: the "flat," surface, which lacks action (motion), and the indescribable, visceral level of Lauren's trauma under it.

The inconsistency and the uncertainty that the text offers the reader are the product of DeLillo's experimental representational technique, the effect of which is hardly calculated by the author. I assume that the undecided, fragmented plot patterns can be understood as the conceptual metaphors cognitive linguists explained, and that they have their own relationship to the experience of human embodiment: the source of these patterns might also be a lower, nonpropositional level of consciousness, where the structures of bodily experience dominate.

The overall quality of the novel, which I depicted earlier as confusing and seemingly unsystematic, is therefore the result of the incompatible information, the constant questioning and correcting of the actions and experiences of the story. The experimental representational technique, which is observable in the whole text of *The Body Artist*, designates the position of the reader. The experience of reading is built from this position, hence it is articulated through the narrative schemas and therefore through our bodily experience. The reader is unable to negotiate between what he or she reads and what actually happens: the actual plot remains inconsistent and fragmented, even in retrospect.

The reading of this novel might result in an experience similar to that of processing incompatible cues from different sense organs. This rarely happens, since different senses usually show different sides of the same experience. But in certain cases we are confronted with incompatible input from different sense organs, for instance when we experience kinetosis. The sensing of space and motion is built from diverse sources (Millar 2008, 3), and therefore discrepancy in spatial processing is possible. Kinetosis, or motion sickness, is a condition that is caused when one senses motion through the vestibular system in the inner ear, but does not see it. The condition is independent of the person's knowledge about the movement.

The reader of *The Body Artist* is affected by different levels of meaning, as well as the rest of the incompatible cues provided by the plot pattern, and just as in the case of motion sickness, one experience is caused by different cues. What I assume is that the textual representation of a traumatized mind which is confused, fragmented, and unbalanced might be organically grounded in confused, fragmented and unbalanced bodily experience. The processing of incompatible inputs may have a similar effect on the body of the perceiver, whether they are direct bodily sensations or the representational techniques or underlying structures of a piece of fiction. The somatic effects may not be as strong in the second case, and they may not even be experienced by everyone. The experience of reading *The Body Artist* may be dulled because the processing of the input happens over a prolonged time, but in my view, the direct relationship between the world, human perceptions and cognition which Noë referred to remains observable.

Conclusion

The purpose of the present study was to provide an account for the somatic experiences of the reader of literary fiction, as well as to place this experience in the process of reading. My hypothesis was that there are observable structures in certain narratives, not unlike conceptual metaphors, which are also traceable to a preconceptual level, where bodily experiences are dominant models of cognition. I assumed that the narrative and the bodily experience are related because they are structured by the same dynamism on the preconceptual level.

I have analyzed Don DeLillo's *The Body Artist*, which has a peculiar structure on the textual and representational levels, and also on the level of the plot. I have concentrated on the representations of space and movement, explored in the themes of movement and inertia, as well as in the corrections and hesitations in the narration, and in the depicted experiences of the protagonist. What I have found is that no consistent experience of space and movement can be constructed from the text, not even in retrospect. This results in an uncertainty of the reading experience which is generated by the uncertainty of (metaphoric and actual) movement in the novel. Characteristically, the representations of space and movement in the novel are fragmented, partial and occasionally false, presented on more than one level. Since I considered the dynamism of the narrative on the preconceptual level—as fueled by bodily experience—my next step was to seek a real life experience where the perception of space and movement would be equally problematic. I found it in *kinetosis*, or motion sickness, which is a condition that occurs when the brain receives conflicting sense cues: motion is felt but not seen, or vice versa. At this point in my reading, the interpretive focus has been transferred from the text to the reader. In *The Body Artist*, in the course of reading, as I have posited, the narrative gives the reader a position from which he or she has to build the reading experience; as narrative structures are processed, the experience that serves as their model reemerges in the body of the reader—as the experience of *kinetosis* suggested itself to me. The process of building the experience is, then, a circle that is kept up by a loop-effect of the somatic reactions which influence, and are influenced by, the text. Thus, narrative fiction, as I believe and as I tried to show, should be understood as a multimedial art form, for the narrative is not only written on the paper and in the mind of the reader, but in his or her body as well.

References

Bonca, Cornel. 2002. "Being, Time, and Death in DeLillo's *The Body Artist.*" *Pacific Coast Philology* 37 (1): 58–68. DOI: 10.2307/4142090.

Bridgeman, Teresa. 2007. "Time and space." In *Cambridge Companion to Narrative*. Edited by David Herman, 52–65. Cambridge: Cambridge University Press.

Caracciolo, Marco. 2014. "Tell-Tale Rhythms: Embodiment and Narrative Discourse." *Storyworlds* 6 (2): 49–73. DOI: 10.5250/storyworlds.6.2.0049.

Dannenberg, Hilary P. 2008. *Coincidence and Counterfactuality: Plotting Time and Space in Narrative Fiction*. Lincoln: University of Nebraska Press.

DeLillo, Don. 2002 (2001). *The Body Artist*. New York: Picador.

Gibbs, Raymond W. 2005. *Embodiment and Cognitive Science*. New York: Cambridge University Press.

Hampe, Beate, ed. 2005. *From Perception to Meaning Image Schemas in Cognitive Linguistics*. New York: Mouton de Gruyter.

Holland, Norman N. 2009. *Literature and the Brain*. Gainesville: The PsyArt Foundation.

Horváth Márta, and Szabó Erzsébet, eds. 2013. *Helikon irodalomtudományi szemle: Kognitív irodalomtudomány* [Helikon review of literary studies: Cognitive literary theory] 2. Budapest.

Johnson, Mark. 1992. *Body in the Mind*. Chicago: The University of Chicago Press.

Kakutani, Michiko. 2001. "*The Body Artist*: A Marriage Replayed Inside a Widow's Mind." *The New York Times*. Accessed April 4, 2014. http://nyti.ms/2kSMAcb.

Kövecses Zoltán. 1998. "Metafora a kognitív nyelvészetben" [Metaphors in cognitive linguistics]. In *A kognitív szemlélet és a nyelv kutatása* [Research on the cognitive approach and language]. Edited by Pléh Csaba, Győri Miklós, 50–82. Budapest: Pólya Kiadó.

Lakoff, George, Mark Johnson. 1999. *Philosophy in the Flesh: The Embodied Mind and Its Challenge to Western Thought*. New York: Basic Books.

Menary, Richard, ed. 2006. *Radical Enactivism: Intentionality, Phenomenology and Narrative*. Philadelphia: John Benjamins Publishing Company.

Merleau-Ponty, Maurice. 2005. *Phenomenology of Perception*. Translated by Colin Smith. Taylor and Francis e-Library.

Millar, Susanna. 2008. *Space and Sense*. New York: Psychology Press.

Noë, Alva. 2004. *Action in Perception*. Cambridge, Massachusetts: The MIT Press.

Ryan, Marie-Laure. 2012. "Space." In: *The Living Handbook of Narratology*. Edited by Peter Hühn et al. Hamburg: Hamburg University. Accessed December 3, 2014. http://bit.ly/1Eh9Xfh.

Szabó, Erzsébet. 2012. "A narratívák olvasásának kognitív modellálása" [Cognitive modelling of the reading of narratives]. *Literatura XXXVIII*, no. 2: 115–25.

Varela, Francisco J. et al. 1993. *The Embodied Mind: Cognitive Science and Human Experience*. Cambridge, Massachusetts: The MIT Press.

Wilson, Robert A., and Lucia Foglia. 2011. "Embodied Cognition." In *The Stanford Encyclopedia of Philosophy* (Fall 2011 Edition). Edited by Edward N. Zalta. Accessed December 3, 2014. http://stanford.io/2krMNCd.

Notes

[1] I am grateful for the help of Marco Caracciolo, who was kind enough to read an earlier version of this paper and provided me with numerous insightful critiques, comments and suggestions.

[2] See, for instance, DeLillo 2002, 117.

[3] See DeLillo 2002, 23.

[4] See DeLillo 2002, 107.

[5] See DeLillo 2002, 33.

CHAPTER NINE

SYN-AESTHETIC EXPERIENCE:
TOWARDS A SOMATO-POETICS OF READING

ZUZANNA KOZŁOWSKA

Somato-poetics of Reading

Philosophy, aesthetics and cultural practices have long privileged the content over the form. The dualism that underlies every idealistic approach assumes that the textual embodiment of the idea is secondary to the idea itself, and that it can be replaced with another one, hence the minor status of the translator in copyright law (Venuti 1999, 47–67) and the longstanding neglect of corporeality in academic reflection. The "return of the body" (Jay 1994, 152) initiated by the end of the 19th century, along with rise of anti-ocularcentric tendencies, triggered an avalanche of changes in the understanding of corporeality and its role in artistic expression and representation. The somatic (Cooter 2010) and the affective (La Caze and Lloyd 2011) turns, which account for the present expansion of somatic and sensual issues in the humanities, introduced new categories to arts criticism. Richard Shusterman's idea of *soma*, "the living body" (Shusterman 2006, 3), conceptually close to John Dewey's notion of "body-mind" or the subsequent "mind-body" (cf. the use of the terms in Dewey 1988a and 1988b), refers to the unity of human experience, both mental and corporeal. Defying the dualistic vision of experience, somatism proposes a holistic view of human nature, based on the notion of bodily consciousness as a perceiving, experiencing somatic self.

Though the literary form has been exhaustively studied, especially within the formalist and structuralist paradigm, hardly enough attention has been paid to the somatic reaction that the sensual component of literature causes in the reader. Most literary reception theories[1] have conceptualized the reader as an incorporeal being, exerting its interpretative or creationist competences upon a text. In the majority of Polish reader-response studies, the reader has remained a "theoretical construct" (Rembowska-Płuciennik 2012, 267),[2] often considered merely as a potential, virtual component of a literary work. Textual or actual, the reader has been conceived essentially as a pure consciousness, a truly Cartesian *res cogitans* contemplating a textual *res extensa*. Yet isn't aesthetic attention and judgment based, primarily, on somatic responses to specific stimuli? Doesn't a powerful musical composition or a strikingly beautiful poem send shivers down our spines?[3] Doesn't a reader succumb to an oddly irresistible state of trans when immersed in the fictitious reality of a great novel? Can't the rhythmic texture of dramatic monologue hypnotize its spectator? The importance of the emotive, somatic dimension of aesthetic experience is suggestively rendered in Richard Shusterman's (2000, 31) hypothetical juxtaposition of automatized and human ways of processing the "aesthetic content": though the machine may effectively decode the perceptual input, presenting a probable interpretation of the data, in no way can its internal computing process be identified with human aesthetic experience, biased and shaped by its pleasures (Barthes 1975), emotions and sensory qualia.[4] It is evident that the notion of "interpretation" does not convey the complexity of aesthetic experience,[5] which cannot be described in cognitive terms only, and explained regardless of its somato-sensory and emotive dimension, crucial to the phenomenon herein discussed.

The empirical approach to the phenomenon of literariness, combining methods and insights of cognitive studies, psychology and the neurosciences, focuses on the sensory, somatic, cognitive and affective aspects of art reception and perception. As a branch of neuroaesthetics, it aims at discovering the neural basis of aesthetic behavior. Somaesthetics plays a vital role in the process of re-corporealisation of arts criticism, thus encouraging external contributions to the field, notably, from the representatives of "natural" sciences that are traditionally viewed as disciplines concerned with matter, and thereby with the body, and opposed to the humanities, which became primarily concerned with "mind," "soul" and thought. The philosophical landscape outlined by somaesthetics, together with empirical data elaborated by neuroaesthetics, exhibits great potential as a refreshing and enriching perspective on literary studies.

Although empirical studies of literary response (Nardocchio 1992) have been conducted and developed in Western interdisciplinary research fields for several decades now, they remain practically non-existent in Polish academic reflection. One of the noteworthy exceptions is Magdalena Rembowska-Płuciennik's recent study *Poetyka intersubiektywności. Kognitywistyczna teoria narracji a proza XX wieku* (Poetics of intersubjectivity: Cognitive narratology and the 20th century prose, 2012), "intended to connect research on narration with the empirical science of embodied mind" (355). Its last chapter discusses the "psychosomatic aspect of a reading experience" (357), in which a narrative is considered as it intersubjectively "stimulates multisensory processes, multisensory mental imagery and the emotional reactions." The book, which describes the cognitive and affective impacts of narrative inventory on a reader's embodied mind,[6] such as the implications of "sensory focalisation" technique (Rembowska-Płuciennik 2006), heralds a methodological turn towards empirical inspirations in literary studies (2012, 10). Another attempt to introduce the somatic dimension into literary studies in Poland was made by Jarosław Płuciennik (2002) and Anna Łebkowska (2008) who have investigated the phenomenon of empathy[7] in literature, thus—in contrast to the critical practice upheld by the reigning tendencies—re-corporealizing the reader. Łebkowska introduced to literary studies a new discipline of "somato-poetics" (2011) which traces strategies of "embodying the body" in literature. When it comes to the pure sensuality of literature, Polish researchers have given most attention to the melic qualities of a piece: its musicality, its rhymes and rhythm.[8]

Indeed, literary studies have traditionally focused on discursive forms of audience responses, analyzing their mental content regardless of their bodily foundations, thus reinforcing the dualistic view of human nature. Yet even if determined to separate the mind from the flesh, notwithstanding their natural unity, one would have to conclude that every mental (viz. cerebral) representation of an aesthetically grasped object is necessarily mediated by the ultimate medium (Shusterman 2007, 73–92): a touching, seeing, smelling, tasting and hearing body. The above-mentioned empirical studies of reading define the literary experience as a neurologically distinctive type of interaction between the reader and the text,[9] neither discrediting the recipient's fundamental role in the aesthetic realization of a piece of art, nor ignoring the specificity of a literary impulse, studied in all its complexity as a synthesis of beautiful form and compelling narrative. This trivial yet elusive fact is of basic importance for the following considerations of somato-emotive aspects of aesthetic experience. Shouldn't literary studies contemplate the proprioceptive experience of beauty (Shusterman 1999), enabled and guided by contact with a poem or a piece of prose? The somato-poetics of reading proposed herein, drawing on the philosophical insights of somaesthetics and integrating factual data of neurological arts-reception research, would investigate the ways in which the text influences *soma*, or, more precisely, ask how a textual body, inscribed in a textual object by an embodied creator, affects the reader's corporeal experience.

In sum, engaging the ideas of Richard Shusterman's somaesthetics and acknowledging the conclusions of empirical reader-response research, literary studies should re-embrace the body as a "locus of sensory-aesthetic appreciation (*aisthesis*)" (Shusterman 2006, 3). Art is a part of the physical world we perceive with our senses, hence the need to probe the obvious yet underestimated reality of the primarily sensual and emotive nature of artistic experience, considered not only from the creator's, but also from the audience's, perspective. This paper constitutes a preliminary step in the recognition of the potential of a somato-poetics of reading (viewed as reversed somato-poetics) for future exploration in literary studies. By exploring the *syn*-aesthetic experience, this article points towards possible somatic effects induced in the reader by various forms of artistic expression.

Syn-aesthetic Experience

The phenomenon of synaesthesia can be considered interdisciplinarily as a neurological condition (Hochel and Milán 2008), a hypothetical impulse of natural language genesis (Ramachandran and Hubbard 2001), an antiocularcentric cultural tool (Kozłowska 2014), a sensory compensation[10] and cognitive development mechanism (Richardson 2009), and finally, as an artistic device and an intersensual metaphor integrated into the tissue of literary text. In clinical terms, synaesthesia consist in the mingling of the senses—synaesthetic perception occurs when a given sensory stimulus automatically activates a redundant perception within another sensory modality. This peculiar neurological condition permanently links separate sensual pathways, thus producing augmented intersensory perception in response to a single-modal stimulus. Colors can become audible, words may be tasted. Statistical reports by S. A. Day indicate a diversity of roughly eighty types of synaesthesia.[11] Among the most frequent ones, Day cites a grapheme-color synaesthesia (in which letters and numbers are tinted with color);[12] among the rarest—a synaesthesia pairing sounds with temperatures.

A synaesthetic connection of two sensory modalities proves stable and idiosyncratic: while distinctive and individual, a supplementary reaction to a given stimulus remains unchanged throughout the entire life of a synaesthete.[13] Essential for our consideration of synaesthetic responses to art are two features of the condition: enhanced memory and affective perception. Synaesthetes are endowed with superior mnemonic skills (Luria 1987); they obtain better results on the Wechsler Memory Scale (Cytowic 1997) compared to non-synaesthetic subjects. The link between clinical synaesthesia and hypermnesis is self-explanatory: supplementary synaesthetic perception, such as spatial visualisation of time units (Jarick et al. 2009), gustatory lexicon (Jones et al. 2011, Ward and Simner 2003) and the graphic representation of speech in ticker-tape synaesthesia constitute an additional reference system, facilitating and accelerating the stimuli-identification process. Sensualisation of abstractions (for instance, colored numbers) facilitates efficient memorisation, storage and retrieval of information.

As mentioned above, synaesthetic perception is emotional. Neuroimaging techniques provide evidence that a single-modular stimulation activates not only the sensory areas involved in the processing of synaesthetically combined modalities, but also the limbic structures responsible for emotional reactions. Mirror-touch synaesthetes,[14] experiencing "mirrored" tactile skin sensations while observing the tactile behavior of others, exhibit unusual empathetic sensibility (Banissy and Ward 2007). In 2001, Vilayanur S. Ramachandran and Edward M. Hubbard formulated a hypothesis of "hyperconnectivity between the sensory cortex and amygdala" (Ramachandran and Hubbard 2001, 3) in synaesthesia, which may explain the emotive nature of intersensory perception and the "heightened aversion synaesthetes experience when seeing numbers printed in the 'wrong' colour" (3), inconsistent with their own synaesthetic patterns. Synaesthetic per/reception is in fact highly intuitive. Richard E. Cytowic (1997), referring to *The Varieties of Religious Experience* by William James, compares synaesthetic experience to ecstasy, pointing towards their shared qualities of epiphany and wonder. *Noesis*, an illuminative insight into the essence of phenomena, constitutes a common principle of ecstatic and synaesthetic experience. The noetic and ecstatic nature of intersensory perception predisposes synaesthetes to aesthetic experience. Scientifically and aesthetically analyzed synaesthetic-reception poetics would require systematic research; the aim of the present draft is only to suggest possible directions in the reflection on synaesthesia as located in the field of literary reception.

The specificity of the synaesthetic experience of art consists primarily in its hyper-sensuality. For instance, in the vision-sound type, a painting does not trigger solely visual, but also auditory perception, obviously altering its reception. Painting becomes musical—not in a metaphorical sense, but literally. Such a perceptual faculty opens up a vast range of semantic and somatic modalities of aesthetic experience. Hypersensuality, which undoubtedly constitutes the most conspicuous trait of synaesthetic per/reception of art, may either enhance, modify or hinder the process of reading. For instance, in grapheme-color synaesthesia the color and its distribution on a given page of a literary text may be considered an additional aesthetic feature, contributing to the experience of reading a literary piece. Words having taste—as in lexical-gustatory synaesthesia— also may alter drastically the semantics of literary text. As stated by Daniel Tammet (2011), the author of *Born on a Blue Day: Inside the Extraordinary Mind of an Autistic Savant*, a "high-functioning autistic savant," and a synaesthete: "different kinds of perceiving create different kinds of knowing and understanding." As an equally vivid illustration of Tammet's thesis, I recall a chance encounter at a conference: during a conversation revolving around Wassily Kandinsky's art,[15] my interlocutor commented with deep conviction: "Those paintings are full of music." In an attempt to look adequately convinced, I assumed a dignified expression and nodded pensively; whereas in reality no such understanding emerged in my subjective experience of the abstract colorful compositions. A synaesthete himself, my interlocutor possessed an intuitive grasp of the deliberately melic content of the piece,[16] contrasting with my non-intuitive, analytical understanding of it.

The second trait of a synaesthetic experience of art is an enhanced sensitivity to an artwork's formal features. During his speech on TED, Daniel Tammet (2011) self-analyzed the gains of intersensory perception:

> My worlds of words and numbers blur with color, emotion and personality. … But it's not only numbers that I see in colors. Words too, for me, have colors and emotions and textures. And this is an opening phrase from the novel *Lolita*. … Nabokov was himself synesthetic. … My perception of the sound L helps the alliteration to jump right out.

Synaesthetic instant perception of phonetic regularities (as in the opening line of *Lolita*[17]), is an example of sharpened perceptive sensibility to literary (and, presumably, also other artistic) devices.[18] The sensual tissue of literary work is seized immediately, without cognitive effort. No deliberately applied analytical method is needed to *see* right through the textual matter, the body of the text:

> Another example: a little bit more mathematical. And I wonder if some of you will notice the construction of the sentence from *The Great Gatsby*. There is a procession of syllables—wheat, one; prairies, two; lost Swede towns, three—one, two, three. And this effect is very pleasant on the mind, and it helps the sentence to feel right. (Tammet 2011)

The feeling of aesthetic approval (or aversion) is key to synaesthetic per/reception of art, as the affective value constitutes its third characteristic. As a response to a questionnaire sent to the members of S. A. Day's

Synaesthesia List, "an international e-mail forum, founded in 1992, for connecting synesthetes with each other and with those researching synaesthesia,"[19] I've received a personal description of a highly affective synaesthetic reception of Robert Motherwell's abstract painting:

> ... this piece was weighted perfectly and I feel like I could never tire of seeing this simple black on white work. I felt an instant connection to Motherwell and as if his painting had a depth and life perception that I had never seen before.[20]

The sensation of aesthetic exactness and the subsequent feeling of intuitive closeness is triggered by a supplementary synaesthetic sensory perception—one that the author could not possibly predict or project. The idiosyncrasy of *syn*-aesthetic experience is both emotive and noetic. As witnessed by a respondent, a powerful *syn*-aesthetic appreciation occurs when the artistically rendered or aroused sensations are consistent with the synaesthete's individual intersensory experiences:

> ... when I see art, even art that is not necessarily in a style that I am crazy about, and that art has the same weightedness as a beautiful sound that I might experience as a synesthete, then I am crazy about that piece.

The quality of aesthetic experience relies clearly upon a reader's (viewer's, etc.) somato-sensory constitution, engaging one's perceptual capacities, extensions, intersections and limitations of the senses, sensory memory, and perceptual biography involving things touched, smelled, heard, tasted and seen.

Those particularly strong *syn*-aesthetic experiences prove deep and memorable, being remembered and recalled over a lifetime: "I still think about that painting and hope to come across it again." Interestingly, synaesthesia can also be purposely applied—as described by another respondent—as a mnemonic strategy in artistic performance:

> Insofar as memorizing text (specifically Shakespearian parts), I used my synaesthesia as a memorizing aid. I discovered that, in many lines I had to learn, there would be a specific colored letter which would then also begin a change or shift of thought that the character had to say. It usually was the first letter of the third word before the end of a sentence ... the next shift of thought would start with that same letter, not always but often enough for it to be a tool for me to use as a mnemonic device.

Employed by the above-quoted synaesthete as a memory enhancement mechanism in theater performance, this fascinating perceptual skill can be also viewed as a display of synaesthetic sensitivity to the materiality of language, to the sensual tissue of textual objects that can—quite literally—be smelled, tasted, seen, heard and felt. The mnemonic potential of inter-sensuality and its consequences for art creation and reception is yet to be fully discovered.

As opposed to non-synaesthetic cognition, a synaesthetic judgement seems both more intuitive and more radical, and the synaesthetic experience, if compared with its non-synaesthetic counterpart—more intense. The "colored beauty" of words in grapheme-color synaesthesia can please as well as displease: "poetry carries its colorful schemes and sometimes can be jarring based on word choices and colors." The chromatic composition of a literary text—the synaesthetic hues and their layout on a page or a screen—can drastically alter its reception, adding to the overall artistic effects involved in the reader's experience. On the other hand, this process can be reversed: synaesthetically perceived color can also guide verbal expression and thus navigate creativity:

> I also recall from my high school days … that I would write essays for required topics and happily write along, choosing a colorful bunch of words that I thought were quite lovely, and when the essay was returned to me, there were many comments asking me to clarify my points. The reason for this was that I would use the prettiest or most matching word, chosen for its colors, rather than its clarity.

The aesthetic criteria prove predominant in a grapheme-color synaesthete's experience of language. The chromatic disposition of the letters carries its own aesthetic value, which overshadows the pragmatic relevance of writing. A written composition becomes pictorial; a grapheme-color synaesthete resembles a painter experimenting with hues and shades of language. Linguistic creation and reception are both strongly influenced by aesthetically-biased synaesthetic perception.

The latest insights of empirical reader-response studies specify two possible neuropsychological indicators of literariness. The first one is the foregrounding (Miall 2008b), viz. the formalist notion of "stylistic variations" that "hypothetically prompt defamiliarization, evoke feelings, and prolong reading time" (Miall and Kuiken 1994, 389). The second one is a distinctive process of feeling (Miall 2008a), including empathetic interaction. Thus, if analyzed within the framework of hypotheses proposed by neuro-aesthetics, synaesthetic perception proves intrinsically aesthetic, or aesthetic-prone.

It should be reiterated that synaesthetes seem predisposed to an aesthetic experience. Synaesthesia itself could be viewed as an aesthetic state, since it involves perpetual aesthetic judgement of perceptive qualities of experience. Synaesthetic perception is *per se* emotional, evaluative, and thus aesthetic. It is almost as if synaesthetes possessed, due to an altered perception (often related in aesthetic terms, such as "beautiful," "magical"), an artistic "sixth sense," shaping both their engagement in artistic creation and strong standpoints on art and its quality—hence the higher incidence of synaesthesia among artists.[21] As Daniel Tammet (2011) claims, "aesthetic judgments, rather than abstract reasoning, guide and shape the process by which we all come to know what we know." As a synaesthete, Tammet adds: "I'm an extreme example of this."

The idiosyncrasy of the synaesthetic reception of art can be viewed as both an argument and a counter-argument on behalf of the singularity of the reader's response. On the one hand, synaesthesia constitutes an uncanny example of highly individual, *quasi* ineffable experiences of art that evade any standard notion of aesthetic experience. On the other hand, the synaesthetic perception of art, with its heightened sensual awareness, unveils the fundamentally corporeal *substratum* of any artistic experience, since synaesthesia could be considered, as R. E. Cytowic once suggested (1997, 27), an early stage of standard perception. If considered in relation to hypothetical neuro-indicators of literariness, the reader's synaesthetic response must be viewed as a hyperbolic yet universal model of aesthetic sensibility. Furthermore, synaesthetic experience proves that a standard art per/reception is hardly transparent, as it derives from a specific categorisation and representation strategy, which itself is shaped by cultural determinants, as witnessed by divergences in hierarchical structuring of senses in different cultures (Sendyka 2011) and diverse sensory metaphors and idiomatic expressions in various languages. Paradoxically, an "absurd," "abnormal," "bizarre" synaesthetic per/reception unveils the fundamental "strangeness" of any per/reception, which remains, in each case, merely the product of a cerebral recreation of reality, conditioned by the limits and capacities of a singular body, by its idiosyncratic corporeality, its perceptual skills and impairments. Perception is also programmed by a culture that teaches us, from our early—and in fact synaesthetic[22]—years, to abandon nebulous holism in favor of segmentation and labelling of pieces of reality as "visible," "audible," "olfactory," "gustatory," or "palpable." As a matter of fact, perception of the external world, including those purportedly fictitious "worlds" (and isn't the whole social reality fictitious?) is far more subjective and co-fictive, confabulated collaboratively by singular and collective bodies that constitute culture. If then a synaesthetic per/reception of the world and art—which constantly intersect in a synaesthete's experience—seems exotic, it's only because we were, developmentally and culturally, encouraged to overcome the holistic perception experienced in early childhood. As a result, the majority of adults divide the real into several separate and usually discrete sensory categories. And yet "standard" perception is fantasy; in fact, no "normal," "full" perception exists. Various species perceive the world differently. Evidently, these deliberations lead us to the fundamental question of the definability of "reality"; I would assume, provisionally, that the (animal, human, vegetable etc.) "world" is always a world in quotation marks, always fictitious, made up. Perception is illusive. Synaesthesia proves it clearly by shattering the notion of pure, "godly" perception. As Richard Shusterman pointed out:

> Though our bodies unite us as humans, they also divide us (through their physical structure, functional practice, and sociocultural interpretation) into different genders, races, ethnicities, classes, and further into the unique individuals that we are. (2006, 4)

Clinically synaesthetic experience of art, both idiosyncratic and universal, is an ultimate illustration of a corporeal perception of beauty, able to uncover the general mechanisms underlying any aesthetic judgment.

Once implemented in literary studies, somaesthetic reflection, as a meliorative practice, could lead to a deeper self-awareness of the somatic effects of aesthetic interaction, promoting knowledge of reader-response mechanisms. It would reinvigorate reception theory by pointing towards the body as a center of *aisthesis*. Due to an augmented perception, synaesthetes may prove more conscious of those effects, and their per/reception of art should be further examined.[23] In particular, as presumed in the field of empirical literary studies, one of the purposes of reading is the search for the somatic pleasures of absorption—of proprioceptive sympathetic sensations and of tension-and-release fluctuations—and thus the contact with art must be considered a self- and other-directed somaesthetic practice. Inspired by somaesthetics, a somato-poetics of reading should advance awareness of the somatic reception of art, developing and perfecting a sensibility and consciousness of the body reacting to aesthetically perceived objects. Such reversed somato-poetics should consider the very nature of aesthetic perception and the specificity of its somatic features through the integration of empirical data provided by literary response research into the very core of its disciplinary interests. How does the body react to art? Shivers, goose bumps, chills and tears, as well as the states of absorption and trance, and the feeling of empathy—

even the Aristotelian *catharsis*—should be re-examined with regard to conceptions developed within the discipline of soma- and neuro-aesthetics.

References

Banissy, Michael J., and Jamie Ward. 2007. "Mirror-Touch Synaesthesia Is Linked with Empathy." *Nature Neuroscience* 10 (7): 815–16. DOI: 10.1038/nn1926.

Banissy, Michael J., Roi Cohen Kadosh, Gerrit W. Maus, Vincent Walsh, and Jamie Ward. 2009. "Prevalence, Characteristics And a Neurological Model of Mirror-Touch Synaesthesia." *Experimental Brain Research* 198 (2–3): 261–73. DOI: 10.1007/s00221-009-1810-9.

Baron-Cohen, Simon. 1996. "Is There a Normal Phase of Synaesthesia in Development?" *Psyche* 2 (27). Accessed February 5, 2017. http://journalpsyche.org/files/0xaa3f.pdf.

Barthes, Roland. 1975. *Pleasures of the Text*. Translated by Richard Miller. New York: Hill & Wang.

Chaberski, Mateusz. 2015. *Doświadczenie syn(estetyczne): Performatywne aspekty przedstawień "site-specific"* [(Syn)aesthetic experience: Performative aspects of the site-specific performance]. Kraków: Księgarnia Akademicka.

Cooter, Roger. 2010. "The Turn of the Body: History and the Politics of the Corporeal." *ARBOR Ciencia, Pensamiento y Cultura* 186 (743): 393–405. DOI: 10.3989/arbor.2010.743n1204.

Cytowic, Richard E. 1997. "Synesthesia: Phenomenology and Neuropsychology. A Review of Current Knowledge." In *Synaesthesia: Classic and Contemporary Readings*. Edited by Simon Baron-Cohen, and John E. Harrison, 17–39. Oxford, Cambridge: Blackwell Publishers.

Day, Sean A. 2002. "A Brief History of Synaesthesia and Music." *Theremin Vox*. Accessed January 3, 2015. http://bit.ly/2kTOG8f.

—. 2008. "Regarding Types of Synaesthesia and Color Music Art." In *Synesthesia: Commonwealth of Senses and Synthesis of Arts*. Edited by Bulat M. Galeyev, 282–88. Kazan: Izdatelstvo KGTU.

Dewey, John. 1988a. "Experience and Nature." In *The Later Works of John Dewey*. Vol. 1. Carbondale: Southern Illinois University Press.

—. 1988b. "Body and Mind." In *The Later Works of John Dewey*. Vol. 3. Edited by Jo Ann Bodyston, 25–40. Carbondale: Southern Illinois University Press.

Doucleff, Michaeleen. 2012. "Anatomy of a Tear Jerker. Why Does Adele's 'Someone Like You' Make Everyone Cry? Science Has Found the Formula." *The Wall Street Journal*. Accessed January 3, 2015. http://on.wsj.com/2kU3Yd5.

Dziadek, Adam. 2014. *Projekt krytyki somatycznej* [A proposal for somatic criticism]. Warszawa: Wydawnictwo IBL PAN.

Fitzgibbon, Bernadette M., Peter G. Enticott, Anina N. Rich, Melita J. Giummarra, Nellie Georgiou-Karistianis, and John L. Bradshaw. 2012. "Mirror-Sensory Synaesthesia: Exploring 'Shared' Sensory Experiences as Synaesthesia." *Neuroscience and Behavioral Reviews* 36 (1): 645–57. DOI: 10.1016/j.neubiorev.2011.09.006.

Handtke, Ryszard. 1982. *Utwór fabularny w perspektywie odbiorcy* [The narrative from the reader's perspective]. Wrocław: Zakład Narodowy im. Ossolińskich.

Harbisson, Neil. 2012. "I Listen to Color." Accessed January 3, 2015. http://bit.ly/1cSlIdo.

Hochel, Matej, and Emilio G. Milán. 2008. "Synaesthesia: The Existing State of Affairs." *Cognitive Neuropsychology* 25 (1): 93–117. DOI: 10.1080/02643290701822815.

Ione, Amy, and Christopher Tyler. 2003. "Was Kandinsky a Synesthete?" *Journal of the History of the Neurosciences* 12 (2): 223–26.

Jarick, Michelle, Mike J. Dixon, Mark T. Stewart, Emily C. Maxwell, and Daniel Smilek. 2009. "A Different Outlook on Time: Visual and Auditory Month Names Elicit Different Mental Vantage Points for a Time-Space Synaesthete." *Cortex* 45 (10): 1217–28. DOI: 10.1016/j.cortex.2009.05.014.

Jay, Martin. 1994. *Downcast Eyes: The Denigration of Vision in Twentieth-Century French Thought*. Berkeley, Los Angeles, London: University of California Press.

Jones, Catherine L., Marcus A. Gray, Ludovico Minati, Julia Simner, Hugo D. Critchley, and Jamie Ward. 2011. "The Neural Basis of Illusory Gustatory Sensations: Two Rare Cases of Lexical-Gustatory Synaesthesia." *Journal of Neuropsychology* 5 (2): 243–54. DOI: 10.1111/j.1748-6653.2011.02013.x.

Kozłowska, Zuzanna. 2014. "Synestezja – wyzwanie dla kultury wzrokocentrycznej" [Synaesthesia: Challenging the vision-obsessed culture]. *Ogrody Nauk i Sztuk*, no. 4: 225–31. DOI: 10.15503/onis2014-225-231.

La Caze, Marguerite, and Henry M. Lloyd. 2011. "Editors' Introduction: Philosophy and the 'Affective Turn'." *Parrhesia*, no. 13: 1–13.

Łebkowska, Anna. 2008. *Empatia. O literackich narracjach przełomu XX i XXI wieku* [Empathy: Literary narratives at the turn of the 21st century]. Kraków: Universitas.

——. 2011. "Jak ucieleśnić ciało: o jednym z dylematów somatopoetyki" [How to embody the body: One of the dilemmas of somatopoetics]. *Teksty Drugie*, no. 4: 11–27.

Luria, Aleksandr R. 1987. *The Mind of a Mnemonist: A Little Book about a Vast Memory*. Translated by Lynn Solotaroff. Cambridge: Harvard University Press.

Markiewicz, Henryk. 1979. "Odbiór i odbiorca w badaniach literackich. Perspektywy i trudności" [Reception and the recipient in literary studies: Perspectives and difficulties]. *Ruch Literacki*, no. 1: 1–15.

——. 1988. "Problemy odbioru i odbiorcy w polskiej teorii literatury" [The problems of reception and the recipient in Polish Literary Theory]. In *Z polskich studiów slawistycznych* [Questions in Polish Slavic Studies]. Edited by Jan Basara, 193–203. Warszawa: Państwowe Wydawnictwo Naukowe.

Meschonnic, Henri. 1982. *Critique du rythme: Anthropologie historique du langage* [A critique of rhythm: A historical anthropology of language]. Lagrasse: Verdier.

Miall, David S. 2008a. "Feeling from the Perspective of the Empirical Study of Literature." *Journal of Literary Theory* 1 (2): 377–93. DOI: 10.1515/JLT.2007.023.

——. 2008b. "Foregrounding and Feeling in Response to Narrative." In *Directions in Empirical Literary Studies: Essays in Honor of Willie van Peer*. Edited by Sonia Zyngier, Marisa Bortolussi, Anna Chesnokova, and Jan Auracher, 89–102. Amsterdam, Philadelphia: John Benjamins Publishing Company.

Miall, David S., and Don Kuiken. 1994. "Foregrounding, Defamiliarization, and Affect, Response to Literary Stories." *Poetics* 22 (5): 389–407. DOI: 10.1016/0304-422X(94)00011-5.

Nabokov, Vladimir. 2000. *Lolita*. Penguin Books: London.

Nardocchio, Elaine F., ed. 1992. *Reader Response to Literature: The Empirical Dimension*. Berlin, New York: Mouton de Gruyter.

Płuciennik, Jarosław. 2002. *Literackie identyfikacje i oddźwięki. Poetyka i empatia* [The literary identifications and resonance: Poetics and empathy]. Łódź: Wydawnictwo Uniwersytetu Łódzkiego.

Ramachandran, Vilayanur S., and Edward M. Hubbard. 2001. "Synaesthesia—A Window into Perception, Thought and Language." *Journal of Consciousness Studies* 8 (12): 3–34.

Rembowska-Płuciennik, Magdalena. 2006. "W cudzej skórze. Fokalizacja
    zmysłowa a literackie reprezentacje doświadczeń sensualnych" [In the
    other's skin: Sensory focalisation versus literary representations of
    sensual experiences]. *Ruch Literacki*, no. 6: 51–67.
—. 2012. *Poetyka intersubiektywności. Kognitywistyczna teoria narracji a
    proza XX wieku* [Poetics of intersubjectivity. Cognitive narratology
    and the 20th century prose]. Toruń: Wydawnictwo Naukowe
    Uniwersytetu Mikołaja Kopernika.
Richardson, Laura S. 2009. "Seeing the Future Synesthetic." Accessed
    January 3, 2015. http://bit.ly/2jZPx99.
Rothen, Nicolas, and Beat Meier. 2010. "Higher Prevalence of
    Synaesthesia in Art Students." *Perception* 39 (5): 718–20. DOI:
    10.1068/p6680.
Sendyka, Roma. 2011. "Antropologia zmysłów" [Anthropology of the
    senses]. *Autoportret* 3 (35): 20–27.
Shusterman, Richard. 1999. "Somaesthetics: A Disciplinary Proposal."
    The Journal of Aesthetics and Art Criticism 57 (3): 299–313. DOI:
    10.2307/432196.
—. 2000. *Performing Live: Aesthetic Alternatives for the Ends of Art*.
    Ithaca: Cornell University Press.
—. 2006. "Thinking through the Body, Educating for the Humanities: A
    Plea for Somaesthetics." *Journal of Aesthetic Education* 40 (1): 1–21.
    DOI: 10.1353/jae.2006.0010.
—. 2007. "Somatoestetyka a problem ciało/media" [Somaesthetics and the
    body/media issue]. In *O sztuce i życiu. Od poetyki hip-hopu do filozofii
    somatycznej* [On art and life: From hip-hop poetics to somatic
    philosophy]. Edited and translated by Wojciech Małecki. Wrocław:
    Wydawnictwo Atla 2.
Skov, Martin, and Oshin Vartanian, eds. 2009. *Neuroaesthetics*.
    Amityville, NY: Baywood.
Sontag, Susan. 1994. "Against Interpretation." In *Against Interpretation
    and Other Essays*. London: Vintage.
The Synesthesia List. 2016. Accessed January 8, 2017.
    http://www.daysyn.com/index.html.
Tammet, Daniel. 2011. "Different Ways of Knowing." Accessed January
    3, 2015. http://bit.ly/1BBfFtA.
Tompkins, Jane P. 1980. *Reader-Response Criticism: From Formalism to
    Post-Structuralism*. Baltimore: Johns Hopkins University Press.
Venuti, Lawrence. 1999. *The Scandals of Translation. Towards an Ethics
    of Difference*. London: Routledge.

Ward, Jamie, and Julia Simner. 2003. "Lexical-Gustatory Synaesthesia: Linguistic and Conceptual Factors." *Cognition* 89 (3): 237–61. DOI: 10.1016/S0010-0277(03)00122-7.

Ward, Jamie, Daisy Thompson-Lake, Roxanne Ely, and Flora Kaminski. 2008. "Synaesthesia, Creativity and Art: What is the Link?" *British Journal of Psychology* 99 (1): 127–41. DOI: 10,1348 / 000712607X204164.

Notes

[1] See Tompkins 1980; see also Polish discussion of the reader-response theories summarized in Handtke 1982, Markiewicz 1979 and 1988.

[2] My translation. All translations of quotations from non-English sources, unless otherwise stated, are mine.

[3] See an analysis of the "chills-and-tears" effect as a response to musical compositions sharing several identifiable formal features (Doucleff 2012).

[4] Shusterman juxtaposes "two visually identical art viewers who offer identical interpretations of the very powerful paintings and poems before them." Only one of them, however, is a sentient human being that is capable of experiencing emotions; the other is a cyborg, endowed with immense perceptual capacity and an ability to instantly connect the perceived data within an interpretative proposition. Nevertheless, even if the interpretation computed by the cyborg would be more exact, Shusterman asserts, "we would still say that the human's general response to art was superior." This preference comes from the human ability to feel. Whereas the human response involves understanding—which arises not only from intellection, but also from feelings and emotions—cyborg's is limited to an interpretation. "For this reason," Shusterman states, "even if the cyborg's interpretive propositions were descriptively more accurate than the human being's, we would still say, … that [he] does not really grasp what art is all about" (2000, 31).

[5] See also Susan Sontag's call for "an erotics of art" in Sontag 1994.

[6] Including socially and developmentally valuable cognitive simulation (and stimulation) of interpersonal scenarios, a powerful and satisfying feeling of immersion and participation in fictitious reality, as well as activation of the imaginative processes of a reader, such as mental visualisation.

[7] Rembowska-Płuciennik's "intersubjectivity" is a broader term than Łebkowska's and Płuciennik's "empathy." See Rembowska-Płuciennik 2012.

[8] See the application of Meschonnic's (1982) notion of rhythm as a category of somatic criticism proposed by Dziadek (2014). Dziadek's broad understanding of rhythm embraces yet does not limit itself to the melic qualities of a text.

[9] See Skov and Vartanian (2009, 3).

[10] Consider this brilliant synaesthetic sensory compensation mechanism, an "electronic eye"—a device converting color frequencies to sounds, used by colorblind subject (Harbisson 2012).

[11] See Day 2008. Updated statistics (incidence of particular types of synaesthesia) are available on Sean A. Day website: http://bit.ly/2jZK7e6.

[12] Grapheme recognition occurs in the fusiform gyrus; the adjacent V4 area is responsible for color processing.

[13] Though some researchers suggest that certain tendencies in association types can be observed (for example in colored hearing synaesthesia), no case of identical sets of correspondences has been described.

[14] On mirror-touch synaesthesia, see Banissy et al. 2009 and Fitzgibbon et al. 2001.

[15] On Kandisky, see Ione and Tyler 2003.

[16] On Kandinsky's elaborate tone-to-color correspondence system, see Day 2002.

[17] See Nabokov 2000, 5.

[18] Many similar questions arise in relation to synaesthetic interaction with an artwork: How do the words having taste in lexical-gustatory synaesthesia alter the semantics of a literary text? Does the mirror-touch effect ever work while confronting a work of art? These issues should be addressed within more systematic research.

[19] http://www.daysyn.com/synesthesia-list.html.

[20] This and the following citations refer to the responses to my Synaesthesia List questionnaire, mentioned above. The herein anonymously quoted respondents' testimonies will not be accompanied by further endnotes.

[21] See Rothen and Meier 2010; Ward et al. 2008 and Ramachandran and Hubbard 2001, 17.

[22] On neonatal synaesthesia see Baron-Cohen 1996, 22.

[23] In Mateusz Chaberski's recent publication (2015), the term "(syn)aesthesia" has been re-employed in the domain of art reception, following the example of Josephine Machon's (Syn)aesthetics: Redefining Visceral Performance. Both studies refer to the performing arts. In his book, Chaberski argues that the notion of a "spectator" or even "participant" should be dismissed in favor of the term "(syn)aesthete" with regard to contemporary site-specific theatrical performances, which entail a distinctive mode of art reception that redefines the status of "audience." The author recognizes the potential of the specifically construed notion "(syn)aesthesia" in regard to other domains of cultural practices, pointing towards future developments. In my article, however, syn-aesthesia is examined through its actual perceptual roots, which Chaberski barely mentions in his study.

CHAPTER TEN

LITERARY HISTORY
AS ORAL-HISTORY PERFORMANCE:
THE CASE OF STANISŁAW BEREŚ'S
POLISH LITERARY HISTORY IN CONVERSATIONS

JOANNA MAJ

The story is always subjective—this is an assumption of the majority of contemporary humanistic methodologies, which treat each statement within literary studies as the expression of the researcher's subjectivity. The subjectivity of the literary historian manifests itself in many ways: in the selection of material, in the interpretation of facts, in the choice of a plot through which the story of a particular literary tradition is presented, in the language and style of the narration, etc. A special case of historic narration is the oral history that emerges in the course of conversation, at the meeting point of two subjectivities, whose specificity is also demonstrated in their physical features and in the physical attributes of their behaviors.

I would like to analyze the case of Stanisław Bereś's *Polish Literary History in Conversations: 20th–21st Centuries*, which is a case of that kind of history. This volume of conversations was created on the basis of audiovisual materials recorded for the television broadcast *Not Only About Books*.[1] I will consider the role of the embodied subjects in the creation of oral literary history, which is variable depending on the medium (*record–book*). I am interested in the performative character of the record and its transcription: the performativity of interlocutors, the performativity of their conversation, the performativity of the perception of the conversation and the performativity of the literary history which is created in the conversation—performative literary historiography.

I regard Bereś's *Polish Literary History in Conversations* as an attempt at constructing a performative form of the genre of oral literary history.

Teresa Walas states that "commonly comprehended 'literary history' is usually a mix of biography, bibliography, the history of literary forms, aesthetic evaluation, and the history of political and social ideas" (1993, 16).[2] Bereś's historiography contains all of these elements. Each chapter consists of an interview with a writer, a biographical note and the writer's photograph. The book contains 23 conversations, making it a multi-subjective history; the literary historian Stanisław Bereś is the persona who connects all of the interviews.

Bereś is a significant figure in the development of this form of literary history. One of the creators of the *extended interview* genre in Poland, he has published volumes of interviews with Tadeusz Konwicki (Nowicki 1986) and Stanislaw Lem (Bereś 1987). As an interviewer, Bereś is deemed to be more of a partner, an interpreter, with whom the writer has to argue about the matter, to polemicize, rather than one to whom he just gives answers in the form of a monologue.

Comparison between the video and its transcription evokes the question of the role of the medium in setting the story. Bereś also pays attention to that difference in the medium, commenting on the practice of transcription of the interviews done for Literary Television News. When speaking about creating the archive of interviews which, for practical reasons, could not be stored any longer by Polish Television, he separates the reality of a recording and the word. He says, "if there are no ways and assets to preserve the words with the images, we should rescue even just the words" (Bereś 2002, 9). He stresses the performative aspects of the conversations with writers: footage shows emotions, mimicry, gestures—it bares those things, which are instinctive and true for the authors. I am interested in how the transcriptions—despite the change of medium—keep their performative character, how this literary history could be understood as a performance, that is, as Hymnes views it, as a type of behavior enacted within the realm of culture and by a person aware of an audience (1995, 18).

In my paper I will focus on two examples—I will consider two excerpts of audiovisual recordings from which the conversations Bereś had with Czesław Miłosz and with Kazimierz Brandys were written down. Admittedly, it is not possible to capture the video material with any transcription. To create the coherent chapters in Bereś's book, the material of the interviews was (sometimes heavily) reedited and illustrated with photographs of writers' faces. In order to show the topic of these dialogues, and to familiarize my reader with the course of the described conversations, I quote the transcriptions of the excerpts in question below.

I have also included information on the availability of the videos on the Internet.

Embodied Subjectivities

VIDEO I: Stanisław Bereś and Czesław Miłosz (book version: Bereś 2002, 15-42)

"I've got one more question about this 'Lithuanian' character. To be perfectly frank, the declaration of your Lithuanian national identity surely troubles some readers… listeners, or more generally Poles, especially because the problem of national identity has recently become much more sharply accentuated. Do you understand those fears? Have you encountered any comments like that?"

"I understand. Yes. I absolutely understand those fears, but my provocations were intentional. Because… I was creating various barriers not to allow [the audience—J.M.] to consume me; unfortunately I am still being consumed… There is no way… Is there? But at least there will be some resistance. I maintained it intentionally and I still maintain it… What kind of a Lithuanian? But it is sheer ignorance of the social conditions that existed there to say that I could have been a Lithuanian. Well, the division there came according to the language. There is no way…. If somebody spoke Polish, he or she was a Pole, not a Lithuanian. But as to my declaration that I am of Lithuanian descent… I was born there, wasn't I? When Lithuania was occupied, when the people were taken away from there, I was deeply affected; there were people from my near neighborhood, who were taken away, weren't they? There were the villages that I used to know… You understand what I mean."

"How do Lithuanians, in turn, treat your Polish connections?"

"Well then, they have accepted that. They have accepted it to the extent that sometimes they write my name Czesław Miłosz, not Czeslavas Miloszas. And that means a lot." (see 10.01–12.08)[3]

Comparing the video source materials with the chapter of Bereś's literary history entitled *Ręka Opatrzności* (The Hand of Providence) (Bereś, 15–42; the conversation's transcription), it is possible to draw a few simple conclusions about the performativity of each form (*recording–transcription*). The material written down from the audiovisual source has been reduced in length and limited in its expressiveness. The context of the spoken words has been changed, and the meaning of the relationship between the interviewer and the interviewee has been simplified through the erasure of the emotional undertone.

The conversation between Bereś and Miłosz takes place with only minimal scenery: just a lamp and a desk with a few books. There is no information about the location of their meeting, nor is any other external context provided in the book-version of the conversation. The camera focuses mainly on the sitting profile or face of the almost ninety-year-old Miłosz. Bereś, who asks the questions, is shown infrequently, and he appears in one frame together with the writer. It seems that the transcription of dialogue is more egalitarian, even if the questions occupy less space in the text, and the hierarchy of the relationship between the interlocutors is less perceptible than in front of the camera.

Because of its interactional character, its me-you relationship, the conversation begins to acquire the unique character of an observable communication, and creates a bond between the interlocutors, which is limited because of the presence of audiovisual equipment. The camera allows us to follow the speakers, or to record the embodiment of the speaking subjects, which involves various factors significant for the perception of the dialogue. The behaviors of the interlocutors, the reactions of their bodies, are closely related to the dialogic situation. Oral communication is also a matter of bodily reaction—indeed, it is based on it. Bodily reflexes give the speech acts their personal, somatic features and create the individual, mediated, bodily character of a conversation between two literary figures.

In the selected video clip, Miłosz responds with great emotional engagement to the question about the Lithuanian context of his work and biography, and this is related to his change of body posture, his waving of hands, and his facial expressions. The nature of speech has the character of a gesture which is hard to describe using words. Some non-verbal behaviors, such as the ways of making an utterance, or its emotional differentiation, were marked by Bereś in brackets while he was writing down the interview: "laughter" (Bereś 2002, 16), "tartly" (18), "he is singing" (126); but it is not possible to express "word for word" the somatic character of oral and bodily communication, which can only be observed during the visual recording. The descriptive attempts to represent the aspect of actual speech—the emotional states, attitudes, and bodily movements—are rendered in the form of objective accounts. They are curt and matter-of-fact. But individual realizations of some behaviors are not translatable from body language to written language; the images allow us to capture them better.

The prosodic factors of the speech also disappear in a transcription of the conversation; but they are important in the oral form of communication—they allow us to read the modalities of the speech act, its rhythm and power. Miłosz utters his words very slowly, but with much reflection and conviction and—which is significant—he realizes some phonemes singly, which is a characteristic way of speaking for Poles from the East. The audiovisual recording allows us to observe the conversation in its physical, original form, to watch the expressed words as a body function. The conversation between Bereś and Miłosz shows that literary history also has a somatic potential—because the interviewee's reminiscences, which he uses to answer questions, are the experiences of the embodied subject. In the videoed conversation there is no medium—in the form of a script or other mnemonic means—intervening between Miłosz and his story.

The performativity of subjects is vestigial in the written form of a dialogue when compared to the video, but the interactivity of conversation remains even in its transcribed form and has an effect on the reader of Bereś's literary history. The performed conversation exerts a powerful influence on the readers even when it appears in the written form of an interview: it demands of the readers that they reconstruct the original situation of the interview, and thus it controls their reading practice. Both forms (video and transcription) have to give the reader a sense of co-presence—the impression *that you are there.*

The performativity of the viewers, when they are following the camera recording, is limited to the acts of listening and watching. The interview transcription stimulates the imagination and senses. It makes the reader reconstruct the course of the conversation using the information from brackets—about laugher, emotional reactions, a specific way of articulation; the reader reconstructs them, recalling the known body reactions of his own somatic experiences. The reader has to interpret the performative practice from the items that s/he sees, hears, reads—experiences.

Performative Stories

Pollock observes that to tell a story is to perform. The same refers to a story told during an interview, which is a *sui generis* performance, with an interviewee playing a role in the context partly determined by the scenario written with the interviewer's questions (Pollock 2005, XI). The context is of significance. In the case of Bereś's conversations with writers—which amount to creating an oral literary history—it is important to investigate how literary history is shaped by the embodied speaking subjects and by the context in which it arises. I will analyze part of a recording of an interview with Kazimierz Brandys, as an example.

VIDEO II: Stanisław Bereś and Kazimierz Brandys (book version: Bereś 2002, 43–68)

"The idea to leave Poland at the age of 65 seems to me extraordinary. People rarely decide to emigrate so late. You didn't just go abroad and you haven't come back."

"I was forced to go abroad. But, in a certain sense, I went abroad of my own will, as a tourist... ... Nobody believed that there would be any martial law or ... a military incursion of the Soviet Army. Somehow we ignored that... ... But the winter was coming. My wife had been ill, in bad health, and we had to choose... I have even written about that somewhere... ... I went abroad for two months with my wife... ... Anyway, we had to choose whether to go to Konstancin to the ZAiKS[4] house or to New York. But the connection with New York was at that time easier, because of the snow... ... Anyway, there was no petrol... So the transport to Konstancin was much harder than buying... buying the tickets. We flew directly to Kennedy Airport in New York, where our friends were waiting for us. It was the invitation from our friend and from my American publisher. But after eight days... my wife found out from a phone conversation that tanks were on the streets of Warsaw. We went then very quickly to the LOT office in New York; they already had there the newspapers with the text of the declaration of martial law. When we read this declaration—then our hair stood on end. We decided not to go back, because it was an obvious attack on Polish democracy, which already existed in the form of the opposition... but, but... it was a freedom movement. And it was crushed. So we started to try to get permission to stay longer in the West." (see 00.31–3.23)[5]

Polish Literary History in Conversations is mostly based on the writers' auto-thematic stories. Brandys, asked about his reasons for emigrating, treats that question as a pretext to get involved in a specific activity, to perform. Performance is a form of communication. The writer speaks about his two weeks' journey abroad in 1981, after which he didn't return to Poland. The actual telling of a story is not fully foreseeable; it is not possible to fully plan the performance—for example, Brandys does not want to comment on his work abroad; he leaves that for the literary critics. In fact, Bereś does not manage to get Brandys to discuss that topic. The lack of predictably in the relationship between Bereś and the writers means that it is impossible to plan the consequences, so the final form of oral literary history is not known during the activity itself. Oral literary history is a process of making history in dialogue; it affirms the original meaning of the conversation where the story first comes into being. The meeting of two people helps them to escape the monologic quality of history in the act of actually speaking to each other. It causes the story to become intersubjective. Additionally, during the transcription stage and editing, it is possible to model the story which has been heard by a historian.

The somatic component, which I highlighted with reference to the interview with Miłosz, plays a big role in the historic story. Della Pollock observes that oral history consists of the knowledge passed on during close mutual encounters, stories being swapped between embodied subjects (2005, 3). It is an act of saying and hearing. Pollock proposes to understand oral history as the type of knowledge which is embodied (2005, 3), the epistemology that lives. She sets conventional models of knowledge and representation against the power of open telling, mind against body (Pollock 2005, 3). She also indicates that stories that record the past acquire their significance from their present relevance. They matter if they are told and retold (Pollock 2005, XII). Thus, Bereś asks Brandys questions and encourages him to answer, because otherwise this story could not even exist. It would simply remain the writer's own experience. The things that are remembered by Brandys are his private experiences, which become public in the act of speaking and then are incorporated into official historic discourse (literary history). Bereś asks Brandys how he feels about specific historical moments, asks him to share his literary opinions, pushes him to explain his choices, his behaviors in the past (his decision to emigrate and his adherence to leftwing ideology). The personal history is being incorporated into public memory; it is a chance, to use Pollock's words, to recontextualize official history. Oral literary history, as Pollock has it, contains the potential for change— because of its performative potential, an important feature beside *praxis* (Pollock 2005, 2–3). A change can occur when a private story is incorporated into an official discourse (its political body), but also during the historical speech act, when the other listeners hear the story.

In these interviews, literary history has been transformed (or remade) through the voices of the writers (or subjectivities) that, thus far, have not been regarded as the authors who write the history of literature. This way, the conventional framework of official academic literary history has been challenged in Bereś's literary history. The writers who had been described in textbooks, here receive the right to speak. Oral literary history complies with memory discourse. With the book's title—he uses the word *history*, not *memory* or *memories*—Bereś really challenges the form of literary history.

Performative Historiography of Literature

Oral literary history corresponds with other cases of new history (microhistory, regional history, etc.), which look for alternatives to so-called *grand histories*. They eschew the objective angle for the perspective of individual historic voices. Oral literary history affirms the reminiscences and witnesses' testimonies. A personal insight into the story allows us to look at the historic event from a new perspective; it allows us to fill in the historic "blank spaces" and also to concentrate on historic details. Anecdotes and rudimentary narration replace the panoramic description of events. Oral literary history, because of its performative character, has a strong element of contingency; the narrative forms and the historical content are formally open, a fact which is willingly used by editors during the transcription and editing stage. For example, the final version of the conversation with Miłosz published in the book consists of several interviews which Bereś carried out with the writer over the course of four years (1996–2000). Also the order of questions is different from that in the video interview; it has been changed to create a more coherent dialogue.

Polish Literary History in Conversations is a multi-subjective form of history. Firstly, because there are 23 interviews in the book, and each writer presents a personal piece of the history of his/her life and his/her vision of a fragment of 20th- and 21st-century literature. Secondly, but perhaps more importantly, because oral literary history arises at the point of the meeting of two subjectivities. The literary past is being negotiated in the dialogue. Performativity is very important for that negotiation, and the performativity dictates the form of that kind of history, so Bereś tries to capture it in the form of narration. The problem is that it is not possible to express the performativity of the embodied subjects in written history, because of the language gap—the problem of translatability. In his book, specific marks of performativity can be found: for example, at the beginning of each chapter there is a photograph of the writer's face, whose function is to compensate for the impossibility of observing the writer's body on video. I think that it could be a good idea to enclose a DVD containing all interviews with Bereś's book. However, the advantage of a change of medium (from video to transcription) is that we do not have to acquaint ourselves with videos in "real time," which can be cumbersome, even if we have better tools to search databases at our disposal (Frisch 2010).

Each history is a kind of subjective narration, a kind of manipulation of the past, and the oral literary history is the reflection of a lively conversation. It is true that in the monologic narration, we can find poorer performativity—a performativity after the change of medium. Still, the traditional way of gathering historical knowledge has been questioned here and it was done with a preoperative tool. Besides, using the conversation as a way of historical communication involves the affects of the reader, and thus engages her/him performatively. Indeed, oral literary history is just one of the possibilities of performative historiography. But it seems to be an interesting form, which tries to address the question of how to write literary history nowadays.

References

Bereś, Stanisław. 1987. *Rozmowy ze Stanisławem Lemem* [Conversations with Stanisław Lem]. Kraków: Wydawnictwo Literackie.
—. 2002. *Historia literatury polskiej w rozmowach: XX-XXI wiek* [Polish literary history in conversations: 20th–21st centuries]. Warszawa: WAB.
Frisch, Michael. 2010. "Historia mówiona i rewolucja digitalna. W kierunku post-dokumentalnej wrażliwości." [Oral history and the digital revolution: Toward a post-documentary sensibility]. Translated by Michał Kierzkowski. In *Teoria wiedzy o przeszłości na tle współczesnej humanistyki*. [Theory of knowledge about the past in the context of contemporary humanities]. Edited by Ewa Domańska, 295–317. Poznań: Wydawnictwo Poznańskie.
Hymnes, Dell. 1995. "Breakthrough into Performance." In *Folklore. Performance and Communication*. Edited by Dan Ben-Amos, and Kenneth S. Goldstein, 11–74. The Hague, Paris: Mounton.
Nowicki, Stanisław [*pen name* of Bereś, Stanisław]. 1986. *Pół wieku czyśćca. Rozmowy z Tadeuszem Konwickim* [Half century of purgatory: Conversation with Tadeusz Konwicki]. Warszawa: Oficyna Wydawnicza.
Pollock, Della, ed. 2005. *Remembering: Oral History Performance*. New York: Palgrave Macmillan.
Telewizja Literacka TVL. *Czesław Miłosz* [posted August 22, 2012]. *Czesław Miłosz*. Retrieved from http://bit.ly/2kSOeKA. Accessed January 10, 2017.
Telewizja Literacka TVL. *Kazimierz Brandys* [posted August 2, 2012]. Retrieved from http://bit.ly/2kX5NVR. Accessed January 10, 2017.
Walas, Teresa. 1993. *Czy jest możliwa inna historia literatury?* [Is another history of literature possible?]. Kraków: Universitas.

Notes

[1] *Not Only About Books* [Nie tylko o książkach] as part of the programme *Literary Television News* [Telewizyjne Wiadomości Literackie] was broadcast on TVP Polonia and TVP-2 from 1996 to 2001. The program host was Stanisław Bereś.

[2] My translation. All translations of quotations, unless otherwise stated, are mine.

[3] Telewizja Literacka TVL. *Czesław Miłosz* [posted August 22, 2012]. *Czesław Miłosz*. Retrieved from http://bit.ly/2kSOeKA. Accessed January 10, 2017.

[4] ZAiKS—Związek Autorów i Kompozytorów Scenicznych [Polish Association of Authors and Composers].

[5] Telewizja Literacka TVL. *Kazimierz Brandys* [posted August 2, 2012]. Retrieved from http://bit.ly/2kX5NVR. Accessed January 10, 2017.

CHAPTER ELEVEN

INVESTIGATING THE CANON AND HOW IT IS MADE: RICARDO PIGLIA'S READING OF THE ARGENTINEAN LITERARY TRADITION

ALEKSANDER TROJANOWSKI

This paper discusses the problem of the recreation of the Argentinean literary canon, as a process performed in Ricardo Piglia's novel *Artificial Respiration.* The novel was published in 1980, in the period of the most restrictive censorship, when both discursive and physical repression was carried out by the military dictatorship that had taken power in the country in 1976. The fact of its publication is surprising given its controversial and subversive content. One explanation of this omission on the part of the censors might be that the novel's political message is coded by being transferred into an intellectual and literary setting, where the characters discuss their readings of canonical literary works. So the political critique is rather *implicit*. The literary canon is definitely the major theme of the text, and the acts of subversion, as well as the political statements, occur in the non-canonical interpretations of canonical texts. Following Eric Hobsbawm's theory of the invention of tradition in modern societies (Hobsbawm and Ranger 1983), I claim that the establishment of the literary canon and its implementation in the educational system is one of the ways in which the ruling class—in this case, the military government—creates and imposes a certain identity as valid. An excerpt from a document produced by the Argentinean Ministry of Culture and Education in the 70s serves as a clear demonstration of how the teaching process and the literature involved in it were openly oriented towards imposing certain values and seen by the government as a field of ideological battle against the Left:

> In this sense, recently there has been noticed a significant Marxist offensive in the area of children's literature. Its goal is to emit a message that would actually come from the child and that would enable the child's "self-education" on the basics of "liberty and alternative." ... This ideological conduct intensifies at the end of primary education, and tends to modify the traditional value system (family, religion, nationality, tradition, etc.). (quoted in: Bravo 2003, 122)[1]

There was, of course, a number of means to identify and overcome the "Marxist threat" in primary schools and impose the right, traditional values. Piglia's novel emerges in a context that consists of a number of symbolic practices—including the creation and maintenance of the literary canon—that impose the traditional values supported by the military government. This system is enforced with political repression and torture. But there is also another discursive aspect of the practices of the government. One may call it performative, since it is about the creation of the political opponent as a "subversive agent," "a terrorist," to exclude him or her from the realm of Argentinean identity (Bravo 2003, 112–19). Therefore, from the performative perspective, the context in which the novel was created can be described as outlined by the military *junta* which was involved in a large scale performance. The performance was about carrying out a policy of torture and terror and, at the same time, convincing the audience in Argentina, and especially outside Argentina, that the terror did not violate human rights, because the victims were not Argentineans. The *junta* maintained a performance that created its own enemies, ruling them out of society (Bravo 2003). And then *Artificial Respiration* was published, referring to the same books and texts, the same literary canon, but containing interpretations that were totally different. If the practice of maintenance of the literary canon is in the repertoire of the power's means to legitimate itself, I would like to examine how the acts of reading and writing may be seen as examples of individual resistance. Indeed, they constitute a counter-practice that operates on the same discourse to establish different meanings. But before I investigate the meanings as they change in Piglia's writing and reading, I would like to describe how the concept of the canon is used in this paper.

The Concept of the Literary Canon

I would like to start with a broadly accepted definition of the canon as a collection of works that are regarded to be lasting and of superior artistic merit (as they are described, for example, in the Oxford Dictionary of English). If we go deeper into this short definition, it turns out to be an effect of a compromise between the two poles of the theoretical debate on the status of the literary canon that took place in the 1980s and 1990s: the debate between traditionalists and relativists (Grishakova 2004, 23).

For the purpose of my analysis I propose an understanding of the concept of the literary canon which reflects a different approach in the sense that it goes beyond the problem of the ontological status of the canon. This understanding draws on the concept of performativity, as it is conceptualized in the work of Richard Schechner (2013) and, in the context of literary studies, as proposed and applied by Anna Burzyńska (2013). Instead of posing the essentialist question of what the signal features of the great, canonical works of art are—but also instead of abandoning this problem as a relativist would do—the performative perspective shows interest in the practices that establish the canon as such and in the ways they do it. I assume that in the case I am examining here the establishment of the literary canon has to do with the authoritarian, political practices of the military government and, in the symbolic sense, with the creation of a strong, self-contained national identity as well as with the creation and exclusion of the (political) Other. But if the existence of the canon is in fact the result of the persistence of a determined set of practices (and I claim that the crucial practice is reading—the canonical mode of reading literature), there is always space for error, misunderstanding, negotiation of meaning, and misreading, in other words, ideological counter-practices. Therefore, I will refer to the canon as an intertextual space—where space is not a set of works of art in the structuralist sense, but a field of relations such as the act of writing, (mis)reading, interpretation and so forth—that is (re)created in all literary texts, as it is their reference and context, *explicit* or *implicit*. If we understand writing as a performative act, the canon is the field of the struggle for identity and values. In this paper I am going to analyze how Piglia's novel, in the particular context in which it was published, disturbs and decentralizes the unity of the literary canon that was being used as the basis of national identity. I will discuss four readings of the Argentinean literary canon made in *Artificial Respiration*. The first is the reading of *Facundo* by Domingo Faustino Sarmiento, followed by the readings of the works of Jorge Luis Borges, Roberto Arlt and Leopold Lugones.

The Readings. Narrative Context

Artificial Respiration is not a historical novel of the Walter Scott type. However, history is a theme of the novel, and, perhaps, the most important one. The mode of narration elaborated by Piglia creates a world in which the reader moves from one historical setting to another—from the 19th century and the beginning of the Argentinean state to the beginning of the 20th century and the culmination of the liberal/conservative conflict, the times that are contemporary for Piglia. The way the historical setting is changed is the text itself, since different pieces of the text—letters, diaries and conversations—are the very construction material of the novel. In a sense, Piglia is more interested in the documents of history than in the history itself. Having constructed the novel with fragments of diaries and letters, Piglia made visible the textual aspect of history—its testimony, which is the sign of how human beings experience it. This feature of the writing certainly puts the textuality at the center of attention. In the novel, a young writer, Emilio Renzi, receives a letter from his fugitive uncle, a professor named Marcelo Maggi. He gets involved in an intellectual exchange, but he also gets to know the complicated biography of Maggi. Invited to visit the professor at his home, he travels to meet him, but never gets the chance—by the time Renzi gets to the town where he lives, the professor has disappeared. Renzi can only meet his friend, a Polish philosopher in exile, Vladimir Tardewski, who leaves Renzi a legacy—some manuscripts and notes of Prof. Maggi.

This is all by way of plot that the novel contains. But of course, there is much more to it—the reflections the characters share in their letters and conversations. Piglia does not simply fictionalize his views. The point of this discursive prose is that the reflexive aspect of the writing is put into dialogic situations. In other words, the fiction does not simply hide the views of its author. The views that I am going to present in the part that follows result from a process in which the characters, the readers and the narrator seem to investigate the reflexive sense—searching, losing the trace and, then, surprisingly, finding it.

Sarmiento

Facundo takes the reader back to the 19th century, to the time of Argentinean romanticism. In that period, contrary to the tendencies in Europe, it was the essay which was the most important genre (and after it, epic poetry). The author of *Facundo*, the work which was absolutely crucial for the development of literature in Argentina (Piglia 2001, 130), as we read in *Artificial Respiration*, was a politician and he saw literature, as did many others of his time, as a tool for political struggle (Piglia 2001, 136). Sarmiento was a member of the liberal elite, a progressive class that sought to civilize Argentina by imitation and implementation of European culture. His essay had the subtitle *Civilization and Barbarism,* which occasions Piglia's reading. But first he focuses on a detail. The book has an epigraph: *On ne tue point les idées* (Piglia 2001, 130), which means "ideas cannot be killed," but of course, as we see, and as Piglia underscores several times, the epigraph is in French. The subtitle suggests the need Sarmiento and his followers felt for civilization imported from Europe: it was barbarism that they observed in the lower social classes in Argentina. For Sarmiento, the *gaucho*—comparable to the North American cowboy, living on the *pampas* (lowlands typical of South America), anarchic, brutal and behind the times—was a representative of the lower classes of the society. This is how he saw them. But what is so interesting for Piglia is the fact that a book that, one may say, starts the literary, national canon of Argentina, which is the foundation of modern national identity (Piglia 2001, 130), begins with such a gesture of exclusion (Piglia 2001, 131). It is a performative gesture of exclusion, one may add, because although in the material form of the signs the social distinction implies that a knowledge of French marks the boundary between civilized people and Barbarism, there is more to it than that. The statement acts in a double way—not only exclusive, but also creative: it projects the barbarian social world, its features and character. And on the basis of such performative effect, material exclusion proceeds. Piglia analyzes *Facundo* and draws the conclusion that it creates national identity on the basis of a radical rejection of the lower, and thus uneducated, classes of society. The point here is that the projection is performative—it works only if *Facundo* is maintained as a part of the canon, and so has it been.

But then Piglia's reading becomes more complex. Tardewski, a character in the novel, proves that there is a certain error in Sarmiento's epigraph. It is a quote which Sarmiento attributes to Fourtol. But the quote is not from Fourtol; it is from Volney. The foundational work of the Argentinean identity, and thus, of the canon, begins with a mistaken attribution—this is how Piglia puts it. At this moment, a decentralization of the text is put into play. The text itself implies social exclusion—of those who cannot read the epigraph and, consequently, of those who need to be taught: the barbarians need a translator from universal culture (Piglia 2001, 130). Piglia does certainly not represent an authoritarian tendency; like Sarmiento's romantics, who fought against the dictator Juan Manuel de Rosas, Piglia, through his writing, performs an act of resistance against an authoritarian and military government. And it is from this place that Piglia reveals the dangerous tendencies in the progressive thinking that founded the literary canon: the idea and the will to control and dominate, with—and thanks to—the power of universal reason. And then, the reason collapses: the author of the foundational text, the leader of the elite of the Enlightenment, makes an error in his quotation (Piglia 2001, 131). Specifically, he makes a mistake in naming the author of the quote (this error was later to be reflected in the ironic practice of false attribution by Borges). The civilization imposed by the romantic generation is, in the reading proposed by Piglia, contaminated by ignorance and, therefore, barbarity. The Other, the ignorant lower class, is seen in Piglia's writing on the Argentinean canon to have been appropriated and used by the progressive elite. The ignorance and barbarity attributed by the romantics to ordinary folk, and to the dictator Juan Manuel de Rosas, are seen as the reverse of the romantic project of national identity. Effectively, the Argentinean identity is formed by the peripheral position of the Argentinean literary world, its contact with only mediocre European intellectuals (Piglia 2001, 127) and an inferiority complex towards European culture. If Piglia reads the romantics this way it is because the identity that they built upon the conflict presented above still persists in Argentinean culture. This is what Piglia says in his writing when he develops the reading of Sarmiento. In *Artificial Respiration* he creates the character of Enrique Ossorio, a national hero from the 19th century. He was a private secretary to the dictator Rosas and a romantic conspirator. It is never clear in the novel whose spy he was, and whom he betrayed. As a character he is built upon the opposition between the romantics and the dictatorship, but the effect is the ambiguous decentralization of both. It is never clear where actually Ossorio belongs, because, in Piglia's reading, Argentinean romantic progressive thought and the regressive dictatorship are connected. Piglia illustrates this shameful alliance by creating the character of Ossorio.

Borges

There is another example of the appropriation of the lower-class Other by literature. It is the *gaucho*, the Argentinean cowboy who was turned into a national hero by 19th century epic poetry. Piglia highlights this problem in his reading of Jorge Luis Borges. In quite a paradoxical fashion, Emilio Renzi claims that Borges was the best Argentinean writer of the 19th century. Borges is the founder of the modern national tradition, but he is not a modern writer himself. According to Piglia, Borges understood the two crucial literary tendencies of the 19th century—romantic nationalism and progressive universalism—and he synthesized them in his work. In fictional conversations in *Artificial Respiration*, Emilio Renzi enumerates a number of Borges's short stories. The majority of them are parodies. In the Borgesian method of false attributions and wrong quotations Piglia sees a parody of the romantics and of the ignorance behind *Facundo*. But there is also the second element of the tradition in the works of Borges: the poetry about the *gauchos*. He writes short stories using typical situations and dialogues from that literature. Piglia is concerned with Borges's treatment of language. In Borges, as read by Piglia, there is a rupture between the literary language of romantic poets and the oral language of the lower class. Piglia recognizes his position as that within the literary tradition, but also within the political tradition, that he finds in Borges. The tradition consists in reading the canon as a space of appropriation of the language of the Other and therefore, as a performative space of invention and exclusion of the Other. The aim of writing, the responsibility of an author to such a reading, is to write in order to restore the authenticity of spoken language. Thus, eventually, the aim is to open the literary canon to the reality (this is to say, the oral use) of the language—speech.

Arlt/Lugones

The tension between the appropriation and the liberation of language reappears in the following reading of the canon in Piglia. Once again it is Emilio Renzi who, this time, contrasts two 20th-century Argentinean writers: Leopoldo Lugones and Roberto Arlt. Both are canonical, but the status of Arlt is somehow special. As Renzi puts it, there is a consensus that Arlt needs to be read, that he is important, but that he was not a good writer (Piglia 2001, 134). The problem that the critics have is that Arlt was a journalist, and therefore they tend to read him as a journalist. He was someone who had a lot of important things to say, many social issues to draw attention to, but it is felt that his writing was really bad in aesthetic terms (Piglia 2001, 134) What Piglia wants here is to draw a picture of the position of Roberto Arlt in the canon: he remains there because of the content of his books, but in spite of his (bad) style (Piglia 2001, 138). Arlt is, then, presented as a contrast to Leopoldo Lugones, the model of the national poet. Piglia shows, in relation to the bad style of Arlt, what good style was. With obvious irony, Piglia says that the style of Lugones is made with a dictionary in the hand (2001, 136). And then he, or rather his character, Emilio Renzi, portrays Lugones as an administrator who translated Homer without knowing Greek (Piglia 2001, 120). The dull but beautiful Lugones is set against the interesting but filthy Arlt. But if we consider, as Piglia does, that the interesting topics of Arlt's writing were the lower strata of society, the question of style becomes problematic. As

Piglia puts it, Arlt is not an important writer despite his style (which is the way he was consecrated); Arlt's writing is his bad style (2001, 138). From this point on, the reading that Piglia makes (or, the one he creates) is an attempt to deconstruct the notion of style as an intrinsic literary value. Piglia can do this only from the perspective we have seen in his reading of Borges—the author that is interested in the language of the Other, in the dialogue rather than in appropriation. According to Piglia, Arlt is the only modern Argentinean writer who succeeded in the construction of the language of the Other—especially the social Other—without appropriating it. He was listening to it and quoting it (without sublimating it) in his novels. That is why for the critics who remained in the realm of high culture, as opposed to mass culture, the style is nothing more than bad. However, Piglia seems to claim, the only ethically responsible reading of Arlt takes into account the style itself, the process behind it, and nothing more.

The same style-oriented reading applies to Lugones. But the question here is why someone would elaborate a literary style with a dictionary. Piglia draws out the historical context, in which Lugones's writing is another type of response to the process related to Otherness. Piglia draws attention to the fact that the period in question was the time when immigration was at its peak (2001, 135). The newly, but not yet entirely, built national identity was changing again. The language was also undergoing significant changes. Piglia proposes to see both styles as competing attempts to create the national identity. The one proposed by Lugones is a monologue—resistant to changes, focused on the cultivation of language the way it is reproduced in dictionaries. On the other hand, and at the same time, Arlt tried to develop a dialogue of different idioms in his novels. The idea here was rather to let Otherness speak and not exclude it from the norms of style.

Thus far, the canon as understood by Ricardo Piglia has taken the form of an intertextual space in which national identity is created and maintained. The process of the making of the Argentinean canon is intrinsically related to the problem of Otherness, and Otherness, historically speaking, has left traces of its existence in the language of this country. In his literary commentaries on the canon, Piglia reveals that the tension that is performatively hidden is the one between the language of the Other and its appropriation by the dominant culture. Therefore the canon as such has the structure of a monologue. However, there have been examples of readings that would open that canon up to more dialogic writing. Piglia finds such a tradition and incorporates himself in it. Such a gesture reproduces the canon, but also marks a critical difference which consists in the exposure of the relations of power that maintain the canon (as in the case of Lugones), or by showing the non-textual, political effect that the canon has (as in the case of Sarmiento).

The analysis of Piglia's practice of reading and writing can be connected with the theoretical aspects of performativity. I understand these theoretical modalities in two ways. Firstly there is a deconstructionist aim in Piglia's reading: by taking up the issue of the canon, Piglia reveals the power/knowledge relations that established the texts in the aspect of their creation (they were created against the ideological background that is revealed) and also maintained the canonical reading that was persistent in the Argentinean culture. This reading itself was a performance that repeated the act of exclusion which is seen as formative for the national identity. The exclusion may be then connected with the propaganda of military *juntas* that used to present dissidents and political opponents as non-Argentineans (Bravo 2003, 107–23). But the interesting thing is not only what is claimed by Piglia, but *how* it is claimed. A deconstruction might take the form of an essay, it may be an academic investigation, but in the case of Piglia it is a novel—a fictional text. From the performative perspective it is interesting how in Piglia's work the reading of the canon seems to lie on the margin of his stories and the plots of his novels—it is not just a message, but rather the condition of the stories he narrates. Because the narration responds to the critical reading of the canon, the speech of the Other is the core of Piglia's narrative. It is essential for me to analyze Piglia's texts as performances (as acts) because the point I have tried to make is that his texts do not communicate or transmit his critical views—they practice the critique. The fictional space he constructs is based on the critique of the literary canon and, within its scope, the plot and the narration respond to the critique. To discuss this aspect would mean to digress from the actual topic of the paper, but I can just briefly indicate that the response of the Piglian narrative to the critical issues I have analyzed lies in the narrative effort to bear witness to the experience of the Other, who remains a mystery for the narrator.

The first performative aspect of Piglia's writing which I would like to underscore lies in the overlapping of reflection (critique) and invention (narrative) within the same texts. Without the reflection one cannot follow the narrative and to internalize the critical roots of the narrative is to trace the difference Piglia would like to make, opening the canonical text to the Other. In this sense, the text makes a difference (acts)—it is constructed in the tradition that has been displaced; as a result, the history is read in a different way and literature is written in a different way, too.

Performative Writing

Now I would like to focus on a different aspect of performative writing—writing as the constructing of reality—to show the textual conditions of making the difference and of the reconstruction of the literary canon. I have already said that Piglia opens the canon up within the fictional realm he constructs in the novels. Now I would like to ask to what extent the canon itself is performatively created in the text. It is a seductive prospect to analyze Piglia's reading of the canon and then to compare it with the canon as it exists objectively: to see the way it really is, and then to trace the difference. But I claim that this is impossible since the canon we can speak of exists only within the scope of Piglia's reading. To study it in a different text would be to trace "a different difference." The conclusion I draw is not that Piglia "invents" the canon in the sense of choosing suitable examples for his ideas. Nor do I claim that the historical processes Piglia analyzes did not happen. By saying this I do not want to suggest that Piglia is subjective and misled. I only claim that a reading should be understood as reading—in its own terms. Therefore, the validity of the sense it creates is intrinsic to the practice of the reading and writing itself—these are, for me, the consequences of studying texts as performances. There are two aspects of performativity in Piglia's narrative that seem to come to the foreground: the first one is the creation of reality and the second is auto-reflection.

In the foregoing passages I have tried to highlight the motif of history as one of the recurrent themes of Piglia's novel. My claim is that the historical perspective is one of the effects the texts produce. There are certain figures that constitute writing on history in *Artificial Respiration*. The state seen as the enemy of civil society, or even a machine of terror rather than a common institution, would be one of them. Consequently, Piglia will trace victims of political terror to establish for himself a perspective to write from. He believes, as did Walter Benjamin, that official history is the process of the imposition of silence on those dominated by the winners. Writing about the 20th century, Piglia would describe Auschwitz as the global metaphor of the key historical processes of modernity (2001, 215). This means that the state is seen as an alien force whose practice is to impose terror on the civilians who lack the language in which they could describe their experience of being oppressed—the victims are silent; the terror, unspeakable. Such a general historical perspective is connected with his view of the modern history of Argentina as a cycle of recurrent violence towards the people. Since the

19th century, both progressive and conservative political struggles in his homeland have resulted in a dictatorship or violence.

To say that such a view of history is constructed is not to undermine it. On the contrary, it is an attempt to understand it. And if we read it this way, we may find that Piglia's texts invite such a constructive reading. The way the text is constructed, the concept of history is linked to the specific context in which it is produced. In other words, Piglia connects his understanding of history with a specific intellectual perspective. In a way, he shows his reading of history as relative to the position from which he reads—and, at the same time, he also reveals this position. I see this practice as another feature of performative writing—an auto-reflection practiced in the text.

The issue of auto-reflecion is, for me, the question of the identity of the performer. Here I would like to mention the main character and the narrator of *Artificial Respiration*. Significantly, the full name of the author is Ricardo Emilio Piglia Renzi. However, I am not going to suggest that the character is simply the *alter ego* of the author. Susana González sees here an example of a play of identities: Renzi, the narrator, and Piglia, the author, are rather subjects of a game whose main principle is multiplicity (2012, 177–78). Although I would not say that Renzi is a mask of Piglia, I would claim that in this character Piglia constructs himself as a performer—this is to say that Renzi is his identity maintained within the scope of the text of the novel. As a textual figure, Renzi combines, thus, the features of the narrator and the figure of the author. We can add now that the character that performs the reading of Arlt and Lugones is Renzi. Renzi is thus a writer, a passionate reader, an intellectual. And he is, as well, the bearer of the legacy of Prof. Marcelo Maggi, the figure of a historian and an intellectual persecuted by the authoritarian state. If we turn to other characters in the novel, we can find out that a feature that they share is that they are all part of the world of intellectuals. Tardewski is a philosopher, Renzi a writer, Maggi a historian. The main topics of the novel are history and ideas; and consequently, the social world that is created in the novel is precisely the world of intellectuals. Moreover, it is a world that combines reflection with political and social commitment. It is certainly not so written because Piglia does not want to present himself as a committed intellectual. It is rather because he creates the world that is his world anyway—the world that he identifies himself with. My claim here is that the underlying textual practice that connects both aspects of Piglia's novel, the concept of history and the figure of the committed intellectual, makes visible the relativity of the text itself. In the novel Piglia creates a certain tradition, a literary canon and a historical narrative, and he reveals the *locus* of construction—the place from which the history and the canon are being analyzed. In doing so he invalidates neither his concept of history nor his critique of the canon. It is a dual practice of claiming and simultaneous practice of reflection on the conditions of veracity of such claims. A story that Piglia tells may be true or not—but the critical point the text makes is that its validity or veracity should be judged in terms created and presented in the text. Ultimately, what the text offers is not a general, abstract judgment, but a judgment rooted in the experience of its performer—and such is, in my opinion, the reflexive foundation upon which rests the whole opening up of the canon that I have presented in this paper.

The fact that the above-mentioned reflection is an auto-reflection is the last important issue I would like to comment on. The *locus* of the reading of the canon, which for me is a performative space that makes the reading possible, is not a theoretical perspective. Instead, it is grounded in the personal experience of Piglia (as well as, the claim follows, of any other performer). By attributing a personal quality to the reading of the canon, I follow the idea of performative writing as developed by Peggy Phelan, who sees it as an affective, as opposed to descriptive, mode of writing (Schechner 2013, 123). Anna Burzyńska moves in the same direction when she speaks about the experience of trauma—which cannot be fully represented—and literature (2013, 481). She repeats the notions of Shoshana Felman, Dori Laub and Walter Benn Michaels, who claim that performative writing is not about representing and teaching about the Holocaust, but rather about the construction of textual experience in which readers who had not gone through it could get involved. Then she points out the existing doubts as to whether it is possible to perform a textual action that would create a reading experience comparable to the experience of trauma (Burzyńska 2013, 482–84). Whatever the answer is, the same claim is made in the texts of Ricardo Piglia. The title of the novel *Artificial Respiration* raises this question. There is no space within the scope of this paper to analyze other aspects of the novel, but I would only like to link its title with the context I have already mentioned: of living under dictatorship. One of the main narrative nodes of the novel is the secret of the disappearance of Prof. Maggi, who, as the reader may deduce, has been murdered for political reasons, just as many civilians were at the time. To live in such conditions is an experience that Ricardo Piglia has had. The novel deals with the experience. However, it is not about telling a story, nor informing the reader about repression. Just as the title suggests, it is an attempt to resuscitate the experience in the text. The reader, in the performative mode of reading, is confronted with the disappearance of

Maggi in an affective way—it is about living the loss, the fear, and investigation of the crime, rather than about information.

I decided to close my remarks on performative writing in Piglia's text with the notion of experience as a central node of reading, because, in my opinion, it makes the practice of opening up the canon and auto-reflection coherent. I mean that, in the novel, the idea of the textual struggle to open the literary canon to Otherness and the notion of history that makes it possible are conceived from the perspective of the committed intellectual, because this is, indeed, the perspective outlined by the personal and historical experience of Piglia. The work on the canon has explicit political effects on the life of an intellectual living in a state of terror. And the fiction that Piglia writes from this experience is a call for Derridian responsibility: he constructs his narrative as the Other who tries to leave in his texts traces of the experience that makes him different. The stake here is the understanding within a dialogue which is performed in the course of writing and reading. Instead of claiming a truthful testimony, Piglia offers a fictional staging of his experience. Such a reading—artificial, textual enactment of the experience of the Other within the scope of his performance—and a response seem to be, according to Piglia, the only way of understanding, or opening, towards Otherness, political, cultural, social, and so forth.

Conclusion

In this paper I have drawn a performative perspective of analyzing literature to read in this manner a novel by Ricardo Piglia, in which he proposes a performative reading of the Argentinean literary canon. My main conclusion is that his reading of the canon can be interpreted with regard to two sets of problems. The first one clusters around his attempt to decentralize the canon by establishing an ethical relationship with the word of the Other. Piglia reveals the acts of appropriation of the language of the Other and looks for textual ways to bear witness to the word of the Other. He finds them in the texts of Borges and Arlt, and it is the tradition in which he wants to participate. His project to decentralize the canon is also connected with another intention: to reveal relations of power that organize and legitimize the canon.

The second set of considerations is connected with the characteristics specific of Piglia's novel, which is both a piece of fiction and a reading of literary tradition. I focus on the constructive aspect of his writing, on the way he constructs the reality he refers to—history and its relation to a national literature. Then, there is the auto-reflexive aspect of his writing, revealed in Piglia's constructing of the figure of a committed intellectual as the point of view from which he reads and writes. Ultimately, I claim that the focal point of Piglia's writing is the notion of experience. He sees his texts as traces of experience and, therefore, the reading they invite is about an artificial recreation of experience in the text, as a form of an encounter with the Other. The issue of Otherness leads to the last remark. Piglia sees the text of his novel, in comparison to Mario Vargas Llosa's "total novel" (Vargas Llosa 2007, 9–12), not as a closed, autonomous reality, but as a part, or a fragment, of a broader social reality. In this sense he does not aim at universality at the level of the text. The universality is rather in the dialogue in which his text is introduced, of which it is a fragment. This universality is exactly the intertextual space in which the canon exists. There are criteria that performatively limit the space; and Piglia offers a textual practice of displacing such boundaries. He traces the acts of exclusions of Otherness in the literary canon to speak of the exclusion that was taking place at the moment in the Argentinean history he was writing the novel. So his text constituted a local counter-practice in the environment of symbolic repression in which reading fiction was proposed as a space of liberty, where Otherness could be symbolized again. And the Other that Piglia tries to speak of are millions of political dissidents and social activists, thousands of whom were killed by the *junta*. But he cannot do it openly. This is the theme that links the literary and historical investigations in the novel with the story of Marcelo Maggi, the uncle of the main character, who disappears because of his political engagement. If we count the years that pass between the historical settings in the book and the disappearance, it turns out that the temporal context of the story is crucial—Maggi disappears at the end of the 1970s. In other words, the symbolic power behind the foundational exclusion of the literary canon and national identity is not just a mere topic of abstract reflection, but has, as Piglia shows it, a very material realization.

References

Bravo, Nazareno. 2003. "El discurso de la dictadura militar argentina (1976–1983). Definición del opositor político y confrontamiento—valorización del papel de la mujer en el espacio privado" [The Argentine Military Discourse (1976–1983). Definition of the political opponent and confinement—"appraisal" of the role of women in private space]. *Revista Internacional de Filosofía Iberoamericana y Teoría Social*, no. 22: 107–23.

Burzyńska, Anna. 2013. *Dekonstrukcja, polityka i performatyka* [Deconstruction, politics, and performatics]. Kraków: Universitas.

González, Susana. 2012. *Ficción y crítica en la obra de Ricardo Piglia* [Fiction and criticism in the work of Ricardo Piglia]. Medellín: Universidad Nacional de Colombia.

Grishakova, Marina. 2004. "Poetics of the Return: On the Formation of Literary Canon." *Senoji Lietuvos Literatura*, no. 18: 23–29.

Hobsbawm, Eric, and Terence Ranger, eds. 1983. *The Invention of Tradition*. Cambridge: Cambridge University Press.

Oxford Dictionary. Accessed December 10, 2014. http://bit.ly/2jWJwHD.

Piglia, Ricardo. 2001. *Respiración artificial*. Barcelona: Anagrama.

Schechner, Richard. 2013. *Performance Studies: An Introduction*. London: Routledge.

Vargas Llosa, Mario. 2007. "Realidad total, novela total." *Cuadernos Hispanoamericanos*, no. 68: 9–12.

Note

[1] My translation. All translations of quotations, unless otherwise stated, are mine.

Part III

Literary Interpretations: Soma and Text

CHAPTER TWELVE

THE THEATRICALITY OF VIOLENCE IN THOMAS HARRIS'S *THE RED DRAGON* AND ITS ADAPTATIONS

ANDRÁS BERZE

The present paper aims to investigate the use of the term "theatricality" in relation to violence and empathy and the relation of these concepts to corporeality in the novel *Red Dragon* by Thomas Harris, and its visual media adaptations: a movie of the same title, and the running television series entitled *Hannibal*. The *Red Dragon* is the first of four novels[1] written by Harris on the work of the FBI Behavioral Analysis Unit in capturing serial killers. These novels introduced the famous character of Dr. Hannibal Lecter, a psychiatrist who turns out to be the serial killer called the "Chesapeake Ripper" and was incarcerated prior to the events of *Red Dragon*. The television series depicts the events leading to Lecter's arrest, much of it is based on information available in *Red Dragon,* and the other three books, although the series can be viewed as a complete reinterpretation of the entire canon formed around the four books and their movie adaptations.

This study sets out to build a theoretical foundation for a term introduced and used in the series: theatrical serial killer. This designation of serial killers is not based on a real definition in criminology, nor is it used in the books or in the movies. However, in the series it is used to describe methods of murder and staging of murder that are already described in the books. My concern with the term theatrical is the potential it has for inserting these works into a fertile theoretical framework in which they can be subjected to observations that are otherwise inaccessible. This theoretical framework is established by Samuel Weber in his book, *Theatricality as Medium* (Weber 2004). I will start with providing an outline of this theory. The general outline will be followed by an attempt to define what is meant by theatrical serial killer in the analyzed works and how the term can be related to the theory presented earlier. I will base this analysis on depictions of the methods of the Chesapeake Ripper (Hannibal Lecter before his capture), which are frequently designated as theatrical. The concept of empathy plays a major role in these works, because people endowed with a greater degree of empathy are contrasted and in conflict with people who lack empathy in the sense I will clarify in the present paper. Therefore, I will spend some time on discussing a phenomenological account of empathy. This account is not exhaustive; for the purposes of the present paper I will focus on the phenomenological theories of Edmund Husserl and Martin Heidegger, because these are sufficient to establish a connection between phenomenology and Mark Johnson's theory of embodied cognition (Johnson 2007)—a link to corporeality. However, for later research, outside of the scope of the present paper, it would be necessary to discuss the phenomenology of Maurice Merleau-Ponty and Emanuel Lévinas. After connecting the phenomenology of empathy with theories of embodiment, and showing the role that the concept of empathy plays in these theories, I will move on to establish how this concept is used and played with in the primary sources I have specified above, by pointing out certain contrasts between key characters. In this process I will disclose a metaperspective employed in these works, which helps us to understand the way these works employ (the concept of) empathy in order to provide not just an aesthetic, but also an ethical critique of the representation and theatricalization of violence.

A Theory of Theatricality

First it is necessary to elaborate on the term *theatricality* and its relevance to the present study. For this I will rely on Samuel Weber's use of the term in his book, *Theatricality as Medium* (2004). Weber presents a conception of theatricality that is not derived from the experience of theater in the strict sense, but rather belongs to that experience in the same way as it belongs to several other phenomena (2004, 1). Indeed, it is one of the main arguments of Weber that, while theater as an art form seems to be in a decline, theatricality as a concept is becoming more and more widely applied to a diverse set of phenomena. To define theatricality as a medium that appears to mediate always along with other media, first I will need to separate it from the more traditional idea of theater, seen as a set of events observed audiovisually from a distance (Weber 2004, 4–8). Theatricality is essentially characterized by involvement. Indeed, in a certain sense that will have to be touched upon here, involvement is what theatricality as a medium mediates. Secondly, the relationship between theatricality and spatiality—the experience of space—needs to be determined, in order to show the operation of theatricality as an opening up of spatiality, which in other words can be described as the creation (or rather, the coming about) of scenes. Later in the present study I will return to the phenomenological basis of the connection between theatricality and spatiality, and shed light on the connection between spatiality and involvement.

The easiest way to disclose theatricality as something different from the audiovisual mediality of theater (or the screen) is probably through investigating the relationship between a theatrical event and its audience. However, this investigation requires certain precautions. The terminology of 'event' and 'audience' must not suggest the separation of two ontologically distinct entities. These are structural elements of theatricality, and therefore an event in itself cannot be taken as theatrical without an audience, nor is an audience really an audience without an event. Furthermore, it is inadequate to suppose that the audience, or theatricality as a whole, is a product of the synthesis of the different perspectives observed by the different spectators that make up the audience. All these presuppositions would interpret theatricality as something arising from an event that is interpreted or constructed as theatrical by the 'subjects' that make up the audience. That is, these presuppositions derive theatricality from the institutionalized experience of (mostly Western) theater—they imagine it as a sequence of audiovisually transmitted scenes observed by a homogeneous audience.

In opposition to this traditional view of theatricality, I will now propose involvement as an essential element in theatrical events. First of all, I contend that membership in an audience is purely coincidental and does not necessarily require any institutionalized establishments like theaters. This is in line with Weber's argumentation when he implements Walter Benjamin's term, *Grouping*. Grouping means that media can bring together people in structures that are not expressions of essential or natural or even institutional characteristics (like nationality or class), but rather are determined by accidental, historical situations (Weber 2004, 118–19). The audience of a theater is an example of a grouping, but grouping does not require theaters. It is in these accidentally formed groupings that an event can become a *shared* experience—and in a more "personal" sense than simply observing the same thing. However, I would like to point out that it is entirely possible for a single human being to become a grouping alone. This phenomenon of becoming a witness is something essential to lay out in the present study. A grouping involves the possibility of sharing the experience of an event. What this means is that becoming witness to something theatrical is never reducible to a purely subjective "fancy"; it is always already public and shareable, even if it is witnessed alone.

Becoming a witness—or a member of a grouping—is becoming involved in an event. In a later part of the present study which is concerned with phenomenology, I will pay more attention to the nature of this involvement. For now I will point out some of its most fundamental features, which will help reaching an understanding of theatricality. A witness or a grouping of witnesses to something theatrical is not simply observing something from a distance, they are parts of the event taking place—they are *in* the events. This does not simply mean that they share the same physical place where a theatrical event is happening (the spatial experience of theatricality is not reducible to the experience of physical surroundings); it rather means that they are in a certain sense—and more often than not involuntarily—actors in the theatrical event they experience. Theatricality is an interaction of grouping of witnesses and of events, which happens as a result of a change. This change—a deviation from everyday experience—is what calls for an involvement that allows new and different (theatrical) ways of experiencing and of sharing experience. Theatricality makes involvement conspicuous. Even if everyday experiences or events that generally do not count as theatrical still require involvement (something that I will elaborate on later), the transparency of involvement is lost in theatricality—or, rather, theatricality can be defined as the loss of transparency of involvement.

This conspicuousness of involvement manifests itself as an awareness of spatiality that is otherwise not reflected upon. Members of a grouping can be defined as people who find themselves in a scene or on a stage— theaters of audience involvement may be the best example of this, when the audience realizes that they are actually partaking in a scene, or that they are on the stage. However, finding oneself onstage is an experience that can also arise when someone partakes in a "staged" event, or if someone witnesses a staged murder. Being in a scene or on a stage means that elements of the environment and certain possibilities of dealing with them that did not previously manifest themselves appear, or that their significance changes.

A scene or a stage is a locale in the sense in which Weber defines theater:

> *Theater* is thus a locale whose status as determined place depends upon external intervention, and thus upon a relation of forces that can never be contained within the place in question. (2004, 314–15)

That is, scenes are places that arise from the space we generally go about as a result of an intervention. This place is demarcated from a more general environment, but its boundaries are not clear. Events, acts, and things become saturated with significance: they gain additional possible meanings—like, for example, in a murder scene, where all the things surrounding the scene suddenly become possible evidences and traces. Since the demarcation is an effect of an intervention that precedes the disclosure of the scene, the intervention is both external and internal to it. The traces at a murder scene lead to something always already outside of the scene. The scene cannot contain the forces that carve it out of the environment. The trace that is both inside and outside becomes the tool, in an investigation, to deconstruct the locale of a murder scene and de-stabilize its spatiality.[2] A murder scene's theatricality is always eventually destroyed by the investigation of the murder. Conversely, everything theatrical loses its theatricality once it is subjected to careful scientific or investigative reflection.

For the subject of the present study, I have chosen the theatricality of violence. This is a limitation on the more general study of the nature of the interventions that make the demarcation of theatrical scenes possible. The study of violence as intervention makes it possible to study the role the human body plays in theatricality in general. In order to investigate the specific case of theatrical violence in Harris's novel and its adaptations and its connections to Weber's theory of theatricality, I will continue by outlining a definition of "theatrical serial killers," based on *The Red Dragon*, and the film and the series it inspired.

The Provisional Definition of a Theatrical Serial Killer

The term "theatrical serial killer" is not used in real life criminology. However, it is frequently used in the series *Hannibal* as a description of the main antagonist, Dr. Hannibal Lecter, the Chesapeake Ripper. The employment of the adjective "theatrical" can be interpreted as the description of an accidental attribute of the murders or the perpetrator, rather than an item of a typology of serial killers. Whatever the case may be, since I have already established that murder scenes in general can be theatrical, and the deployment of this adjective is not redundant, it may be useful to investigate what those attributes are that make necessary the designation of certain murders or murderers as theatrical.

The FBI's Crime Classification Manual defines serial murder as the murder of three or more victims in separate events, separated by cooling off periods. However, there is no general characteristic that can be used to describe all serial killers and be applied in the investigation of each individual case (Douglas et al. 2006, 461). Therefore, in the fictional case of the Chesapeake Ripper, the description of his methods as theatrical will refer to a characteristic of his individual case, without any specific intent of categorization.

While the novels and, to an even greater extent, the movie adaptations are rather enigmatic about the deeds of Hannibal Lecter before his capture, the books contain bits and pieces about them, which are more or less unified into a narrative in the ongoing television series. It is in fact the main aim of the series to put together the fragmented information on Dr. Lecter's life in America before his capture, which is found scattered mostly in the first three novels, and use it in an adaptation that can stand on its own. As an interesting side effect that I will look into later, the series visualizes things that are only mentioned in passing in a very evasive fashion within the books. Because of the continuity of the narrative, I will rely on the series in my account of Doctor Lecter's murders.[3]

The victims of the Chesapeake Ripper were severely mutilated (*ante mortem*, at least in some cases) and had some of their organs removed, and their bodies were left on display in a manner that is consistently described as theatrical. Since putting a corpse on display is already in itself theatrical—an intervention of an external force that redefines the spatiality of its location—the relevance of description of the manner of the display as theatrical needs some explanation. An example of the Ripper's victims described in the 7th episode of the 1st season of the series, and also mentioned in *The Silence of the Lambs* (novel) (Harris 1988, 15), may shed some light on this. One of the Ripper's victims was found in a church pew, with his tongue as a bookmark in the Bible he was holding. His thymus and pancreas had been removed. Another case mentioned in the same episode, and also in *The Red Dragon* (novel) (Harris 2009, 69), is that of the Wound Man, where a medieval anatomy book illustration of battlefield injuries was reenacted on the victim using the tools in his workshop.

The purpose of putting the victim of any kind of homicide on display is humiliation, a characteristic of sadistic serial killers (as are *ante mortem* mutilations), but the fact that the Ripper selected his victims with complete disregard to race, gender or external features, and the distinctly asexual nature of the murders, indicate that he would not entirely fit the category of sexual sadist (Douglas et al. 2006, 226–30). Nevertheless, humiliation plays an important role in the Ripper's murders. A further motive for turning the bodies into spectacles is that it hides the significance of the removal of organs—all the removed organs are edible. Although Dr.

Lecter does engage in cannibalism, he often does this by serving the stolen organs at high society dinners—the purpose of this is the further humiliation of the victim as well as of the guests and not the performance of some kind of ritual.

Taking all these things into consideration, it seems that the theatricality of the crimes of the Chesapeake Ripper consists in the way the bodies are turned into tools of representation, the way they are emblematized. As a result of this, their (former) humanity is not so much the issue in witnessing them, it is rather the way their de-humanization saturates them with meaning. The way they are turned into a spectacle is an intervention into the regular course of dealing with witnessing a murder victim. The violence perpetrated against these victims does not simply consist of their murder. They are further violated after death. The Chesapeake Ripper is a theatrical serial killer, because he commits violence upon his victims even after their death by turning them from corpses into puppets that are only the traces of his forceful intervention on the murder scene, from which he is absent. To be a witness in such a scene is to be involved in the violence, but in such a way that the witness is also violated. It is intuitively obvious that this reaction is reached because the "puppet" in the scene is a human body. However, some explanation is needed as to how exactly corporeality contributes to this experience of theatrical violence.

The Phenomenology of Empathy

Empathy will prove to be a key concept in the present study as that which connects corporeality with the theatricality of violence, and allows for the demonstration of certain aspects of theatrical violence in the primary sources. Before I can set out to fully expose the role of empathy in the *Red Dragon*, I should first provide a concise theoretical overview of the way empathy is thought of in the phenomenological tradition, how it is connected to corporeality, and how that can be fit into the theory of theatricality that I have presented. For the purposes of this overview, I will start with Edmund Husserl's account of empathy, since he is the one who introduced the term into phenomenology. Then I will take a look at Martin Heidegger's reasons for his criticism of the use of this term. After this I will demonstrate a connection between Heidegger's phenomenology and Mark Johnson's cognitive theory of embodied meaning, in order to arrive at a definition of empathy that is relatable to corporeality. Finally, I will connect this concept of empathy to the concept of theatricality that I have previously outlined.

Husserl's phenomenology is an attempt to provide an objective and formalized account of the structure and constitution of human experience with the use of phenomenological reductions. The term "phenomenological reduction" stands for Husserl's set of procedures of reducing all presuppositions about experience (e.g. suspending the question of the existence of the world outside of experience), thus reaching, through the transcendental ego, the sphere of transcendental experience—the point where all objects of consciousness are so far reduced from any presuppositions that they become ideal objects (Husserl 1967, 10–11). The overt transcendentalism of Husserlian phenomenology is highly problematic in itself and has been widely criticized ever since the dawn of phenomenology. I will look into some of this criticism later in the present section. However, for now I will dwell on another problematic aspect of the Husserlian method that led Husserl to the introduction of the term empathy.

While trying to reach the transcendental sphere of experience by suspending the "outside" world, Husserl has constantly to deal with the problem of solipsism. His solution is the introduction of intersubjectivity. Intersubjectivity is what transcendental subjectivity is expanded into, through the transcendental act of empathy. Empathy, for Husserl, describes the transcendental (mental) act in which the subject experiences the world while also experiencing other subjects, or "alter egos" that are experiencing the same world (Husserl 1967, 34–36). Therefore experience is, in its very nature, communal through intersubjectivity. To Husserl, empathy is a structural part of human experience because human beings perceive the experiences of others, to use Husserl's term, as "co-experienced," or, as grounded in a perception of likeness (1967, 35). While Husserl here does not elaborate on the nature of this similarity, I put forward that it is founded upon the bodily nature of experience, that is, on the fact that the self and the other are both *similarly* corporeal.

Husserl conceives of the Transcendental Ego as a Leibnizean monad that is closed off from the world but contains within itself the reflections of all other monads, the Alter Egos (1967, 36). It follows from this that empathy, as an experience of others as similar to the self, first requires a certain self-knowledge and that this is reached through the phenomenological reductions. This monadism is criticized by Heidegger in his account of the experience of others designated by him as Being-with (Heidegger 1962, 149–63), which is a structural element of Being-in-the-World (78–86). Before elaborating on Heidegger's account of empathy and the experience of others, I will first try to shed some light on what he means by Being-in-the-World, since this term will be of importance in a later part of this section.

Heidegger does not see human experience as reducible to monads or ideal objects of consciousness. He in fact argues for a holistic account of experience, going against any Cartesian opposition between subject and object. Being-in-the-World is the way human experience always is as a whole (Heidegger 1962, 91–95). The source of intelligibility that in Husserl's case was the monadic Transcendental Ego is an always already shared, socio-culturally determined world in Heidegger. Heidegger makes use of the term "significance" with which he designates the connections of elements encountered in the world that make it possible for human beings to engage in activities in the world (and they are always already engaged) and be *involved* in them. Heidegger also makes it clear that the entities encountered in the world are also involved in it. This is what makes it possible to encounter them (Heidegger 1962, 120).

The Heideggerian concept of involvement is related to the concept of involvement as discussed above—a participation which has an accidental and non-institutional nature, as that of a grouping—although it does not entirely correspond to it. For Heidegger involvements mean the possibilities of being for humans—ways in which one can be involved in the world through activities involving certain tools or other entities. "Significance" is the totality of the relations that make involvement possible. The way I have used the term is less specific and simply means that the states and activities of human beings are in fact always already interactions with other beings. This is something that Heidegger would much rather designate as Being-in, an aspect of the structure of Being-in-the-World. Importantly, both Heidegger and I posit that the interactions described above only become objects of (self-) reflection in special cases and are usually non-conscious and inconspicuous (Heidegger 1962, 102). What I have designated as theatricality is that which makes these interactions conspicuous by distancing them from their everyday being.

Heidegger problematizes empathy in his discussion about Being-with, which deals with the interactions that involve other people. As was the case with the earlier-introduced concept of grouping, Being-with does not necessarily require the presence of other people (Heidegger 1962, 164–66). It is rather an essential characteristic of interactions which discloses that these interactions are public and shareable. In other words, Being-with points out the iterability and performativity of human interactions.[4] What I mean by saying that the interactions are public is that since involvement with them is a possibility that belongs to Being-in-the-World and not to any particular or monadic individual subject, these interactions consist of performative acts that are accessible to and iterable by anyone. Heidegger contends that it is this publicness of interactions that is primary to the self-knowledge required for empathy (Heidegger 1962, 161–63). That is to say, it is only through already given iterable practices of meaning creation that one can establish one's knowledge of oneself, and not the other way around. Involvement in such public interactions is what constitutes human beings, which beings are then endowed with the ability for self-reflection.

I will take my departure from Heidegger by positing that what makes the share ability of these interactions possible is corporeality. To demonstrate this, I will turn to Mark Johnson's theory of embodied cognition, which is described in his book, *The Meaning of the Body: An Aesthetics of Human Cognition* (2007). First I will demonstrate the connections of this theory to Heidegger's, and then I will elaborate on the role of corporeality in theatricality based on the relationship between the sense in which I used the terms involvement and corporeality.

The most obvious connection between Johnson (2007, 1–17) and Heidegger (1962, 122–28) is that they both propose that the Cartesian dualism of mind and body is not simply incorrect in describing these two entities (for example, by not attributing the faculties of the mind to the human brain), but that the very assumption of the independent existence of these entities is a mistake. It follows from this that whatever the faculties of human cognition may be, they are not attributable to either the mind or the body (described in the Cartesian sense). What Johnson sets out to do is the study of meaning but not as something emerging from a self-reflective transcendental subject-mind, but rather as the "result of one organic process, so that all our meaning, thought, and language emerge from the aesthetic of this embodied activity" (2007, 1). For Johnson, the grounds of human being (or being human) are ways of bodily engagement with the environment. He argues, much like Heidegger, that trying to define human beings without an environment with which they can interact is a fundamental ontological mistake.

According to Johnson, the "embodied mind" can be grasped as a continuity (and not a separation) between a human body in the physical or biological sense and the environment with which it interacts. At no point does this mind become entirely detached from the environment, and conversely, the environment as such cannot be defined separately from a body that acts in it, because without such an actor it is just a set of physical things that are in no connection with each other (Johnson 2007, 1–33). The embodied meaning that is always already being produced in this interaction is analogous to Heidegger's structure of involvements and significance. The difference is that Johnson provides a corporeal grounding for this structure. *Embodied experience is Being-in-the-World.* A human being must have a body in order to be involved in the world.

If embodied experience can be taken as a corporeally grounded interpretation of Being-in-the-World, then starting from this, it must be possible to provide a corporeally grounded interpretation of Being-with as well, and from that to derive a sense of empathy that can be defined in relation to corporeality. Johnson points out that all cognition is based on sensomotoric experiences of dealing with the world (2007, 17–33). This means that when I see another human being make a movement with his arm, this is not simply visual information that is somehow processed by my brain. In fact, I interpret that person as a human being, because he makes a movement that I also can make. I experience the other's movement by relating it to my own experience of making the same moves. The publicness of interactions is possible, because the sensomotoric abilities of human bodies are shared by all human beings. This is why the environment is also public; it is something that we can all be involved in.

Following this argumentation, engaging in the study of neurological processes to explain certain aspects of human behavior (i.e. interaction with the environment) is a legitimate way to interpret human being, as long as this study does not get lost in attempts to look for (ideal) mental representations in the brain (as this would be tantamount to equating the brain with the Cartesian Ego), but rather sees neurological processes as structural elements of the essentially corporeal (sensomotoric) interactions with an environment. Neurological processes are impossible without this interaction, as concepts and thoughts are also grounded in sensomotoric aspects of experience through conceptual metaphors (Johnson 2007, 167–68).

If this is so, empathy is not an ability to make judgments about the psychological states of another human being by relating them to our own psychological states. It is a result of the shared sensomotoric basis of cognition. Our bodily ability to imitate the movement of others is what makes it possible for us not only to understand them (in the sense as being involved in the same interactions as them), but to be able to imagine ourselves in their place—or more correctly to imagine ourselves in their body. This displacement of our emotions into others' bodies is what relates theatricality to empathy. It is an intervention of our own involved dealing with our environment in which we become involved in it in a different way than we previously were. This difference is what makes involvement conspicuous.

Violence is the theme of the present study, because it seems that this displacement of empathy is something that happens only when the emotions and sensations of others become obtrusive for us in our interactions with an environment which includes (involves) others as well. This happens most readily when feelings become more manifest than what we are used to, and violence seems to always cause this kind of manifestation. There are several ways in which this can happen, and by laying out a case study of empathy in the *Red Dragon* and the television series *Hannibal*, I will attempt to show some of these ways in the next section.

Metaperspective and the Extension of Violence

It is true especially for *The Red Dragon* and the television series that there is an emphasis on the contrasts and similarities between extreme (almost pathological) empathy and the complete lack thereof, which is defined as psychopathy or sociopathy in the discussed works. If empathy is a fundamental aspect of human beings, it is necessary to discuss now what exactly is meant by the lack of empathy or degrees of empathy in the series and the book. I will start with the investigation of the contrast made between the two characters of Hannibal Lecter (the Chesapeake Ripper) and Will Graham, an FBI consultant, as they are depicted in the television series *Hannibal*, and later I will move on to an investigation of the serial killer Francis Dolarhyde in the *Red Dragon*.

It is obvious that the colloquial (non-phenomenological) use of the term "empathy" refers to the observation implicit in these works (and possibly in everyday life) that in some people the experience of the suffering of other people does not trigger the displacement of their emotional states in the way that it would if they imagined that suffering as happening to them. Conversely, those who are endowed with what is referred to as extreme or excessive empathy do suffer the torments of those they witness suffering. For them being a witness to violence is often the same as being the victim of that violence, in the sense that both are involuntary actors in a scene that came about as an intervention of external force—violence.

It is this involuntariness of interaction, the loss of agency, which is the key to the understanding of what is meant by the lack of empathy. Psychopaths still have an understanding, a Being-with other people, in the sense that they recognize that others are performing the same movements and interactions with the environment that they are also capable of. However, they understand the movement of others as coming from a different source than their own motions. Psychopaths as described in the primary sources understand other people as puppets. The case of the

Chesapeake Ripper, which I have already discussed, clearly demonstrates this tendency. The Ripper uses other people's bodies as props for staging scenes. He kills them because he sees their resistance to his will as an annoying obstacle and not as the effect of an agency that is similar to his own. He sees himself as unique. He wants to become the puppeteer, and he needs to cut the strings in order to do this.

On the other end of the spectrum there is Will Graham, who is described as having an ability to see the killers in a way no one else can (Harris 1981, 2–3). His empathy is so strong that he goes beyond the common reaction of empathizing with the victims and has the ability to empathize with the killer—he can trace back the desire of the killer that produced the scene by reconstructing his interactions which led to the creation of the scene. This ability of Graham is said to be more or less unique. This uniqueness is what attracts Hannibal Lecter to him, and this is why he goes to such lengths in the series to manipulate him. He is a unique puppet.

Of course, since Will Graham is overly empathetic, he is far more affected by the victims too, than the other witnesses (investigators). In fact, it is a peculiar aspect of the series that the corpses are so aestheticized and thus alienated from their (former) humanity that it becomes hard for the audience to identify them as something to empathize with—they are like statues or paintings. What do produce emotional effects are the reactions of Graham to seeing the corpses. The audience of the show gains access to the theatricality of the murders by empathizing with Graham, who empathizes with the victims. While this is a very clear aspect of the television adaptation, the same phenomenon is encountered in *Red Dragon*, when Graham investigates the house of the murdered families. The corpses have been removed by the time Graham gets there and we do not see them, and only find out what happened to them as Graham is checking his notes on the autopsies. What gives this scene shock value is not the sight or experience of the corpses, but the way Graham is shocked as he reconstructs and re-lives the events (Harris 1981, 13–18).

This channelling of suffering and violence reveals an interesting metaperspective employed in the stories under consideration. In *Red Dragon*, a book of narrative fiction, it is Graham's narration that reveals the murder scene and makes it theatrical because of his being shocked by the events. This is a metaperspective, because the novel itself would not have had any other way of describing the murders than by a narrative, and turned it into a narration within a narration. Analogous to this, in the series seeing Graham interact with the scene is what reveals it as an instance of theatricality, and not primarily because of the sight of the corpses, but by the performance of Hugh Dancy, the actor playing Graham in the series, who seems genuinely distressed by the scenes. The movie *Red Dragon* employs both of these devices: in the house investigation scene, we see Edward Norton as Graham narrate the events of the murders into a tape recorder while he inspects the house, and we see that he has to stop in the narration, for example when he arrives at a point where two children were shot, because he is overwhelmed by the idea.

Returning to the previously-used puppet metaphor might prove useful in explicating the full weight of this metaperspective. By committing violence on the victim a psychopath aims to become the puppeteer of the human being (whom he already sees as a sort of puppet). In the case of a theatrical serial killer, the display of the violated body—the puppet—is also a way of violating those who witness it. It is an extension of the physical violence through the (normal) operation of empathy. If violence towards the victims turns them into puppets, and the witness to the displayed victim is also violated, this means that the witness is also turned into a puppet. The scene in the first episode of the series where Hannibal Lecter kills a girl and puts her on a display to guide Graham to a better understanding of another serial killer he is after is a perfect example of this. The theatrical serial killer does not simply hurt his audience but also manipulates it.

This also means that the display of theatrical violence on the screen, or in a narrative, is also a form of violence against the real audience or readers. Also, they may even become puppets in a sense, but only if we accept the assumptions that the psychopath makes about human beings—I will address this issue shortly. The metaperspective, the fact that the violence done to the victims is channelled to the audience through Graham in media (not just audio and video, but also theatricality), reveals this otherwise transparent violence in representing violence. This way, the works convey an important ethical question with regard to the way the press and the news media handle real violence in cases of serial murders or even terrorist attacks. News of attacks and murders are theatrical and they reorganize the spatiality of the private dwelling of the audience where they read newspapers or watch television.[5]

It would be tempting to connect this with the issue of creating puppets via violence and engage in a critique of the ideology of the news media. That is, it is tempting to posit that the news media turn its audience into puppets by violating them by way of showing them violence, the same way as does a theatrical serial killer. However, any such enterprise must take into account that psychopaths with their reduced ability to empathize misunderstand the way human beings are. Even the success of a manipulative attempt is a result of a very different interaction with the environment from that which a psychopath has. I will now turn my attention to this misunderstanding by addressing the way Francis Dolarhyde, the serial killer in *Red Dragon*, tries to explain to Freddy Lounds what he is "really" doing (Harris 1981, 209–17). Freddy Lounds is a journalist, which is significant in the light of the metaperspective laid bare above.

The Cartesian Misunderstanding in *Red Dragon*

In what follows I will briefly describe the method and motivation of the character of Francis Dolarhyde, the serial killer Will Graham tries to catch with the assistance of the imprisoned Hannibal Lecter. Then I will relate his fantasies and methods to the theoretical insights laid out so far, and demonstrate that what I have designated as psychopathy entails a privative mode of empathy, in which the understanding of the motions and acts of other human beings is given, but the source of that motion is misunderstood, and conceived of as something outside and independent of the body—which is analogous to Cartesian dualism. I will demonstrate this using a scene in *Red Dragon*, where Dolarhyde captures the journalist Freddy Lounds and tries to demonstrate and explain to him what he does to his victims. Finally, I will relate this to the insights on metaperspective in the previous section.

Francis Dolarhyde was an unwanted child, born with a cleft palate, who was raised by his abusive grandmother. Because of his deformity he perceives himself as ugly and disgusting (Harris 1981, 244–72). After seeing the William Blake painting, *The Great Red Dragon and the Woman Clothed in Sun,* he becomes obsessed with the red dragon in the painting to the point that he wants to transform himself into the dragon as an escape from his distorted body image. After a certain point this fantasy becomes so strong that he begins to "transform" people in order to help his own transformation (Harris 1981, 279–82). It does not become entirely clear how he imagines this process, but what he does is manifest. At the beginning of *Red Dragon* Dolarhyde killed twice. He attacked families with two children. He broke into their houses, killed the husband and the children, sexually abused the wife, and then killed her too. His signatures included breaking all the mirrors in the house—this is something that Graham sees as a sign that the killer perceives himself as deformed—and placing small shards of the mirrors into the eyes of the victims. Graham contends that the aim of this is to make them look more alive as a result of the reflected light (Harris 1981, 13–23). It is also clear that Dolarhyde uses the murdered family members as an audience to his violation of the women (Harris 1981, 244–72).

As I have already mentioned, the aim of these highly ritualized actions is Dolarhyde's transformation into the Red Dragon. As Lecter points out in the movie, the dragon is ugly, but its strength makes it sublime—this is why it is so attractive to Dolarhyde. However, it seems that the killer needs the lady clothed in sun for his transformation, as well. That is what he transforms his female victims into. He needs the audience because he wants to be seen while he has power, because that is when he is beautiful. While the disturbing way of the handling of the primary victim and its role in this fantasy of transformation is in itself worth studying, for the present purpose I find the way the other family members were used to be more instructive.

I contend that Dolarhyde does not care that his audience is made up of corpses, because he conceives of the motions and acts—the lives of other people—as originating from sources external to their bodies, and after getting rid of this mover (the soul in an ill-defined sense), he conceives of himself as the new source of life for them. He cannot look at himself in the mirrors, but he wants to see himself through the eyes of his victims. He makes them watch his performance, and he has to kill them, because nobody would watch him otherwise. He also needs to first wound and then kill his partner in his performance, because no one would perform with him voluntarily. In a sense his error is obvious: he is not the source of life for his audience, and nobody sees him; his audience is dead. On the other hand, he is also mistaken about the aesthetics of his performance. He sees himself as becoming beautiful and expects awe and admiration—an appreciation of his beauty. Yet when live witnesses encounter the scenes he leaves behind, they are shocked, horrified and disgusted by them. This is because they have an intuitive understanding of the embodied nature of cognition and motion, which means that they see the corpses as human beings deprived of this embodiment, of Being-in-the-World.

This is illustrated in a conspicuously ironic way by the case of the capture and murder of the journalist Freddy Lounds. After the FBI have persuaded Lounds to publish a fake interview about the serial killer, Dolarhyde kidnaps him (Harris 1981, 208). Then he sets out to explain to Lounds that he does not butcher and rape his victims but transforms them. To convince Lounds of that, his captor shows him photos of his (primary, female) victims before and after their death (or transformation). He presents these photos as if they were clear visual evidence of his statement (in the movie adaptation, this is the first time we see the corpses). The presentation seems to indicate that he sees his victims as becoming more beautiful in the process as well (Harris 1981, 209–17). However, Lounds only sees dead women with glass shards in their eyes. Even if, after having seen the photos (and for his own protection) he attempts to reassure Dolarhyde that he finally understands what the killer does, his pathetic plea for mercy reveals that he hardly sees Dolarhyde's work as beautiful (Harris 1981, 216). Scared of having to suffer as much as the photographed people, Lounds, in fact, empathizes with the victims.

This scene is ironic, because Lounds is a sensationalist journalist who reports on brutal murders for their shock value. He tries to justify these reports as being useful or serving the public by keeping it informed; however, the way most people react to his articles is similar to how he responds to Dolarhyde's explanation and presentation. This in turn can be seen as an aspect of the metaperspective: a way the novel and its adaptations address themselves. These works are aware of the way that the effects of violence have multiple layers and that the violence they depict and its depictions are always forms of external intervention. What the metaperspective offers is the chance to make this intervention in a way that allows for a genuine involvement with and clear reflection of the nature of empathy. The works negate the possibility of thinking of people in terms of puppets and puppeteers.

Conclusions

The aim of this paper was to lay out the interrelationships of the concepts of theatricality, violence and empathy in Red Dragon and its adaptations, in a way that these concepts remain theoretically applicable in a broader context. These interrelationships were then used to demonstrate the ethical metacritique that is employed in the novel and its adaptations. The argumentation of this paper leaves several avenues open for further study. Firstly, it is intended to serve as a starting point for further research of the later novels and their adaptations in the same series. Secondly, it aims to create a theoretical framework of the theatricality of violence, which can be applied to other instances of the fictional or non-fictional representations of violence. Thirdly, some of the theoretical questions are left open, for example, the philosophical implications of the parallels between Cartesian dualism and the ways in which the psychopaths in these works misinterpret other people are merely broached here, as a full discussion of this issue would greatly exceed the scope of this paper. Another such question is the relationship between deconstruction and the Derridean term "trace" and the investigation of murder scenes, which is also only touched upon. Since the present paper aims to be a possible starting point for literary interpretations of this nature, hopefully the opening up of these questions will contribute to more elaborate and comprehensive discussions of the field.

References

Derrida, Jacques. 1976. *Of Grammatology.* Translated by Gayatri Chakravorty Spivak. Baltimore and London: Johns Hopkins University Press.
—. 1977. *Limited Inc*. Evanston: Northwestern University Press.
Douglas, John E., Ann W. Burgess, Allen G. Burgess, and Robert K. Ressler. 2006. *Crime Classification Manual: A Standard System for Investigating and Classifying Violent Crimes*. San Francisco: Jossey-Bass.
Harris, Thomas. 1981. *Red Dragon*. New York: Berkley Books.
—. 1988. *The Silence of the Lambs*. New York: Macmillan USA.
—. 1999. *Hannibal*. London: Arrow Books.
—. 2006. *Hannibal Rising*. New York: Delacorte Press.
Heidegger, Martin. 1962. *Being and Time*. Translated by John Macquarrie, and Edward Robinson. Oxford and Cambridge (USA): Blackwell. First published 1927.
Husserl, Edmund. 1967. *The Paris Lectures*. Translated by Peter Koestenbaum. Dordrecht, Boston, London: Kluwer Academic Publishers.
Johnson, Mark. 2007. *The Meaning of the Body: Aesthetics of Human Understanding*. Chicago and London: University of Chicago Press.
Weber, Samuel. 2004. *Theatricality as Medium*. New York: Fordham University Press.

Filmography

Demme, Jonathan, Thomas Harris, and Ted Tally. 2001. *The Silence of the Lambs*. Full screen special edition DVD. Directed by Jonathan Demme. Metro-Goldwyn-Mayer Studios.
Scott, Ridley, David Mamet, Steven Zaillian, and Thomas Harris. 2006. *Hannibal*. Two Disc Special Edition DVD. Directed by Ridley Scott. Metro-Goldwyn-Mayer Studios.
Ratner, Brett, and Ted Tally. *Red Dragon*. Widescreen Collector's Edition DVD. 2006. Directed by Brett Ratner. Metro-Goldwyn-Mayer Studios.

Webber, Peter, and Thomas Harris. *Hannibal Rising*. 2007. Unrated Widescreen Edition DVD. Directed by Peter Webber. Weinstein Company.

Notes

[1] Thomas Harris, *Red Dragon,* New York: Berkley Books, 1981.
Thomas Harris, *The Silence of the Lambs*, New York: Macmillan USA, 1988.
Thomas Harris, *Hannibal*, London: Arrow Books, 1999.
Thomas Harris, *Hannibal Rising*, New York: Delacorte Press, 2006.
[2] For a detailed discussion on the "concept" of trace and its role in deconstruction, see *Of Grammatology* by Jacques Derrida (1976, 18–19).
[3] While these murders provide a frame for the entire narrative of the series, the most informative episodes about them are the first and seventh episodes of the first season, entitled "Apéritif" (first aired on 2013.04.04.) and "Sorbet" (first aired on 2013.05.09), respectively.
[4] For a detailed discussion on the relationship between iterability, a form of repeatability which alters that which is repeated, and its relationship to performativity, see *Limited Inc* by Jacques Derrida (1977).
[5] This intrusion is discussed in relation to terrorism and its dependence on being mediated in a chapter of Weber's *Theatricality as Medium*, entitled: " 'War,' 'Terrorism,' and 'Spectacle': On Towers and Caves" (2004, 326–35).

CHAPTER THIRTEEN

ARCHEOLOGIES OF AFFECT: SHAKESPEARE'S PHANTASM OF LOVE IN *ROMEO AND JULIET*

MATTHEW BIBERMAN

In his recent study, *Antinomies of Realism*, Fredric Jameson hazards the following thesis: modern bourgeois subjectivity is productively understood as an immersive living in a "perpetual present" where "the isolated body begins to know more global waves of generalized sensations, and it is these which, for want of a better word, I will here call affect" (2013, 28). Later Jameson explains that he follows Rei Terada's stipulation that "affects are bodily feeling, whereas emotions (or passions, to use their other name) are conscious states" (32). Finally Jameson wonders,

> Are we to suppose that before the construction of the secular bourgeois body in the course of the nineteenth century, affects simply did not exist, and that an older pre-modern humanity had to do with the various systems of emotions[?] (34)

understood as conscious disembodied states. In this paper I am going to respond to Jameson's question by outlining a tentative genealogy for his notion of bourgeois affect. Fundamentally I will be suggesting that "affect" as Jameson conceptualizes it emerges with the waning of a belief in the "spiritualized body" in western culture. This collapse (or disenchantment), however, needs now to be seen as a site of "creative destruction," one in which the resulting absence of spirituality serves (or served) as ground for the rise of new notions of the body. Chief among these new notions is Cartesian subjectivity and with it, the construction of this new register for the body of the Jamesonian affect. Now as a Shakespearean, I recognize the missing third among this play of signifiers: first the spiritualized body, and last the affective body, leaving in between—what? The theatrical body. The reasoning here is dialectical and resolutely old school: the rise of Jamesonian affect is presented as a compensatory exchange in which the waning of a religious aura formerly presumed to permeate existence creates a lack that then induces the emergence of modern experiential affect. Fair enough, but what do we learn if we pause for a moment on the intermediate phase, the performative or theatrical body?

As a way to begin our exploration, I want to revisit the scene in *Romeo and Juliet* where the young lovers consummate their marriage. Thanks to the scheming of the nurse and the friar, Romeo has returned to the Capulet house and by means of a rope ladder, has climbed to and spent the night in Juliet's room. Now with morning approaching, Juliet expresses her dismay at Romeo's departure. In response, Romeo declares:

> Let me be tane, let me be put to death,
> I am content, so thou wilt have it so.
> I'll say yon grey is not the morning's eye,
> 'Tis but the pale reflexe of *Cynthias* brow.
> Nor that is not Lark, whose noates do beate
> The vaulty heaven so high above our heads,
> I have more care to stay, than will to go:
> Come death and welcome, *Juliet* wills it so.
> How ist my soul, let's talke, it is not day. (3.5.17–25)

I start then, as Shakespeare so often does, with a question: why does Romeo say to Juliet: "How ist my soul, let's talke." As a way to answer, let's cast our eyes back a few scenes earlier in the play—to the famous balcony scene, for there we find the same language. Juliet calls out, "Romeo?" and Romeo, to us and himself, says: "It is my soul that calls upon my name" (2.2.164). This consistency suggests that in Romeo we have a follower of Ficino, who in his treatise *On Love* wrote that when in a platonic love relationship "such men exchange themselves with each other … While I love you loving me, I find myself in you thinking about me … and I recover myself in you, preserving me" (quoted in Wells 2007, 47). It is important to note that here Romeo modifies Ficino's love doctrine, for in Ficino, the lover and the beloved are men. In Shakespeare we see illustrated the cultural development of two key strands of modern sexuality: the extension of the doctrine of platonic love to male-female matches, and the solidification of the concept of companionate marriage (as opposed to the idea of marriage as an alliance tool). Note too that this modern, heteronormative construction of love around marriage flatly contradicted the Platonic ideal that put the love of an older man for a boy at its peak. Yet it is important to note that woven into this now familiar ideological package is a key belief which distinguishes Shakespeare and marks him as pre-modern, and that is his strong conviction that lovers actually exchange souls.

This idea of a soul exchange is not limited to Romeo. We find it throughout Shakespeare's work. Lysander in *A Midsummer Night's Dream* pleads:

Stay, gentle *Helena*; heare my excuse,
My love, my life, my soul, faire *Helena*! (3.2.245–46)

And the attentive reader of the Sonnets will discover that those poems propound this doctrine quite openly: here is the start of Sonnet 109:

O Never say that I was false of heart,
Though absence seem'd my flame to quallifie,
As easie might I from my selfe depart,
As from my soule which in thy brest doth lye:
That is my home of love ...

Shakespeare, here, is not speaking of the soul as a mere metaphor for a love bond between a couple. Or perhaps it is better to say that in Shakespeare the word "soul" increasingly comes to function as a site appropriate for a strict Derridean deconstruction. "Soul" must be thought of as denoting both a spiritual essence and nothing of the sort. The challenge for us is to set aside the reading of soul as nothing of the sort and retrieve a reading of soul as spiritual essence, as an ontological fact, the very ground of human existence and identity.

Let us pursue this thread for a moment: if, for Shakespeare, the soul was approached not as a metaphor but as a scientific fact, how would it have been explained? The exchange of lovers' souls was explained as a transplanting action that occurs through the eyes. For example, when Romeo first sees Juliet, he declares: "Did my heart love till now, forswear it sight, / For I never saw true Beauty till this night" (1.5.52–53). It is critical to recognize that Shakespeare's account is consistent with the science of the day. Again Ficino is a good guide. His *On Love* provides a detailed and widely influential account of vision and its relation to erotic love; in it he writes, "the eye ... shoots the darts of its rays into the eyes of the bystander ... it is shot from the heart of the shooter ... the infected blood becomes sick" (*De Amore*, 1484, quoted in Wells 2007, 51). As a result, a spiritual entity, a phantasm, was said to appear in the brain, implanted via the eyes.

At this juncture our survey of Renaissance science shifts from optics to neuroscience. As Marion Wells explains in her study *The Secret Wound*, the brain science of the period was dominated by faculty psychology. This model, derived from Aristotle, posited that the brain was comprised of three ventricles. The first ventricle was thought of as the site of the imagination—here the external senses produced images for processing. The second ventricle was the site of fantasy: here the estimative faculty manipulated those received images into phantasms, entities able to persist in the mind despite the vanishing of the represented objects in the external world. Finally, the third ventricle was said to house the memory, thought of as a kind of holding tank for the phantasms. As Wells makes clear, this theory of the faculties was profoundly Christianized. The phantasm is thought of as the conversion of the sensible image into a spiritual entity, a phantasmic object able to be perceived by the individual's soul. No doubt it seems odd to us, but the idea was that a human soul could only apprehend other spiritual entities, and for this reason the brain functioned to convert images into phantasms. Thus the second faculty was critical. Wells writes, "the estimative faculty, then, plays a critical factor in formulating motivational feelings about the object" (2007, 42). Typically this was thought of as determining one's intention toward the phantasm, and if this determination was sufficiently positive, the viewer was stirred to desire. Shakespeare uses the word intention precisely this way. In *The Merry Wives of Windsor*, Falstaff tells the audience: "O, she did so course o'er my exteriors with such a greedy intention, that the appetite of her eye did seeme to scorch me up like a burning-glasse" (1.3.65–67). Falstaff's declaration illustrates how this ideology joins spiritualism to science so as to produce embodied emotional states. Vision is presented as working in accordance with the extromission theory: while the woman absorbs the image of Falstaff via her eyes, she then emits beams that are compared to a magnifying glass. Falstaff, in consequence, feels as if light is being concentrated on his skin, burning him. At the same time, the audience understands that inside the woman's brain, her estimative faculty is creating and then doting on this phantasm of Falstaff, her beloved object, or at least that so Falstaff surmises. In *The Winter's Tale*, Leontes rehearses the theory to haunting effect. In one scene the King examines his son, and while doing so, he is unable to beat back the conviction that his wife has cuckolded him and left him to raise a child not his own. Leontes studies his son because he wants to determine if the boy's physiognomy resembles his own. This experience induces a fit of anxious speculation:

> … yet were it true,
> To say this Boy were like me. Come (Sir Page)
> Looke on me with your Welkin eye: sweet Villaine,
> Most dear'st, my Collop: Can thy Dam, may't be
> Affection? thy Intention stabs the Center.

Thou do'st make possible things not so held,
Communicat'st with Dreams (how can this be?)
With what's unreall" thou coactive art,
And fellow'st nothing. Then 'tis very credent
Thou may'st co-ioyne with something, and thou do'st,
(And that beyond Commission) and I find it,
(And that to the infection of my Braines,
And hardening of my Browes.) (1.2.135–46)

On this passage Maurice Hunt comments: "Leontes judges that love combines with dreams and gives birth to fantasies—nothing real" (1990, 92). I submit instead that Hunt's paraphrase accords with what we believe in our secular age. But we live after the death of the soul as a living ideology. Seen from Shakespeare's vantage point, Leontes is describing here in detail how a phantasm appears in the second ventricle of the brain. When an individual over-invests in a fantasy, when "intention" dotes and dwells on that phantasm beyond its spiritual worth, then the brain is thought to become the site of infection, with the result that the individual falls into a state of melancholy. Leontes now believes that his wife has committed adultery and that therefore he has doted incorrectly on her phantasm, a phantasm that is no longer true to reality, and it is this additional untruth that is the nothing that the mind's intention has formed. Leontes muses, "with what's unreall' thou coactive art": a virtual definition of the estimative faculty; then a line follows in which he mobilizes and jokingly inverts the concept: "Then 'tis very credent / Thou may'st co-ioyne with something, and thou do'st, / (And that beyond Commission) and I find it, / (And that to the infection of my Braines, / And hardening of my Browes)." The thinking here goes: if, on the one hand, the estimative faculty can produce spiritual phantasms, then on the other hand it can produce bodily effects—witness Leontes' physical illness, the material hardening of the infected brain. As Wells stresses, faculty psychology embodies an earlier iteration of dialectical thought, one in which the phantasm functions "copula"-like to mark the dynamic synthesis between body and soul. The influential philosopher Giorgio Agamben has written that this nexus of ideas

is so characteristic that European culture in this period might justly be defined as a pneumophantasmology, within whose compass—which circumscribes at once a cosmology, a physiology, a psychology, and a soteriology—the breath that animates the universe, circulates in the arteries, and fertilizes the sperm is the same one that, in the brain, and in the heart, receives and forms the phantasms of things we see, imagine, dream, and love. (1992, 193)

It is telling that the phantasm has received so little attention among modern scholars. This silence needs now to be read in conjunction with the rise of Descartes' cogito. It may seem obvious but it bears explicit stating: the notion that the self grounds itself (cogito ergo sum) has to be read as the successor to this vanishing ideology of pneumophantasmology. Max Weber spoke of religion quite precisely as the vanishing mediator in our ideological construct of modernity. It is helpful then to visualize the vanishing of this pneumophantasmology as constituting the void that then serves as the ontological ground for the construction of the Cartesian ego. It is when the Cartesian ego is apprehended as embodied that we get the experience of subjectivity as affect. With this kept in mind, we can stipulate a definition for theatricality and the theatricalized body. Theatricality is a psychological state which processes reality as a hunt for a lost sense of the sacred. It clings to the collective, it wants to discover the miraculous through the eyes of others watching it. Embodied affect is a subsequent modulation, where the self is conceived foundationally not in terms of an element within a dramatic collective but as a static monad, as what Jameson calls an "isolated body" now shorn of community and immersed in a "perpetual present," that is, locked in a single time frame and as such unable to experience, as before, the waning of the spiritual.

The collapse of this earlier worldview is precisely the repression, the nothing, upon which our modern (and postmodern) notions of subjectivity are grounded. The inclusion of this history is what Jameson wishes to see when he comments that "there is another interpretation of affect which demands comment in passing, and that is the unique status of melancholia among the various kinds of affects presumed or implied by the definition." "Is it," he wonders, "really so that melancholia is the very prototype of affect, as so much contemporary theory seems to believe; or better still that affect is simply another word for melancholia, as such?" (2013, 71–72). My response is that Jameson's definition of the regime of affect is a way to describe the embodied emotional states that evolved after the vanishing of the soul from our mental landscape. Consider how Jameson imagines affect to range

> chromatically up and down the bodily scale from melancholy to euphoria, from the bad trip to the high—from Nietzsche's most manic outbursts to the unquenchable depression and guilt of a Strindberg. And this is, as I have stressed, to be radically distinguished from the play of emotional states as such, even though as modernism develops, their representations will not fail to be tinged and colored, as it were tuned and orchestrated, by the new affective phenomena and the new registering apparatuses designed to capture them. (2013, 42)

This is a brilliantly phrased theory but it gains additional clarity when we conceptualize the registering apparatus of affect as a modification of a prior bodily machine, one that once processed emotional states as part of a spiritual economy, but, that earlier economy being now defunct, has been repurposed to become our modern pathways of affect.

Slavoj Žižek titled a recent book of his on our era (the era of the cogito) *Less Than Nothing*; yet never once does he recognize that what is tangibly under our current nothing, less than our current nothing, is the earlier epoch committed to phantasms, spirit, and most critically, the practice of magic as a means to manipulate the spiritual relations with the phantasms around us. Žižek (2012) stakes out his position in his presentation of Descartes' project. First he quotes Derrida's analysis of Descartes:

> the Cogito escapes madness only because at its own moment, under its own authorship, it is valid even if I am mad, even if my thoughts are completely mad. … as soon as Descartes has reached this extremity, he seeks to reassure himself to certify the Cogito through God, to identify the act of the Cogito with reasonable reason. (quoted on 330)

Žižek then comments that the subsequent tradition of German Idealism will replace God with "the abyss of darkness, the 'Night of the World' " (330). But it is not the case that the philosophical tradition is then just an effort to "think the abyss of madness at the core of subjectivity" (331) but is at the same time an effort to rethink how madness also names the vanishing of the regime of the spirit (Agamben's pneumophantasmology). Consider this account of epilepsy from a well-known medical treatise, Dr. Willis's *Practice of Physick*, published in 1684. His understanding of epilepsy is that "The Spirits inhabiting the middle of the brain are the primary subject of this disease"(69). He adds that disease is not brought so much to the solid parts as to the Sprits themselves. Willis explains that "the explosive particles of the Spirits, and this Copula knocking one against another, stir up the falling fit" (69). Here we see the power of an earlier hegemonic ideology, one where it is possible to imagine that the medical disease of epilepsy is a malady of the soul, and that death is the secondary effect that follows from the death of the soul. This world view, I submit, is best categorized as pre-modern. The modern is where questions of "spirit" have been banished from the discourse of Science by making the soul an intangible entity that is relegated to conversations concerning theology. The postmodern represents a return of the repressed; witness our routine head-shaking at the fundamentalists we now see around us.

As a way to conclude this brief paper I would like to review the ending of one of Shakespeare's most popular comedies in order to use it as an illustration of the change that has been my subject here. In *Much Ado About Nothing*, Claudio jilts his betrothed Hero at the altar: he declares that he will not "knit my soule to an approved wanton" (4.1.44). Claudio bids Hero farewell, pledging that "on my eie-lids shall Coniecture hang, / To turne all beauty into thoughts of harme" (4.1.106–7). Beatrice, Hero's cousin, then utters a signaling line: "Why how now cosin, wherefore sink you down?" (4.1.110). The villain Don John conjectures, "these things, come thus to light, / Smother her spirits up" (4.1.111–12). All the characters now presume Hero dead: her father exclaims, "O Fate! Take not away thy heavy hand, / Death is the fairest cover for her shame / That may be wisht for" (4.1.115–17). My students smile at this device. And they are right to smile. Today we are unable to suspend our disbelief at Hero's fainting spell because we do not live under the regime of the spirit. We do not believe that the death of the spirit can induce mortal death. But of course at the same time, for Shakespeare's plot to function, he and his audience must already be sliding out from under this older regime. Indeed my contention here is that his plots illustrate the coming exhaustion of the older regime while also fashioning its replacement—affect. Once Hero revives, the Friar shares his plan to fake her death. At the play's conclusion, Claudio weds unseen a woman who he is told is Hero's cousin. When this woman is revealed to be none other than Hero, the characters then respond with language that guides us in our collective response. Hero says: "And when I liv'd, I was your other wife, / And when you lov'd, you were my other husband." Claudio exclaims: "Another *Hero!*" Hero responds: "Nothing certainer. / One *Hero* died defiled, but I doe live, / And surely as I live, I am a maid." Don Pedro, the Duke, exclaims: "The former *Hero*, *Hero* that is dead." To which Hero's father concludes: "She died my Lord, but whiles her slander liv'd" (5.4.60–66). Here we see how a theatrical miracle replaces a theological miracle. The proper response to such a device is not an expression of the spirit, but an expression of the theatricalized body.

This halfway house of the dramatized body is then replaced by the fully modernized body of affect when the privileged site for the study of embodied response changes from the theater to the reading room. This shift, the shearing away of the viewer from the collective and his transformation into the solitary reader, is what signals high modernism for Jameson, a movement he finds epitomized in the stream of consciousness technique refined in the novel. Interestingly, the specter of the theater then returns as cinema overtakes literature, but in this next phase, the former collective experience of drama cannot be reconstituted because of the barrier of technology. Film can gesture at the illusion of breaking the fourth wall, but the brute fact that we are watching projected images on a screen frustrates the dynamic effect of that earlier device: the soliloquy. The return to something like early modern theatricality is only made possible with the emergence in technology of the current wave of social digital media. Theorizing our current regime, which we may call the age of the collective mediated body, is an interesting prospect, but for now it must remain only that and serve instead as a place to end.

References

Agamben, Giorgio. 1992. *Stanzas: Word and Phantasm in Western Culture*. Minneapolis: University of Minnesota Press.

Hunt, Maurice. 1990. *Shakespeare's Romance of the World*. Bucknell: Bucknell University Press.

Jameson, Fredric. 2013. *Antinomies of Realism*. London: Verso.

Shakespeare, William. 1609. *Quatro 1. The Sonnets*. London: Thomas Thorpe. Accessed January 20, 2017. http://bit.ly/2kX49DE.

Shakespeare, William. 1623. *First Folio. Comedies, Histories, & Tragedies*. London: William Jaggard, Edward Blount, L. Smithweeke, and W. Aspley. Accessed January 20, 2017. http://bit.ly/2jEzIBo.

Wells, Marion. 2007. *The Secret Wound*. Palo Alto: Stanford University Press.

Willis, Thomas. 1684. *Dr. Willis's Practice of Physick*. London: Dring.

Žižek, Slavoj. 2012. *Less than Nothing*. London: Verso.

CHAPTER FOURTEEN

THE RE-EVALUATION OF FEMALE AND QUEER BODIES IN SELECTED WORKS OF CONTEMPORARY POLISH LITERATURE

KATARZYNA LISOWSKA

The aim of this study is to analyze the role of literature in the re-evaluation of the bodies marginalized in the discourse and culture. The excluded corporeal experiences are often the experiences of women and non-heterosexuals. The main idea of the paper is that literature, by representing the silenced other and revealing problematic issues, participates in the reformulation and the broadening of the discursive and literary imagination. I will analyze these issues by engaging with two theories in which bodily experience plays a significant role,[1] namely, Richard Shusterman's somaesthetics and Judith Butler's idea of gender performativity.[2] The analysis will involve texts selected from contemporary Polish prose writing.

I will start with discussing Shusterman's and Butler's concepts which are to be applied in the study. The main objective of somaesthetics is to emphasize the role and value of our bodily experience. The importance of corporeality is stressed with reference to everyday practice and to philosophical tradition (Shusterman 2000, 139–40). Somaesthetics, which includes an analytic, pragmatic and practical dimension (Shusterman 2008, 23–24, 29), allows for the reinterpretation of the meaning of the body, which was traditionally denigrated in Judeo-Christian culture (Shusterman 2000, 145–47). In my readings, Butler's theory is particularly inspirational for the two ideas which, in her philosophy, are emphasized: that of the artificiality of gender identity, which is considered to be a cultural and social construct (Butler 1990, 136–37), and that of the role of materializing the body in discourse (Butler 1993a, 16). Referring to Butler's ideas, I will also pose a question about the possibility of resignification and reformulation (Butler 1993a, 1993b) of the social norms that regulate our bodily and sexual experience (Butler 1990, 1993a, 1993b).

Femininity in the Masculine Text

From the above philosophical and theoretical perspective, it is worthwhile to look at Szczepan Twardoch's short story *Masara*,[3] which seems to provide a literary illustration of the concepts of somaesthetics regarded with respect to its two dimensions: pragmatic (that is, aimed at suggesting certain styles of perfecting the body) and practical (that is, focused on applying the methods of the improvement of the somatic aspect of the self).[4] Furthermore, this narrative, if viewed in the context of Butler's philosophy, allows us to notice various other dimensions of corporeality.

The short story is divided into two parts. The narrator of the first one is a seventeen-year-old girl, Paulina, who is obese. Her suffering has mainly to do with the social stigma which she experiences. The criticism voiced by her environment, the family and the peer group, determines her view of herself.[5] She has been dubbed "Masara," which in Silesian dialect (the action takes place in Upper Silesia) means "a disgusting, fat fly" (MS, 66).[6]

Although Paulina's intellectual qualities are not highly valued either (MS, 71), it seems that the reason for the prevailing dislike for the girl is her body (71). Female subjectivity, reduced to corporeality,[7] is regarded as an object of evaluation; subjectivity-as-body should undergo various beautifying procedures.

However, it should also be noted that the emphasis on the character's emotions and self-evaluation creates in the story a point of view which is not discordant with the perspective of experiential somaesthetics focusing on individual experience of the body (Shusterman 2008, 26). Therefore, the pragmatic and practical dimensions of Shusterman's concept are, as it were, paralleled by the suggestions voiced by the characters (MS, 73). Also the later transformation of Paulina is inseparable from the emotional background of the narration. This issue is discussed as it is present in both parts of the analyzed short story.

In the second part the narrator and central character changes. The story is told by Marek, Paulina's classmate from secondary school. In this section the adult lives of the characters are described. Marek hears about Paulina, who has become a completely different person in terms of the body and soul (MS, 85). Remorse, combined with unclear anxiety, forces Marek to meet Paulina. Yet again, the woman seems to be described only as an aesthetic object (MS, 96, 98). However, it is clear that this transformation is deeply rooted in her feelings and experiences, namely in the love she used to feel to Marek (MS, 98).

An issue which requires separate analysis is the anxiety that Paulina's behavior and appearance arouse. When Marek confesses that he is afraid of Paulina (MS, 98), it seems that such fear and uncertainty are caused by the power of gender performativity revealed by the woman's transformation.[8] Thus, referring to Butler's ideas, I would like to argue that Paulina's story highlights, but also grotesquely inflates, the mechanisms of embodying the fictional and normative ideal of gender identity. Her gestures and acts, notions which I employ after Butler, serve to create the perfect realization of the female body. Although, as Butler shows, the procedures of building a fiction of the individual identity and sexuality are unavoidable (1993a, 2),[9] and their demonstration, as in Paulina's case, could serve as a disturbing disillusion, it is important to note that the character's behavior is not meant to be subversive. The heroine's practices do not lead to the resignification of the binding norms, the possibility of which was suggested by Butler (1993a, 21–22),[10] but, on the contrary, they hyperbolize the consequences of applying the existing rules. However, in a deeper sense such hyperbole could be treated as a subversion which, while imitating gestures and acts, exposes their artificial, accidental and often interrupted character and, as a consequence, undermines the idea of stable gender identity.

It should be noted that, interestingly, the construction of female characters presented in the foregoing paragraphs could be also treated as a sign of a masculinity crisis.[11] Indeed, the story signals the male anxiety and disorientation caused by the transformation of the traditional hierarchy. As a consequence, masculinity, treated as a performative construct, as this notion was introduced by Butler (1990), is unstable and ambivalent, which allows us to describe the characters in terms of an uncertain, queer identity. Their experience is described and, to a certain degree, re-evaluated, too.

Female Reinterpretation

Attempts to re-evaluate the woman's body can also be found in Ewa Schilling's novel *Akacja* (Acacia, 2001).[12] Similarly to Twardoch's short story, this text describes bodies in pain. However, the suffering of Schilling's heroines differs from the experiences of Paulina in *Masara*; Schilling's novel also reinterprets the motif of female madness. *Akacja* was published together with another short novel, *Wrzosowisko* (The Heath), as a single book. The book, thus, comprises two short novels taking place in the same setting (a small town in Warmia) and at the same time (just after the Second World War), and has the same characters (however, the main heroines in each story are different). The first part, *Wrzosowisko* (The Heath), describes the friendship between a young woman, Emilia, and a teenager, Charlotte, who is epileptic. During the war, Charlotte was raped by a Russian soldier (AK, 10–11) and Emilia was a patient at a German psychiatric hospital. At the end of the war she ran away and hid herself in the forest until she was found by Charlotte. The main subject of the second part (titled *Akacja*) of the book is the friendship between two young women, Małgorzata and Alina. Alina, who was an inmate of the concentration camp Ravensbrück, still wrestles with both the psychic and physical consequences (AK, 183) of having been imprisoned; she is afflicted with incurable tuberculosis. Her health further deteriorates (AK, 245–48) after a few months spent in a Polish prison, where she was confined for political reasons (AK, 215).

By recalling the motif of a woman's madness Schilling's novels refer to a well-known *topos* in female literature (Kraskowska 1999, 211). However, mental disorder—often presented, especially in 19th-century literature, as a typical female disease[13]—is re-evaluated by Schilling as a sign of female community (Iwasiów 1999, 46). I use the word "madness" as a name for various borderline experiences which represent "psychic discomfort" connected with the female condition (Iwasiów 1999, 46). Therefore, it is possible to describe Emilia's illness (which could be treated as a cultural construct),[14] Charlotte's epilepsy and Alina's post-war trauma as women's signatures in the world created in the novel. It is also very important that the "diseases" mentioned in the novels include suffering of both the body and the soul. The characters' reciprocal concern for each other's corporeality can be treated as a sign of breaking free from the dualism of human nature, which makes the ideas presented in the novels similar to those which animate the concerns of somaesthetics and feminism.[15] Through the representation of ugly, suffering bodies, the narration situates itself in opposition to the tendency to idealize and beautify female corporeality (AK, 13, 183).

Schilling's novels also re-evaluate the issue of female sexuality, a significant aspect of the corporeal. The narrative depicts a homosexual desire between the characters.[16] As a consequence, the novel could be considered as a protest against the invisibility of lesbians in culture (Mizielińska 2006, 97–110). In the first part of the book, the homosexual aspect of the friendship between Emilia and Charlotte is only suggested (AK, 86), while in the second part, it is expressed clearly (AK, 210).

Thus, the project of the re-evaluation of female corporeality constructed in Schilling's novel is wide and complex. It includes the reinterpretation of "female diseases," the representation of various women's experiences, the protest against the idealization of the female body and the expression of lesbian desire. These issues can be considered not only from the perspective of somaesthetics but also from the point of view of feminist studies. Schilling engages with such popular motives as female madness and romantic friendship which, rooted as they are in the literary tradition, in her texts reveal their conventional status and therefore recall Butler's concept of gender performativity and artificiality. Her characters perform their femininity and at the same time re-evaluate its discursive and cultural position.

Queer Bodies: Two Perspectives

Recently published literature in the Polish language, including works by Izabela Filipiak and Michał Witkowski, also engage with the problem of the representation of the queer body. I will start with an analysis of Izabela Filipiak's project, which is aimed at the re-evaluation of the biography of Maria Komornicka, a poet and writer who was active at the turn of the 20th century. Although Komornicka died in 1949, she disappeared from public life as early as 1907. The reason for that was her/his decision to consider herself/himself a man and to use the name of Piotr Włast. This gender transformation was not accepted by the poet's milieu. Włast/Komornicka was regarded as a mentally ill person. Therefore, after treatment in various psychiatric hospitals, he/she was isolated from society.

Filipiak's project, rooted in queer criticism, includes the reinterpretation of the author's life and works taken as a whole. What is more, Filipiak uses both literary (theatrical drama)[17] and non-literary (academic dissertation and essay)[18] forms of communication to develop her ideas. I will focus on the first type of text, which is represented by the biographical drama *Księga Em* (The Book of Em, 2005).[19] The non-literary works, for their part, provide a context which broadens the concepts expressed in the drama.

It is important that in her analyses, Filipiak considers corporeality as an integral, and very significant, aspect of Komornicka's existence.[20] Her aim is to present the experience of the poet and the writer as embodied. Therefore, her reinterpretation could be situated in the perspective of somaesthetics. Another important aspect of Filipiak's project, the idea of gender performativity, lends itself to interpretation in the context of

Butler's philosophy. References to these two concepts will be combined in the brief overview presented below.

The corporeal aspect of Komornicka's existence is described in various ways. As noted by Błażej Warkocki, in the drama, Em's/Komornicka's transformation is presented in the form of the erotic scene (2007, 177) of an encounter between the main character and an androgynous incubus (KE, 51–55). The emphasis on the corporeal aspect of the plot's dramatic climax and of Komornicka's biography is definitely worth noting. For Filipiak, the somatic aspect of the embodying of the gender norms is connected with painful experiences, too.[21] This idea is present in the drama, e.g., in the scene of the meeting with the seller of aching-gender plaster (KE, 74–77). Like Schilling, Filipiak stresses also the sexual aspect of corporeality. Therefore, her drama indicates the subtly erotic (KE, 48–50, Warkocki 2007, 176) aspects of Komornicka's texts and biography.[22]

In this way, Filipiak argues that Komornicka's body, which failed to materialize within the framework of heterosexual discourse, aimed at resignifying marginalized corporeal practices or at introducing alternative corporeal behavior.[23] Therefore she presents Komornicka's transformation in terms of subversion. Filipiak claims that the poet could identify herself/himself with neither the feminist nor the misogynist discourse of her times (Filipiak 2006b, 89). The ambiguity of the character can be noticed in the scene of the train journey. The scene metaphorically describes Em's identity, which was not female but not male either (KE, 81).

Furthermore, Filipiak argues that Komornicka's biography reveals that the social constraint to repeat certain acts, gestures and norms gives rise to unavoidable differences between particular practices and therefore deprives gender identity of stability (Butler 1993b, 317).[24] Filipiak indicates that Komornicka turned out to be "a subversive factor" (2006b, 410) which destroyed the binary gender system (410). As Butler stresses, such a transformation is enabled by gender performativity, which allows one to oppose the dominating order (1993a, 241). For Filipiak, the queerness of the subject created by Komornicka/Włast in her/his works and biography is a privilege (2000, 139). She/he can play with gender roles and reinterpret the discourse to describe his/her experience (139).

Filipiak seems to remember that, although such reformulation of gender norms starts from the individual body (Butler 1993b, 317–18),[25] it can inspire changes in the dominating discourse as a whole (Butler 1993a, 241). As a consequence, subversion proves that culture is prone to changes (Chołuj 1995, 73). Filipiak, by creating "a happy queer" (Warkocki 2007, 179), reveals the existence of marginalized subjects and, at the same time, re-evaluates their painful corporeal experience, which is often treated as pathological (Hyży 2003, 242). This is achieved by means of the idea of gender performativity and its subversive power.

The representation of the queer body in Filipiak's texts could be juxtaposed with the treatment that this same topic receives in Michał Witkowski's prose. I will present a short overview of two of his novels, *Lubiewo* (*Lovetown*, 2010)[26] and *Drwal* (*The Lumberjack*, 2011),[27] to analyze the specificity of the perspective adopted in the texts and indicate the similarities and differences between the works of these two authors.

Both novels could be situated in the context of queer studies. This field of study is openly invoked in *Lovetown* (*Lubiewo*) in a passage titled *Theories* (LV, 305–7).[28] However, queer theory is also present in the background of the narrative in both books. The problem of gender performativity is extensively presented in both novels. The main subject of the first of them, *Lovetown*, is a specifically Polish gay subculture. It is created by a group of elderly men whose youth had been passed in the times of the Polish People's Republic. At the beginning of the 21st century, when the action takes place, they are a marginalized (also among other minority groups) and forgotten part of society. However, they still practice a performance aimed at finding sexual partners (LV, 6). The performance is based on acts and gestures which imitate female behavior (LV, 6). Thus they deploy the essentially Butlerian assumption that identity is a fabrication—produced through corporeal and discursive practices (Butler 1990, 136).

The same strategy is present in the second novel, *Drwal* (*The Lumberjack*). Here the notion of gender performativity is widened and includes both hetero- and homosexual (or rather queer) behaviors. The narrator suggests that it is not only acts and gestures that are signs of gender stereotypes, but language too is oppressive and possesses stigmatizing power (DR, 85–86).

Thus, in both *Lovetown* and *The Lumberjack* corporeality is presented as the space of a possible protest against the norms that discipline the body; the same understanding of the bodily dimension—as the space for dissent and personal freedom—can be also found in Shusterman (2000, 140; 2008, 78) and Butler (1993a, 21–22, 223–42). This view of the body as a site for liberation is suggested by indicating the artificial and conventional, and therefore potentially susceptible to change, aspects of gender norms (Butler 1993b, 317–18). What is more, in *Lovetown*, it is old, suffering and sick bodies that are often depicted (Madejski 2005, 9). The narrative includes the story of Di, who has been a prostitute in Vienna

(LV, 132–48) and the story of Jessie/Zdzicha Aidsova who suffers from
AIDS (28–34, 49–51).

However, it seems that, when compared with Filipiak's novels, these
works focus more on the external aspects of gender performativity. As
argued by Warkocki (2013, 119–25), the world presented in *Lovetown* is
not supposed to be revolutionary.[29] The same could be said of *The
Lumberjack*. The problems described above can easily be situated within
the aesthetics of camp (*Lovetown*)[30] or parody and the grotesque (*The
Lumberjack*), and they could to some extent be interpreted from the
perspective of queer theory.[31] But they can also be contextualized within
the broader tendency of the somatic turn in philosophy, of which
Shusterman's somaesthetics is both a fruit and an inspiration, restoring the
notion of the body and stressing the need to introduce alternative corporeal
practices.

Conclusion

If literature has the power to re-evaluate marginalized bodies, this is
because of the special ability of a literary text to reveal and deconstruct
cultural images of corporeality and to combine the collective experience
with the individual one (Łebkowska 2006, 400). The problem of the
representation of corporeality in literature could be analyzed from various
perspectives. My aim was to situate this issue in the context of
somaesthetics and the concept of gender performativity. It needs to be said
that both theories were applied to the texts in different ways. Butler's ideas
apply mainly to texts in which the transgression of the norms of
heterosexual discourse (as in Schilling's and Witkowski's prose, and
Filipiak's drama) is presented. Filipiak and Witkowski refer to the idea of
gender performativity openly. As a consequence, one may argue that
Butler's theory is one of the basic contexts in which these works can be
situated. Somaesthetics, in turn, was treated as a broader frame in which
the issue of literary representation and re-evaluation of the body could be
placed. While the emphasis on the idea of body consciousness and
corporeal development (Shusterman 2008, 29) was the basic somaesthetic
concept applied in the paper, Butler's reflection served as the main point
of reference in the analysis of the texts which describe the marginalized
corporeal experience.

It could be concluded that, by describing various corporeal and sexual
experiences (lesbianism, masculinity crisis, gender transformation), the
analyzed texts demonstrate that these issues should be treated as important
subjects of literary reflection. The presentation of corporeality becomes a

field in which individual and collective perspective can be combined. One should remember that, as Butler observes, representation is also the act of naming a certain phenomenon and therefore materializing it in the discourse (1993a).[32] Thus, by re-evaluating marginalized bodies literature may confirm its ability to support the transformation of culture and discourse,[33] so that both spheres could be broadened[34] and, therefore, capable of including more types of gender identity and experience in the reservoir of social imagination.

References

Badinter, Elisabeth. 1993. *XY—tożsamość mężczyzny* [XY: On masculine identity]. Translated by Grzegorz Przewłocki. Warszawa: W.A.B.

Boniecki Edward. 1998. *Modernistyczny dramat ciała: Maria Komornicka* [A modernist drama of the body: Maria Komornicka]. Warszawa: Wydawnictwo IBL.

Butler, Judith. 1990. *Gender Trouble: Feminism and the Subversion of Identity*. New York: Routledge.

—. 1993a. *Bodies That Matter: On the Discursive Limits of "Sex."* New York: Routledge.

—. 1993b. "Imitation and Gender Insubordination." In *The Lesbian and Gay Studies Reader*. Edited by Henry Abelove, Michèle Aina Barale, and David M. Halperin, 307–20. New York: Routledge.

Chołuj, Bożena. 1995. "Tożsamość płci—natura czy kultura?" [Gender identity—nature or culture?]. *Spotkania Feministyczne: Warszawa 1994/1995*, 68–73. Warszawa: Res Publica Nova.

Filipiak, Izabela. 2000. "W. +M. =M. W." In *Nowa świadomość płci w modernizmie. Studia spod znaku gender w kulturze polskiej i rosyjskiej u schyłku stulecia* [The new awareness of gender in modernity: Gender studies in Polish and Russian culture at the end of the century]. Edited by German Ritz, Christa Binswanger, Carmen Scheide, 111–40. Kraków: Universitas.

—. 2005. *Księga Em* [The book of Em]. Warszawa: tCHu.

—. 2006a. *Absolutna amnezja* [Absolute amnesia]. Warszawa: tCHu.

—. 2006b. *Obszary odmienności. Rzecz o Marii Komornickiej* [Areas of alterity: On Maria Komornicka]. Gdańsk: Słowo/Obraz Terytoria.

Gilbert, Sandra M., and Susan Gubar. 1984. *The Madwoman in the Attic: The Woman Writer and the Nineteenth-Century Literary Imagination*. New Haven: Yale University Press.

Hyży, Ewa. 2003. *Kobieta, ciało, tożsamość—teorie podmiotu w filozofii feministycznej końca XX wieku* [Woman, body, identity: Theories of

the subject in the feminist philosophy of the end of the 20th century].
Kraków: Universitas.
Iwasiów, Inga. 1999. "Gatunki i konfesje w badaniach 'gender' " [Genres
and confessions in 'gender' studies]. *Teksty Drugie*, no. 6: 41–55.
—. 2005."Alexis. Gdzie jest kobiecość?" [Alexis: Where is femininity?].
Pogranicza, no. 1: 27–30.
Janion, Maria. 1996 *Kobiety i duch inności* [Women and the spirit of
otherness]. Warszawa: Wydawnictwo Sic!.
Jarzębowski, Zbigniew. 2005. " 'piszę tę ciotowską księgę…' " ["I am
writing this queer book…"]. *Pogranicza*, no. 1: 19–21.
Kraskowska, Ewa. 1999. *Piórem niewieścim. Z problemów prozy kobiecej
dwudziestolecia międzywojennego* [Written by a woman: Studies in
female prose writing of the interwar years]. Poznań: Wydawnictwo
Naukowe UAM.
Łebkowska, Anna. 2006. "Gender." In *Kulturowa teoria literatury.
Główne pojęcia i problemy* [Cultural literary theory: Main notions and
issues]. Edited by Michał Paweł Markowski, and Ryszard Nycz, 367–
407. Kraków: Universitas.
—. 2012. "Somatopoetyka" [Somatopoetics]. In *Kulturowa teoria
literatury 2. Poetyki, problematyki, interpretacje* [Cultural literary
theory 2. Poetics, questions, interpretations]. Edited by Teresa Walas,
and Ryszard Nycz, 101–36. Kraków: Universitas.
Madejski, Jerzy. 2005. "Żorżeta, przegięcie, literatura" [Żorżeta, drag,
literature]. *Pogranicza*, no. 1: 7–10.
Melosik, Zbyszko. 2002. *Kryzys męskości w kulturze współczesnej*
[Masculinity crisis in contemporary culture]. Poznań: Wolumin.
Mizielińska, Joanna 2004. (*De)Konstrukcje kobiecości. Podmiot
feminizmu a problem wykluczenia* [(De)Constructions of femininity:
The subject of feminism and the issue of foreclosure]. Gdańsk:
Słowo/Obraz Terytoria.
—. 2006. *Płeć, ciało, seksualność. Od feminizmu do teorii queer* [Gender,
body, sexuality: From feminism to queer theory]. Kraków: Universitas.
Pancewicz-Puchalska, Magdalena. 2007. "Performatywność—materia—
płeć. O dekonstrukcji tożsamości Judith Butler" [Performativity—
materiality—gender: On Judith Butler's deconstruction of identity]. In:
Lektury poststrukturalistyczne [Poststructuralist lectures]. Edited by
Katarzyna Liszka and Rafał Włodarczyk, 35–42. Wrocław: Chiazm.
Schilling, Ewa. 2001. *Akacja* [Acacia]. Olsztyn: Wspólnota Kulturowa
Borussia.
Shusterman, Richard. 2000. *Performing Live: Aesthetic Alternatives for
the Ends of Art*. Ithaca: Cornell University Press.

—. 2008. *Body Consciousness: A Philosophy of Mindfulness and Somaesthetics*. Cambridge: Cambridge University Press.
Śmietana, Urszula. 2003. "Od écriture féminine do 'somatekstu.' Ciało w dyskursie feministycznym" [From écriture féminine to "somatext": The body in feminist discourse]. *Przegląd Filozoficzno-Literacki*, no. 1: 153–71.
Twardoch, Szczepan. 2011. "Masara." In *Tak jest dobrze* [It's all right]. Szczepan Twardoch, 61–98. Warszawa: Powergraph.
Warkocki, Błażej. 2007. *Homo niewiadomo. Polska proza wobec odmienności* [A queer: Polish prose and alterity]. Warszawa: Wydawnictwo Sic!.
—. 2013. *Różowy język. Literatura i polityka kultury na początku wieku* [Pink tongue: Literature and the politics of culture at the beginning of the century]. Warszawa: Wydawnictwo Krytyki Politycznej.
Witkowski, Michał. 2010. *Lovetown*. Translated by William Martin. London: Portobello Books.
—. 2011. *Drwal* [*The Lumberjack*]. Warszawa: Świat Książki.

Notes

[1] These theories belong to the broad stream of the contemporary humanities that is focused on re-evaluation of corporeality. For more about this issue with reference to literary studies, see e.g., Łebkowska 2012.
[2] Another important point of reference is feminist studies, which enables me to broaden Shusterman's and Butler's concepts. However, the emphasis will be put on the relations between literary studies, somaesthetics and the idea of gender performativity.
[3] Twardoch 2011, 61–98. Further quoted as MS.
[4] For the discussion of the dimensions of somaesthetics, see Shusterman 2008, 23–24, 29.
[5] See MS, 67–68, 72.
[6] My translation. All translations of quotations, unless otherwise stated, are mine.
[7] For a brief presentation of the issue of female corporeality in the feminist discourse see: Śmietana 2003, 153–71 (especially p. 154).
[8] The following interpretation of Paulina is done mostly in the light of Judith Butler's ideas presented in *Gender Trouble* (see chapter *Bodily Inscriptions, Performative Subversions* in: Butler 1990, 128–41).
[9] I owe this reference to Mizielińska 2004, 192–93.
[10] I owe this reference to Pancewicz-Puchalska 2007, 41.
[11] For more about the contemporary masculinity crisis, see e.g. Badinter 1993, Melosik 2002.
[12] Further cited as AK.
[13] See Gilbert and Gubar 1984, 53.

[14] See the part of Emilia's aestheticized narration about the psychiatric hospital (AK, 50).

[15] Cf. Shusterman 2000, 145–47; 2008, 93–94, and Śmietana 2003, 154, respectively.

[16] I focus on lesbianism, which is an important issue in the novel's narration. However, the reader will find some signs of male homosexuality, too (AK, 94, 199).

[17] It should be mentioned that references to Komornicka's biography appear in Filipiak's novel *Absolutna amnezja*, too. See for example the character named Lisiak, who is a patient at a psychiatric hospital (Filipiak 2006a, 186–92). However, unlike in the drama *Księga Em*, these references are, though important, not the main subject of narration. Therefore, the analysis of Filipiak's literary texts will address *Księga Em* only.

[18] See Filipiak 2000, 2006b.

[19] Further cited as KE.

[20] It needs to be said that the first Polish works on Komornicka's creativity and life analyzed Komornicka's transformation in terms of ideology or individual transformation and spirituality which frees the individual from corporeality. See Janion 1996, Boniecki 1998.

[21] I refer to Butler's concept of materiality understood as violations (1993a, 29) performed on an individual body.

[22] See Filipiak 2006b, 246–80.

[23] This interpretation is made in the light of Butler's idea of the materialization of heteronormativity in individual bodies and her remarks on resignification of the symbolic order (Butler 1993a). Another important context is Shusterman's emphasis on the role of alternative corporeal practices (Shusterman 2000, 140).

[24] I owe the reference to Butler to Magdalena Pancewicz-Puchalska (Pancewicz-Puchalska 2007, 41).

[25] I owe the reference to Butler to Magdalena Pancewicz-Puchalska (Pancewicz-Puchalska 2007, 41). See also: Shusterman 2008, 99–100.

[26] Further cited as LV.

[27] Further cited to as DR.

[28] Another context recalled in the excerpt is camp theory (LV, 305).

[29] However, as I argue above, there are features which make the book participate in the re-evaluation of the literary representation of queer bodies.

[30] See Warkocki 2013, 116, 124.

[31] Queer perspective has been applied to the novel in numerous essays and reviews. See, e.g., Madejski 2005, Jarzębowski 2005, Iwasiów 2005.

[32] See also Mizielińska 2004, 192–93, Hyży 2003, 175–81.

[33] Such conclusion is also to be found in Chołuj 1995, 73.

[34] I refer to the metaphor used by Filipiak, who argued that Komornicka had the tendency to broaden the "previously unowned, systematically familiarized, fields" and "locate herself/himself on the borders" (2006b, 486).

Chapter Fifteen

The Aesthetics of the Body in Mircea Cărtărescu's Prose

Iulia Maria Rădac

The attempt to investigate a literary text from a new perspective, one that employs uncommon instruments, is frequently risky for a number of reasons. It will inspire the skepticism, or even criticism, of the main actors on the literary scene. The authorized voices will always impute to it a lack of direction, and accuse it of straying away from the hermeneutical tradition if the method is completely new. An experimental perspective will be perceived either as partial, in the case of close readings, or, on the contrary, as too general, if the approach is transdisciplinary. In the latter case the main fear is that the literary object loses its particularity.

The decision to carry literature out of its comfort zone is by no means a necessary exercise of validation and innovation for the domain; following the direction of literary studies of recent years, it seems that Romanian critique has understood this. Along with the great opening of literature onto the aesthetics of the body, which began in postmodernism and which can also be perceived in the realms of the last decade's prose and poetry, literary studies have started to pay close attention to corporeality. Body studies are present in Romanian humanities, in psycho-critique and in psychoanalytic critique. In 2008, Simona Sora, known for her journalistic activity in Romanian culture, published a warmly-received study about the body in literature, a result of her doctoral research. Speaking about her book, *Regăsirea intimității* (The Retrieval of Intimacy: The Body in Romanian Interwar and Post-revolutionary Prose), Sora admits to dealing with an unusual problem:

> The body, corporeality, the living body are not popular subjects nowadays in Romania. "The indubitable body," "the body of the soul," "the body alone" seem to be weak concepts, convenient umbrellas for theoretical outpouring, for French-like (or American) seminars, used especially by

doubtful researchers who are looking for peripheries, ambiguous amateurs of interdisciplinary boundaries and those who are splitting hairs. The "tough," actual subjects are from a different area: the mechanisms of repression and censorship during communism, the resistance through culture, memory and (anti)nostalgia, re-education and persecution, the embrace and refusal of ideology, the idyllic and fragmentary mirror of the inter-war period.[1] (2008, 242)

Gheorghe Crăciun (2009), a Romanian postmodern writer and the most important theoretician of the phenomenon, analyzes our prose through the same prism. His book entitled *Pactul somatografic* (The Somatographic Pact) is not a theoretical study, but an essay voicing the author's artistic beliefs. The affinity between Crăciun's thought and Richard Shusterman's somaesthetics is easily observable. It is my intention, in mentioning these two books, Sora's and Crăciun's, to demonstrate that the need to reevaluate the eternal theme of mind-body dualism is recognized in Romanian critique and also to indicate, albeit very briefly, how this theme has been approached.

The aim of my paper is to investigate the representation of the body and its narrative consequences in Mircea Cărtărescu's novel, *Travesti* (Disguise), in which the body functions as an obsession that propels the mechanism of writing, and is also responsible for the modality of constructing the narrator's identity and discourse. The memory of seeing and being touched by a particular obsessive body makes the narrator psychologically and somatically vulnerable. He recalls images, which are basically representations, and emotions, which are a complex of sensations constituting the experience. Cărtărescu's work is about a somatic experience—but it also is a somatic experience embodied in the text, as I intend to interpret it through the prism of Richard Shusterman's somaesthetics. The debate over the limits or possible shortcomings of somaesthetics has involved, on several occasions, even the author of the theory, but a critical approach is not the focus of my paper. I rather intend to look at somaesthetics—abstaining from a critical analysis—as an inspiration for a different possible analysis and interpretation of a literary object, a signal that the literary-text resources are not fully investigated with methods specific exclusively to literary criticism. For instance, the reading of the chosen text in the perspective of somaesthetics reveals that, so far, criticism has ignored the blind spots of what is generally called the ineffableness, or the genius, of Cărtărescu. Cărtărescu's prose, where the references to the body are very important, has a hypnotic effect on the reader. The way he presents somatic experience produces a specific type of text. In his prose works, the narrator becomes a performer who employs various strategies to seduce the reader.

Mircea Cărtărescu is often considered to be the greatest Romanian writer of the present day. Born in Bucharest on 1 June 1956, he is one of the most important voices of Romania's "Blue Jeans Generation." After graduating from the Faculty of Letters and up to the Romanian Revolution in 1989, he had no option but to choose a teaching career in a secondary school in Bucharest, as all his colleagues did. At present he is employed as an Associate Professor in the Romanian Literature Department of the University of Bucharest. Known equally as a poet, novelist, essayist, literary critic, journalist, member of the Romanian Writers' Union and of the European Cultural Parliament, he enjoys great public success but also a warm critical climate. Cărtărescu has published over 25 books and a large number of articles. So far his work has been translated into over fourteen languages; he has won prestigious national[2] and international literary awards,[3] and in the last three years he was nominated for the Nobel Prize in Literature. He was a special guest of the Conrad Festival in Kraków, in Poland, in 2014.

What makes Cărtărescu so widely appreciated is the remarkable force of his narrative and his capacity to use all the registers of the Romanian language, from the lower ones to the more refined. His fluid discourse mixes classical references with elements of fantasy. In the universe of his work one can see the deepest abyss of the human soul and unique metaphysical projections of the individual, all of them expressions of a visionary and ludic imagination. In the *Romanian General Dictionary of Literature*, Cărtărescu's poetry is characterized as representing

> rudimentary urbanism, bohemian Beat, anti-lyricism and anti-metaphor, invasion of objects, everything that is non-poetic turned into poetic, imagistic insurgency, hippy prose, reality buried in poems, devouring psychedelics of the lexical inflation infiltrated into cynic realism, parody of the greatest poetical schools, the cult of derision, associative craziness (biology and gastronomy, neurology and metaphysics, gynecology and cabala etc.)—everything that could startle and drive crazy the dictatorial isolation of Romanian politics of the '80s. (*Dicţionarul General al Literaturii române* 2004, 153)

The same dictionary mentions that in an interview given to the Romanian magazine *Dilema* in 1996, he declares that "he is not bothered with himself as a poet" and that he was "sick and tired of his own poetry" when he was writing one of his most appreciated poems, *The Levant* (1990). He also states that the collective-generational phenomenon is completely out of date and irrelevant, and his novel *Travesti* (Disguise) is a "semi-failure." By contrast, its enthusiastic international reception proves the opposite, namely that Cărtărescu's prose deserves to rest on the first shelf of a symbolic universal library. In the English edition of Cărtărescu's first book of prose—*Nostalgia*—the essayist Andrei Codrescu, the author of the Introduction, compares the Romanian author with the Brothers Grimm, E.T.A. Hoffmann, Franz Kafka, Jorge Luis Borges, Bruno Schulz, Julio Cortázar, Gabriel García Márquez, Milan Kundera and Milorad Pavić. If viewed against other works of Romanian literature, Cărtărescu's prose may be the most appropriate place to start a reflection on the aesthetic of the body. Somatic aesthetics can be studied as related to each aspect of his prose, starting from the generative moment, a textual phase, and going as far as the extratextual consequences of the text upon the reader. Admittedly, Cărtărescu is widely appreciated as original and visionary. However, he understands literature as Umberto Eco has understood it before him: as a creation of a precise universe, as "a cosmological" conundrum. To him, as to Eco, the author is a semi-god projecting, in a detailed and accurate way, a credible world (Eco 2011, 23). Indeed, in an interview given in 2003 to *22* magazine, Cărtărescu (2003) claims: "Some consider my books to be prolix. Actually they are a very concise mapping of the world. Seen closely, my deliriums are maybe too symmetrical and rational constructions."

Travesti (Disguise) appeared in 1994, and was the first novel published by Cărtărescu. Its subject is the universal problem of the experiences that shape a teenager; for that reason his protagonist belongs to same type as the main characters of Robert Musil's *The Confusions of Young Törless*, James Joyce's *Portrait of the Artist as a Young Man* and Herman Hesse's *The Glass Bead Game*. *Travesti* (Disguise) is the story of a 34-year narrator who records his experiences from when he was 17, half of his life so far. During the summer holiday he goes to a student camp with his classmates and there something fearful happens. He is disturbed by the recurring image of his classmate Lulu. When, disguised as a woman, Lulu is willing to touch the narrator, it has a dramatic effect on the latter: it makes him realize that his vague but haunting memory of having a little sister is actually a memory of his own first four years of childhood, when his mother used to dress him, a little hermaphrodite, as a girl. Hence the troubled personality, the terrifying personal drama that the adult tries to overcome by writing out his experience. This experience would fall within the domain of what Richard Shusterman calls analytic somaesthetics, a discipline dealing with various interactions between the body and social power, that is, norms of health, skill and beauty, and gender—all these interactions reflecting and supporting a balance of social forces

(Shusterman 2008, 23). Clothes deeply mark the personality of the young child and this trauma represents the nucleus of the novel. The adult, troubled in his mind, writes the potentially curative text addressed to his double from the mirror, Victor: "I was thinking about you, Victor, squatting there in the mirror, in your closet, in that terrifying limbo" (Cărtărescu 1994, 57). At 17, he has the appearance of a typical teenager and his ambition to write a great book balances against his physical ugliness. The teenage drama is presented in Cărtărescu's novel as a transition from the state of agony—the phase in which the boy feels contempt for everything that belongs to the body—to the stage in which a compensatory solution is found: living for and through fantasy and literature. This is the main reason for his constant feeling of loneliness, even when all his colleagues surround him with songs and jokes. His inability to join the group is perceived as a kind of schizophrenia that, as he fantasizes, could be healed by a practical intervention to remove his brain:

> I wanted to open my skull and peel off the layers of my brain's cortex, to dispose like a slobbery placenta that substance responsible of all our unhappiness, to give away on a channel the barrier between life and ourselves. I wanted to keep only the reptilian brain, to melt myself in love and bruise in hate, drooling, panting, coughing, sneezing, hiccupping, my heart beating and filtering my blood through my kidneys, killing lymph germs, everything together with everybody, with the group, gang or family with breed or species or living world or the Godhead, just so I wouldn't live the schizophrenia of thoughts anymore, this miserable loneliness alias. (Cărtărescu 1994, 127)

Thus far, Romanian prose has not been considered from the perspective of performance studies. On the other hand, the active body—the sensing body and the body in action—is frequently referred to in Cărtărescu's prose. But it is approached by criticism from a contemplative point of view. Corporeality is perceived as decorative, not as an organic function but as a mechanism—thus, not as a somatic system. Therefore, the reasons for and the consequences of Cărtărescu's references to the body remain largely unexplored.

The critical reviews of *Travesti* emphasized the originality of the author in his treatment of two important themes, writing and adolescence, but the book's "exaggerated and unconventional eroticism" (Popovici 1994, 15) has also been remarked on because it seems to be an affront to traditional maidenly modesty of Romanian literature. The critics appreciate the duality that characterizes the central character, who blends the feminine[4] and the masculine principle in his body and mind. But in

Romanian criticism the bodily experience presented in the novel is usually seen from a depreciative perspective, as an inferior level of experience. The contempt for the body in the more general context of European aesthetics is also critically noted by Richard Shusterman. Such disdain, indeed, is clear in the following excerpt of a literary comment by one Romanian critic:

> Starting from a strictly physiologic plan, passing through the labyrinth of contradictory moods and then entering the most profound zones of the subconscious, the writer follows the ascendant curve of the spiritual evolution of someone chosen to discover the bottommost truth. (Gurlui 1994, 8)

In other words, it is a common belief that in order to achieve the highest level of illumination one should transcend the barrier of the organic.

I read Cărtărescu's novel bearing in mind Richard Schechner's idea, from one of his most popular articles, "Performance Studies: The Broad Spectrum Approach" (1988), that one should analyze the performance of the artistic product instead of the critical text. Therefore, I strongly believe W. B. Worthen's opinion to be pertinent to my case. He believes that, from a literary point of view, performance is a function which sheds light on some of the meanings of the work. These meanings would otherwise remain invisible to a traditional reading, although they do exist as delitescent potentials and as a proof of the author's work (Worthen 2007, 12). Delia Pop, the author of a monograph on Cărtărescu, clearly stated that

> Romanian writer Cărtărescu is obsessed with hermeneutics and the aesthetic of the body. In his love poetry, for instance … the being builds itself within the web of the text, as an absolute modality to express freedom; the poet is symbolically giving his organs in exchange for the work of his life. (2010, 304)

And:

> one can derive a body politics from his prose too (*The Dream, Twins, Disguise*) and even from the daily notes from his *Diary*. This politics converts into metaphor, into an aesthetic category, displaying itself through language. Like any text, the body may be written or spoken and enters into dialogue with other speeches (with the Great Text), withstands their oppression … and, in its turn generates infinite meanings. (304)

In *Travesti* (Disguise), Lulu is not significant as a character, but because the author structures the narrator's existence into "periods with

Lulu" and "periods without Lulu, of a beautiful normality" (Pop 2010, 305). In this context, Richard Schechner's thought is illuminating. As he observes (recalling Eugenio Barba's theory), performers continuously play on the fragile line between equilibrium and imbalance (Schechner 1977, xviii). Therefore, performance speaks about how people turn into other people. Lulu is responsible for the way the identity of the narrator is built and expressed. This is how Lulu generates the performance. The record of him is kept both at the mental level—the narrator asks himself: "How can I cut off from my brain…?"—and at the somatic level: "Victor, do you know that my loneliness has on its white skin a boil and that this boil is called Lulu?" Referring to his memory of Lulu, the student from Budila, he declares that he has never understood what happened there: images and emotions are linked in a way that is beyond any coherent explanation. I read the "images" as representations and the "emotions" as the whole complex of sensations that contributed to the experience. Therefore, I associate this dichotomy with an observation that Shusterman (2000) makes in his *The Pragmatist Aesthetics*: art can be defined as experience, as a somatic experience in this particular case. So the narrator keeps the image in his mind, and the experience in his body.

Cărtărescu explores terrifying images and changes their usual meaning. For instance, in an extreme situation, the stopping of his breath is not a metaphor, or a rhetorical figure, but an actual fact. So, when he finds out he never had a sister, he notes:

> My brain, my heart and my sex suddenly exploded! I am torn into pieces! And the pieces are also torn into pieces! God, I cannot breathe because my throat is split ring by ring and cartilage by cartilage. My ribs pierce the skin of my chest and my skull opened in parietals in ethmoid, sphenoid and occiput, wasted away like shards of crockery. My kidneys glow between slices of meat and ribbons of skin. (Cărtărescu 1994, 167)

Writing is the ultimate recourse in the attempt to overcome the trauma:

> What I am trying here is actually the last thing I can do. I am hanging as to the last straw to the thought that maybe it's possible to heal myself through writing. I mean to let loose, as much as I can, this skein, this mess of intestines, this mandala woven into my brain. If writing is, as they say, a kind of therapy, if it can heal, it should be able to do so now. I'll muddy page after page, I'll use them as mulls imprinted not with ink, but with my old wounds' suppuration. Eventually, in the end, everything shall go through them and, as they get more purulent, I'll be drained of venom. (Cărtărescu 1994, 16)

Among the effects of these various incursions into the somatic are the performer-narrator and his powerful message. Cărtărescu's text hypnotizes the reader by using visceral references. His strategy is to make the reader believe that his aim is to obtain the illumination of the mind, but the actual focus is his body.

Bringing performance studies and somaesthetics together may seem awkward for the analysis of a literary text, but I hope that it has been a valuable exercise to highlight the effects Cărtărescu's prose on the reader. A novel critical outlook, this perspective emphasizes new features of the text. It does not 'harm' the text at all, nor does it limit the text. Thus, performance studies, within the perspective outlined by somaesthetics, can provide a challenging alternative to the traditional literary studies in the moment of humanities' crisis.

Mircea Cărtărescu seems to cancel the distance between the body and the letter, so the impression that the reader gets is, in Gheorghe Crăciun's (2009) terms, that of a somatographic pact. He wants the "cruelty and pleasure" (Cărtărescu 1994, 10) seems to of the catching of Lulu in the book, like a butterfly in the entomology display. The typewriter is

> your torture table, and mine too, for I cannot bother you without tormenting myself, as you cannot cut with a scalpel in your own meat, to remove your pus, without screaming and struggling like one possessed. (Cărtărescu 1994, 10)

As Roland Barthes declares, the pleasure of the text begins at the very moment in which the author's body will follow its own ideas, because only then does the concordance between his body and his mind take place. In Mircea Cărtărescu's prose the seduction of the reader is complete when this sensation is transferred from the writer to the reader.

References

Cărtărescu, Mircea. 1994. *Travesti* [Disguise]. București: Humanitas.
—. 2000. "Ca experienta interioara, nu fac distinctie intre poezie si proza. Interviu cu Mircea Cărtărescu" [As an inner experience, I do not distinguish between poetry and prose. An interview with Mircea Cărtărescu]. By Raluca Alexandrescu. *Observator cultural*. May 5. Accessed January 4, 2017. http://bit.ly/2ktvyAn.
—. 2003. "Toate premiile din lume nu fac cat un vers reusit dintr-o carte" [All prizes in the world do not value as much as a successful verse from a book]. An Interview with Mircea Cărtărescu. By Marius Chivu. *Revista 22*. October 2. Accessed January 4, 2017. http://bit.ly/2ks78r5.

Crăciun, Gheorghe. 2009. *Pactul somatografic* [The somatographic pact]. Pitești: Paralela 45.

Eco, Umberto. 2011. *Confesiunile unui tânăr romancier* [Confessions of a young novelist]. Translated by Ioana Gagea. Iași: Polirom.

Gurlui, Liliana Chicu. 1994. "Scrisul ca terapie" [Writing as therapy]. *Cronica*, no. 22: 8–9.

Pop, Delia. 2010. *Provocări ale postmodernității* [Challenges of Postmodernism]. Iași: Princeps Edit.

Popovici, Vasile. 1994. "Omenesc, preaomenesc" [Human, all too human]. *Revista 22*, no. 37: 15.

Schechner, Richard. 1977. *Performance Theory*. London: Routledge.

—. 1988. "Performance Studies: The Broad Spectrum Approach." *TDR* 32 (3): 4–6.

Shusterman, Richard. 2000. *Pragmatist Aesthetics: Living Beuty, Rethinking Art*. Lanham, Md.: Rowman & Littlefield Publishers.

—. 2008. *Body Consciousness: A Philosophy of Mindfulness and Somaesthetics*. New York: Cambridge University Press.

Simion, Eugen, ed. 2004. *Dicționarul general al literaturii române* [General dictionary of Romanian literature]. Vol. II, C–D. București: Editura Universul Enciclopedic.

Sora, Simona. 2008. *Regăsirea intimității* [The retrieval of intimacy]. București: Cartea Românească.

Worthen, William B. 2007. "Disciplines of the Text: Sites of Performance" In *The Performative Studies Reader*. Edited by Henry Biall, 10–25. London: Routledge.

Notes

[1] All the translations of quotations, unless stated differently, are mine.

[2] Some of the most important national awards are: *The Romanian Writers' Union Prize* in 1980, 1990, 1994, and 2008; *The Romanian Academy Prize* in 1989; *The Prize of the Writers' Association in Bucharest* in 2000 and 2003, *The "Book of the Year" Prize* in 2008, and *The National Prize for Literature* in 2008.

[3] In 1992 he was nominated for *Prix Médicis* in France, *Prix Union Latine* and *Le meilleur livre étranger* in France, for the French translation *Le Rêve*. The French translation *Orbitor* was short-listed in 1999, 2000 and 2001 for the *Prix Union Latine*. Also, in 2005 he was honored with the Acerbi Award in Italy.

[4] In an interview given to Raluca Alexandrescu, for "Observator cultural" magazine, Cărtărescu (2000) confesses: "I've always felt hung-up on seeing the world only through the eyes of the man I am. I've always wanted to see it with the other's eyes [the woman], who in a way lives latently in me."

CHAPTER SIXTEEN

UNIMMORTAL MEN
AND THE BODY OF DEATH:
THE SOMATIC EXPERIENCE OF DEATH
IN MILTON'S *PARADISE LOST*

ÁGNES BATÓ

Death as the Key to Understanding the Fall

Death is brought into the Miltonic cosmology as early as the third line of
the epic poem. In spite of the much-argued complexity of the syntactic
structure of *Paradise Lost*, the author outlines quite clearly in the very first
five lines of the work the logic behind the system of reasons and
consequences that serves as the theological basis not only for *Paradise
Lost*, but also its sequel, *Paradise Regained*. Death, in this case, is a
crucial agent in the understanding of the fall and also the universe as
described by Milton, whereby death is not just a mere allegory, but a
fundamental element of the discourse of the epic.

In the eschatological vision outlined by Milton, understanding the fall
equals to understanding the divine plan of reinstating mankind from its
fallen position, and in alignment with the biblical Revelation, creating a
new world. Therefore the epic poem presents not only the event of the fall,
but "All our woe" (1.3). In this sense sin and death must be considered and
studied from different points of view, given that their significance and role
change with the radical change in the universe. As the figures of Adam
and Eve shift from allegorical to individualized, as John Erskine (1917)
noted, both sin and death fulfil figurative and actual roles as well. Entering
Earth through the bodies of the human couple, they are transfigured, and
having become human and individualized, cease to be allegorical entities
standing for the original, essential sin and death. The role of death also
switches in terms of its adjudication, changing from the devil's curse to

men to a divine gift (Erskine 1917). Death, especially bodily death—
which causes also the death of the soul in Milton's understanding—
guarantees the resurrection of the soul and body of "unimmortal" (10.611)
men, that are unlike the fallen angels, whose final doom is eternal death.
Death, as Erskine summarizes, is the ultimate decree of God, but it also
serves as the passage to redemption. As sin, defined as the disobedience
and transgression of Eve and Adam, evolves from the universal meaning
of sin to become a personal vice, embodied in Satan, so do Eve and Adam
too, whose reasons for disobeying differ from one to the other. As the
characters meet their own personal evil, they also meet their own personal
death. During the process in which death becomes a corporeal, flesh and
blood entity and reality in the work, the abstract idea of the fall becomes a
tangible fact, acquires meaning and completes the Miltonic cosmology,
and also accounts for the events related and revealed in the text.

In my study, I have used three separate editions of John Milton's
Paradise Lost. The quotes come from Project Gutenberg's edition of
Paradise Lost. I referred to Barbara Lewalski's edition, but I do not quote
it. In terms of biblical references, I also relied on the meticulously
annotated version by Matthew Stallard, but I do not quote it either. For
further biblical references, I used an Authorized King James version of the
Holy Bible.

In the following I am going to outline a cosmology as explained by
Milton, exploring the position and role of death in it; then I will go on to
study the transcendental origin, and genealogy, of death, both as a
character in the epic and as the divine punishment; after that, on the basis
of Milton's *Treatise on the Christian Doctrine*, I will outline the author's
concept of death, in order to analyze it in relation to the human, divine and
satanic levels of creation. As a technical notice, when talking about death,
as a quality or biological phenomena, I use the word starting with a
minuscule; when I refer to the character, I write it with a capital D.

Death in the Miltonic Cosmology

Beginning with Northrop Frye, many critics have argued that, similarly to
the Scriptures, *Paradise Lost* swarms with cross-references and coincidences.
In order to understand the structure of the Miltonic, post-lapsarian
cosmology, it is necessary to study these relations, wherein death plays an
important role in establishing the order of the epic.

The poles of the order are signified by Heaven and Hell, life and death.
The former are the dwelling places of angelic and demonic creatures,
respectively, and the latter two are qualities, being present in Heaven and

Hell, filling them, providing them an atmosphere. It is no wonder that Hell is described as the "universe of death" (2.622). In the epicenter there is Earth, between the qualities of life and death, available to both. The opposite of life, therefore, is death, but that does not equal non-existence, but the lack of the divine quality which distinguishes matter from organic creatures. It is a conscious-less, senseless form of existence, a constant defect, as is exemplified by the ceaseless hunger of Death. Death is not biological; therefore it cannot terminate spiritual existence, that of the demons. For their order, death is the separation from God, the source. Death therefore is both a quality and an entity in the work, the real antithesis of God, the last enemy to be defeated.

As Milton states in his prose work, *A Treatise on Christian Doctrine* (1826, 178–79) there is no creation *ex nihilo*, because the primal matter is constant: in the cosmology of *Paradise Lost* the opposite of creation is disorder, represented by Chaos. This is a cosmic place that surrounds the entire created world. The dialectics of order and disorder rule the Miltonic universe, and the disorder of life is therefore death. Chaos, anarchy itself, is frightening even for Satan, who stands "unterrifi'd" (2.708) in front of Death; later there is a detailed account of forms of death, and the description of chaos in the Book 2 is also quite scientific. The closeness to God or to Death that (as in the paradigm above) embody the very nature of life and death, respectively, defines the position of each entity within the cosmos. Angels and demons, being immortal, are separated by their being located in Heaven and Hell, respectively; whereas Sin, carrying in itself the nature of death, was born in Heaven and does not dwell in Hell. What is significant in Milton's outlook on the wider universe is that death is not ultimate and irreversible, but only a part of the created cosmology.

The Genealogy of Death

About the existence of death we learn early enough; what is more, the author provides a vivid and mysterious explanation of its birth, as a persona and as a phenomenon as well. The incestuous adventures of Satan, Sin and Death are revolting and exciting in equal measure, the description of such fornication enjoying a certain popularity in the age of Milton. As John M. Steadman (1985) reveals, similar representations appeared in Phineas Fletcher's *The Purple Island* (1633) and Edmund Spenser's *Faerie Queene*, whose common source may be St. Basil's *Sixth Homily on the Hexaemeron*, produced in the fourth century, not to mention the several biblical allusions that relate sin to death, attributing a natural, family relation to them (Jas 1:15).

Death as a phenomenon has a cause and a history, and it is also given a body (Stein 1996). The birth of Death as the son of Satan and his daughter Sin explains the fundamental theological truth that sin brings about death, and they are inseparable, and imputable to the guilty mind of Satan, who, immersed in self-love, inflicted the creation of humankind's destiny. However, the idea of death was born in the divine mind, as the sentence for men if they disobey God's injunction on eating the fruit of the tree of knowledge. The chronological order of the events of the epic is irretraceable, and with a purpose: the atemporality reflects the divine anticipation and foreknowledge of the events in their totality. But in the design of the world it is presumably God who first devised death in the sense that He foresaw its birth. Nevertheless, death does not appear first in relation to God, but according to the logic of creation it existed at least as a possibility.

The actual conception of death took place before even the fall of the rebel angels, but its birth came after, in accordance with the theological fact that it comes into being only in a fallen world. The monstrous being is converted into the instrument of Satan to fulfil his vengeance; upon hearing the divine Decree of the aforementioned ban and punishment, he inspires Eve to sin, therefore allowing death to arrive in the world. Conversely, in Satan's understanding, the idea of death differs from the human notion of it; what he has in his mind is the unnatural figure. Eve, by contrast, when she is tempted, confronts death as an abstract concept, not a particular creature; death is for her a form of transformation, the acquisition of divine abilities. The human experience does not coincide with the satanic; death is an existence and an abstract category.

The identification of the creature with the concept happens after the moment of the deliverance of Death, as Sin recalls her fearful encounter with her firstborn: "I fled, and cry'd out *Death*; / Hell trembl'd at the hideous Name, and sigh'd / From all her Caves, and back resounded *Death*" (2.787–89). Death is created by Sin, his mother calling its name, by the power of the word, relegating to it the attributes that define it. Also, Hell at this moment becomes filled with death, it resounds with it, and reflects the negative quality of this creature, it is where "death lives" (2.624).

Death is, consequently, the result of a complex process, its manifold nature reflected in its multilevel creation. It comes alive, but it is also mortal, its existence intertwined with that of Sin:

His end with mine involvd; and knows that I
Should prove a bitter Morsel, and his bane,
When ever that shall be; so Fate pronounc'd. (2.805–7)

Death therefore would, and will, disappear if and when Sin disappears. In the following I intend to reveal the nature and the degrees of death as Milton explains them in one of his prose works.

The Degrees of Death

Milton in his prose work *A Treatise on the Christian Doctrine* distinguishes four degrees of death; and, in accordance with this distinction, in the epic paraphrase, death appears in different shapes—"If shape it might be call'd that shape had none" (2.667). As it is the somatic symptom of sin, death becomes a part of every body to a certain degree. It might possess no shape, but it possesses and devours bodies, creating the antithesis of the living body.

The precursor of death, according to Milton's prose work, is guiltiness. In the poem guiltiness also obtains a body, as it is represented by Sin, the daughter of Satan, whose incestuous union with his own daughter gives birth to death. I agree with Robert B. White Jr. that Milton presents Sin and Death as coeternal with Satan, as the inversion of the Holy Trinity, since Satan himself is pregnant with the potential for becoming a sinner, a condition that materializes in his daughter. On the same grounds, Satan carries in himself the potential of death; however as an originally heavenly creature, he lacks a physical body. He belongs to a legion of creatures that are

> ... so soft
> And uncompounded is their Essence pure,
> Not ti'd or manacl'd with joynt or limb,
> Nor founded on the brittle strength of bones,
> Like cumbrous flesh ... (1.424 –28)

Nevertheless he suffers the second degree of death, namely spiritual, together with the army of his followers: they lose their divine grace, they are changed. The biblical passage "How art thou fallen from heaven, O Lucifer, son of the morning?" (Isa 14:12) is paraphrased in *Paradise Lost*: "But O how fall'n! how chang'd / From him" (1. 84–85), him referring to God the Lord. The symptoms of spiritual death, as Milton describes them, feature the loss of right reason, a symptom spectacularly enacted by the fallen archangel throughout his soliloquies, leading finally to the total reinterpretation of the divine order and prohibition that prevented Eve from eating of the fruit of the tree of knowledge. He also, as Milton describes it, becomes a "servant of sin," and loses his will to do good.

The third degree of death, bodily death, materializes in the human world as Eve consumes the fruit, putting the seed of death into her own body. The human couple experiences the symptoms of the first two degrees of death immediately after trying the "mortal taste," their newly discovered nakedness being the sign of shame of guilt. Bodily death exists only on the human level of creation or existence, but though it integrates into the human discourse naturally, this does not take place during the course of the argument. Adam contemplates it in a vision and is taken aback with horror: "But have I now seen Death? Is this the way / I must return to native dust?"(11.462–63). In Abel, his son, he recognizes only death; the death, once again, depicted as a son, but also as a horrible independent entity. The scene alludes back to the event in Book 2 when Satan fails to recognize his son: both Satan and Adam, therefore, show the symptoms of spiritual death.

The fourth degree, Death Eternal, is the punishment for the damned after judgment day, represented by hell:

> Rocks, Caves, Lakes, Fens, Bogs, Dens, and shades of death,
> A Universe of death, which God by curse
> Created evil, for evil only good,
> Where all life dies, death lives, and Nature breeds,
> Perverse, all monstrous, all prodigious things (1.621–25)

Hell, then is the negation of existence, not only the extinction of life of a body, but also damnation. Their residence in Hell, the dwelling place of the fallen angels, means that the rebels are damned, destined to suffer eternally in the empire of death, where they will be locked up after Judgment Day. The fallen angels, therefore, experience all degrees of death, except the bodily degree. The bodily degree of death means the union with death, which is not available for the demons.

The several appearances of death, nevertheless, do not mean that death is an ultimate power in Milton's cosmology. In the coordinate system of *Paradise Lost*, death is the condition that stands opposite to God, at the other extreme, but its power is limited by the power emanating from God, affecting only the human degree of creation, the "unimmortal" level. However, bodily death is also temporal, therefore it is not the antithesis of creation. Creation, according to Milton, is not *ex nihilo*; the opposite of creation is Chaos, the lack of the rule of divine order that controls the otherwise boiling elements that constitute the world. Hell and death are "dark materials" (2.916), but still controlled by the ultimate power of the Creator.

Eating Death: The "Unimmortal" Experience of Death

The human concept of death is treated carefully by the author of *Paradise Lost*, given the fact that at the exposition of the epic the human couple cannot exactly grasp the meaning of this phenomenon, but nevertheless are quite aware of it, and they also voice their concerns:

> So neer grows Death to Life, what ere Death is,
> Som dreadful thing no doubt; for well thou knowst
> God hath pronounc't it death to taste that Tree (4.425–27)

To them the only known facts about death, therefore, are its difference from life and its status as a form of punishment on God's part. However, death also arouses curiosity, as they realize its proximity to life. In the logic of the human world, death is closely linked to life and knowledge, meaning that the comprehension of the totality of human existence lies in understanding death. The obvious question is formulated by Satan: "Can it be sin to know, / Can it be death?" (4.517–18).

The answer to this question arrives in the form of a somatic experience: it is their nakedness that they become conscious of after tasting the fruit, leaving them to confront the vulnerability of the naked body (9. 1053–69). In the typically Miltonic way—through a play of opposites in which Milton depicts how they move from the state in which they were protected, or "shadowed," by innocence from the knowledge of evil to the state of having their eyes opened, but their minds darkened— Adam and Eve recognize their material existence, which creates in them a new sense of perception. They understand that they are not spiritual beings but that they possess a body, and the awareness of corporeal experience generates guilt. Guilt, as Milton describes it in the *Christian Doctrine*, is the first sign of death. By hiding their body, humans hide their imperfection; covering and clothing are associated with shame, enmity, confusion; and the power of Satan, deceit (Psalms 109:29).

Death is also interpreted as a transformation: disguised as the serpent, in Book 9, Satan, argues that he owes his own transformation from a beast to a human to the power of the tree of knowledge, and the threat of death is nothing but the transition from human to divine (9.679–732). Eve, in fact, undergoes a wild transformation as well; as Neil Forsyth (2003) noted, she carries out the first interpretation in sacred history, and rereads God's words. Also, she becomes similar to Death, as she experiences great hunger and devours the fruit, anticipating the monstrous, Death's insatiable despoiling of the world (Kermode 1960). Thus, eventually, death becomes a part of the human body, and is "brought" to the world through the female body, wherein its seeds are planted, although she "knew not eating Death" (9.792). From then on, death is elicited in several ways and, in association with the loss of happiness, becomes part of human discourse, as it is of everyday speech. The profanation of the word and the frequent conjuring of death also predict how it becomes part of human consciousness, and becomes related to loss.

This sentiment of loss has also somatic symptoms, as Adam perceives Eve affected by her mortal transformation; nevertheless he cannot avoid sharing the crime with her:

> ... yet loss of thee
> Would never from my heart; no no, I feel
> The Link of Nature draw me: Flesh of Flesh,
> Bone of my Bone thou art, and from thy State
> Mine never shall be parted, bliss or woe. (9.906–16)

What is an emotionally charged confession also explains the human perception of life—and death. That Adam feels the bond between Eve and himself to the bone, their similar nature, their corporeality, makes him accept and share the destiny of Eve—who also decided to share her fate with Adam, whatever it brings with it. Therefore human death, up to this point, serves as an expression of the feeling of loss and fear of the unknown, but meanwhile as the human couple explore the meaning of it, they learn about their bodies. In the process the image of Eve appears to be the mirror of Sin, as both are accompanied by death: "if Death / Consort with thee, Death is to mee as Life" (9. 953–54). This is a reference to Satan's meeting with his own tempter, Sin, who is also followed by Death in the second Book.

The bodily experiences do not cease at this point, since Adam, after eating his share of the fruit, and therefore death, is as sexually excited as upon his first meeting with Eve, and they engage in sexual intercourse as wild as the epic description allows. Their lovemaking differs from their former sexual encounters registered in Book 4 in that it is charged with lust, a carnal feeling, as opposed to pure love, which is sacred. In Book 4 the human couple is also depicted as naked, but their nakedness invokes no guilt or shame, and their lovemaking is described as the opposite of hypocritical celibacy.[1] There Milton recalls the biblical teachings of marital due, godly procreation and the sacred mystery of matrimony, whereas the depiction of their union in Book 9 paraphrases the description in the biblical Proverbs (7) of a prostitute seducing a young man. This new kind of bodily experience reduces sex to a tradable luxury, committed under the shadow of death.

Yet further experience still awaits man. Adam, while wondering about the nature of death, arrives at the conclusion that it cannot be the separation of soul and body, given that it is not the body which is sinful, and if the soul survives, it "shall die a living Death" (10.788). He imagines the souls wandering in hell, but he discards the image as unnatural, reflecting Milton's own idea elaborated in *A Treatise on Christian Doctrine* (279–80). He also begins to understand the impossibility of "deathless Death" (10.798), a death that is eternal, given that it contradicts nature's law, so he begins to envision redemption. But at this stage he only fears that:

> That Death be not one stroak, as I suppos'd,
> Bereaving sense, but endless miserie
> From this day onward, which I feel begun
> Both in me, and without me, and so last
> To perpetuitie; Ay me, that fear
> Comes thundring back with dreadful revolution
> On my defensless head; both Death and I
> Am found Eternal, and incorporate both (10.809–16)

Adam recognizes the double significance of death, that in the bodily sense it is an event that comes to pass, ending cognitive processes (an alienation from the created world). As he becomes aware and certain of death, he experiences feelings and symptoms which death entails. This new awareness, and the richness of feelings, thus, is occasioned by the human being's mortality. The man becomes of one body with death, as death coexists within and with man: as Adam says, "make death in us live" (10.1028).

The understanding of the nature of death culminates in Adam's contemplating it for the first time: in the vision of the first killing, the murder of Abel committed by Cain. When Adam is allowed to see the future of mankind, he first must face death, and cries out in dismay: "But have I now seen Death?" (11.462). Indeed, what Adam sees is how the image of God is "Rowling in dust and gore" (11.460) and returns to its "native dust" (11. 463). The alienation from the divine source is complete, and even the divine image, the body, is destroyed, becoming the image of death. Contrary to Lucifer, Adam never sees death as a bodiless shape, but only through the human body. He also must behold an encyclopedic list of ailments and diseases that wreck the human body, and learns about the symptoms of old age, but also learns how to keep fit. Understanding death, thus, leads to the understanding of the fall and the new human existence.

Death his Deaths Wound Shall then Receive:
The Divine Perception of Death

The divine definition of death means that it is a punishment for the disobedience of the human couple, a result of their newly acquired knowledge of evil. The realization of having committed sin makes man guilty; it equals the knowledge of evil, and causes death to ensue, that is, distances humans from the source of life, and drives them to a negative world, Hell. However, from God's point of view, death is not eternal, and the dead may be ransomed by the death of an immortal creature. In the sacrifice of Christ, his death must be realized through the body, he needs to become incarnate, obtain a human body, and suffer death; but being exempt from sin, he can recover from death:

> Thou wilt not leave me in the loathsom grave
> His prey, nor suffer my unspotted Soule
> For ever with corruption there to dwell;
> But I shall rise Victorious, and subdue
> My Vanquisher, spoild of his vanted spoile;
> Death his deaths wound shall then receive, and stoop
> Inglorious, of his mortall sting disarm'd.
> I through the ample Air in Triumph high
> Shall lead Hell Captive maugre Hell, and show
> The powers of darkness bound. (3.247–56)

Death can be put to death, therefore, and limited to the level of existence which is farthest from God. Christ envisions the ritual of dying and resurrection, predicting the promise of a second life for men. As the biblical Revelations predict, those whose names are omitted from the book of life, will suffer the second death, and will be cast into the lake of fire at the Last Judgement (Rev 20:12–14). After that a new world is born, free from sin and death.

Death as a punishment befalls humankind for one reason: for not appreciating the divine image in themselves. As the archangel Michael explains to Adam in Book 11:

> Therefore so abject is thir punishment,
> Disfiguring not Gods likeness, but thir own,
> Or if his likeness, by themselves defac't
> While they pervert pure Natures healthful rules
> To loathsom sickness, worthily, since they
> Gods Image did not reverence in themselves. (11. 520–25)

The decay of the human body is due to its being alienated from its divine essence, losing the likeness. Sin and death exist as a disruption of the divine order within creation, death originally being the elimination of flaws from within the matrix of existence, with the death of the human couple following upon the tasting of the fruit. However, since they do not die immediately, flaws trigger more flaws, which is why they are set loose in the mortal world, where they are brought through the human body. Thus, allowing for the mortal existence of humankind means channeling death into the world. The human body pregnant with death causes the decay of Earth. But eventually the rule of Death on Earth is only temporal, which is why his power is limited to the mortal bodies, and outside of the Earth it is confined to a shapeless form.

Satanic Experience of Death

Contrary to the human, somatic experience of death—in which death appears solely in the figure of the human body—the satanic death is depicted as an independent entity, as if being a black hole, consisting of antimatter, possessing nothing reminiscent of a living creature. Within the divine order, death is placed furthest from life in the system of coordinates of the Miltonic cosmology, representing a gap which the divine power does not reach, causing a total lack which provokes insatiable hunger. The evil of death, in fact, is only the gravity that attracts and devours everything that lives, depriving creatures of what life is, returning them to earth.

It is Satan who first comes across death in the epic:

> … The other shape,
> If shape it might be call'd that shape had none
> Distinguishable in member, joynt, or limb,
> Or substance might be call'd that shadow seem'd,
> For each seem'd either; black it stood as Night,
> Fierce as ten Furies, terrible as Hell,
> And shook a dreadful Dart; what seem'd his head
> The likeness of a Kingly Crown had on. (2.666–73)

The sight of death is terrible for Lucifer—himself being the son of God as well—because it defies visual expectations and possibilities, having no shape, that is, a body with discernible body parts. The image of God therefore cannot be discovered in him. It is horrible because it is unimaginable, yet Satan must witness its existence.

The encounter of Satan and Death, no matter how terrible it might be, contains a set of allusions that reflect the divine power illuminating even this cursed corner of the universe. Death, in accordance with biblical and traditional imagery, carries the signs of power, a dart and a crown, as a presage of his future reign in the mortal world. On the other hand, Lucifer still shines as the angel of light, preserving something of his former glory, and appears as a comet, and as Ophiucus, the Serpent Bearer, a celestial body that portends war and pestilence.[2] In spite of being depicted as a bearer of ill omens, Lucifer is still associated with light, and the comet predicts the fall of kings, represented by Death. The reader-listener therefore is reminded, even at this point, of the power and the final victory of Divine Providence.

The actual figure of Sin and Death are often considered to be allegories; however, they are not more allegorical than any other characters in the work. The importance of Sin and Death being depicted as separate entities in the work is the key to the notion of immortality. For the rebel angels, when they are exiled from Heaven and cast into a fiery lake, theirs is an eternal suffering, unlike men's of which God says, "Man therefore shall find grace, / The other none" (3.131–32). The punishment of the demons, as they themselves realize, lies in its infinite nature; they cannot unite with death, mortality is alien to their nature, but for this reason their suffering is also eternalized. Death, which serves as a rite of passage for humankind, is unreachable for Satan, although visible, and therefore he can contemplate it in its full form, unlike Adam and Eve, who only sense it via their own bodies, or by the sight of the dead body of Abel.

The importance of Sin and Death lies in the fact that, together with Satan, they represent the antithesis of the Holy Trinity of Heaven, thus creating a negative pole in the universe. As Robert B. White argues, the fatherly self-knowledge embodied in the Son turns into self-ignorance when Satan fails to recognize his former love and the fruit of their incestuous union (1973, 340). Sin, the negative equivalent of the Holy Spirit, stands for the misdirected self-love that Satan feels for his own "perfect image" (2.764), the young and beautiful Sin, whom he would rather forget and deny when they meet again. The formal discrepancy arising between the employment of allegorical figures and the conventions of the epic poem seems problematic. However, taking into consideration the Miltonic universe as a whole, it becomes clear that these figures are not mere personifications that serve as vehicles to enhance our understanding of abstract notions. They exist as epic characters on their own. For example, the relationship of Sin and Death with Satan cannot be viewed as a negative reflection of the union of the holy Trinity: instead, it subverts the idea of consubstantiality. Besides, Sin and Death participate in corporeality; and in this respect they are distinguished also even from incorporeal angels. Death cannot exist as a phenomenon in the universe outside Earth, since other creatures are not mortal; but according to the Miltonic doctrine, as a figure, he is also delivered, given birth to, and therefore acquires a shapeless, bodiless existence. The relationship of Satan, Sin and Death also refers to the perverted union of Adam and Eve, whose mortal love will give birth to Cain and Abel, of whom the former becomes a murderer. Since the love of the first human couple is lustful, they deliver imperfect creatures, and as a result, the first death in sacred history is an unnatural death. Notably, the first birth in the Miltonic sacred history is that of a being named after God's designed punishment for sin— Death. The newborn creature assumes his role because, indeed, he coincides with the divine plan. The destructive, painful event of Death's birth is also an omen that predicts the physical reality of delivering a child, with labor being a punishment for women for Eve's transgression. In the physical sense, Sin is in constant labor due to being violated by Death, and Satan witnesses the terrible reality of the tormented, distorted female body as the result of childbearing. It is Sin herself who relates her essentially bodily experiences:

> Thine own begotten, breaking violent way
> Tore through my entrails, that with fear and pain
> Distorted, all my nether shape thus grew
> Transform'd: but he my inbred enemie
> Forth issu'd … (2.782–87)

The abuse of Sin's body by both Satan and their son, Death, may be an obscene parody of the Holy Trinity, but her physical disfigurement also indicates the immortal experience of death. Although immortal creatures cannot die a bodily death, they are subjected to decay and deformation, which comes with the separation from God. Sin's constant suffering is a reminder of the infinite torments that the demons must endure, and which will be their destiny after the last day.

Conclusion

The Miltonic death, in the end, is "unimmortal," limited, only temporal in the universe, and to be destroyed by the victorious Son. Although it is able to "unimmortal make / All kinds" (10.611–12), the prefix itself suggests that in the divine morphology the root of the world is not "mortal" but immortal, being the natural form of existence. Similarly, God calls "mortal foe" (3.179) the enemy of mankind, which has double connotations as well. Throughout the poem "mortal" is used as "giving death" and "subject to death"; therefore, sin and death can be viewed in two ways: they are destructive, but they are also predicted to be destroyed when they receive a deadly strike from the Redeemer.

Milton carefully designed the representations and appearances of death to teach about the essence of the fall, the separation from God, and also to remind his readers, constantly, of the promise of redemption. Death, however terrible, is nevertheless limited, tied to the human body, but not indestructible; therefore it is acceptable, serving the divine design as a passage from mortal to immortal existence. The physical depictions and supposed personifications humanize the epic, imparting to it its uniquely sublime quality, of which death is an organic part.

References

Erskine, John. 1917. "The Theme of Death in Paradise Lost." *PMLA* 32 (4): 573–82. DOI: 10.2307/456939.

Forsyth, Neil. 2003. *The Satanic Epic*. Princeton: Princeton University Press.

Holy Bible. Authorized King James Version [1611]. 1984. Grand Rapids, Michigan: Zondervan Publishing House.

Kermode, Frank, ed. 1960. *The Living Milton: Essays by Various Hands*. London: Routledge & Kegan Paul.

Milton, John. 2007. *Paradise Lost* [1667]. Edited by Barbara Lewalski. Malden: Blackwell Publishing Ltd.

—. 2009. *Paradise Lost* [1667]. In *The Poetical Works of John Milton*. Urbana, Illinois: Project Gutenberg. Retrieved January 22, 2017, from: http://bit.ly/2krNLyG.

—. 2011. *Paradise Lost* [1667]. Edited by Matthew Stallard. Macon: Mercer University Press.

—. 1826. *A Treatise on Christian Doctrine* [1659]. Translated by Charles R. Sumner. Cambridge: Cambridge University Press.

Steadman, John M. 1958. "Milton and St. Basil: The Genesis of Sin and Death." *Modern Language Notes* 73 (2): 83–84. DOI: 10.2307/3043042.

Stein, Arnold. 1996. "Imagining Death: The Ways of Milton." *PMLA* 30: 77–91.

White, Robert B., Jr. 1973. "Milton's Allegory of Sin and Death: A Comment on Backgrounds." *Modern Philology* 70 (4): 339–41.

Notes

[1] In the Biblically Annotated version of *Paradise Lost* edited by Matthew Stallard, there are collected the biblical references to unnecessary abstention as being a hypocritical and satanic thing: 1 Tim 4:1–3, 1 Tim 3:2.

[2] Barbara Lewalski's notes in the footnote to lines 709–11 on page 57 of her edition of *Paradise Lost*.

CONTRIBUTORS

ÁGNES BATÓ is a student of the Graduate School of Literary Studies, University of Szeged, Hungary. She majored in English and Spanish languages and literatures. She wrote two M.A. theses, at the English and Spanish Departments, titled *Mirrors of Paradise Lost* (2013) and *Góngora and the Sublime* (2014). Her research interests comprise epic poetry and visual culture, focusing on the mirror metaphor and the attitudes to perception and mirroring in literature, visual arts, and literary criticism.

ANDRÁS BERZE was born in 1989, in Senta, Yugoslavia. He obtained an M.A. degree from the University of Szeged in 2013. In the year 2016, he completed the pre-doctoral course at the University of Szeged. His research interests include theatricality, film adaptations, and depictions of violence. He is writing his dissertation on the adaptations of Thomas Harris's Hannibal novels. He is currently employed as a technical writer in Budapest, Hungary.

MATTHEW BIBERMAN, a Professor of English at the University of Louisville (USA), is the author of the scholarly monograph *Antisemitism, Masculinity and Early Modern English Literature* and of the memoir *Big Sid's Vincati*. With Julia Lupton he is the editor of the essay collection *Shakespeare After 9/11*. His study *Shakespeare, Adaptation, Psychoanalysis* is forthcoming from Routledge.

ANNA BUDZIAK teaches literature and literary theory at the University of Wrocław, Poland. Her research interests include British Decadent Aestheticism and Modernism. She has authored two book-length studies: on T. S. Eliot (in Polish), and on Walter Pater and Oscar Wilde. The latter, *Text, Body and Indeterminacy: Doppelgänger Selves in Pater and Wilde*, was shortlisted for the biennial ESSE Book Award, 2008–2010. She has also published articles exploring the interface between literature and philosophy.

ALEX CIOROGAR is a Ph.D. candidate in Comparative Literature, Babeş-Bolyai University (Romania), from which he also earned two M.A. degrees, in Comparative Literature and Romanian Literary Studies. He has authored a number of book reviews and articles, and has co-edited two volumes of critical analyses dedicated to Dimitrie Cantemir's *Istoria Ieroglifică* (The hieroglyphic history), regarded as the first Romanian novel. His current research interests include contemporary literary theory, digital humanities, authorship theories, and life-writing.

LILLA FARMASI is a Ph.D. student at the Institute of English and American Studies, University of Szeged, Hungary. She focuses on the ways human embodiment, text, and narratives influence each other. Her research interests include cognitive theories, postclassical narratology, the phenomenology of perception, and postmodern American prose. Recently, she has also explored various applications of narrative theory in non-literary contexts, especially in the fields of psychology and psychiatry.

ZUZANNA KOZŁOWSKA is a Ph.D. student at the Faculty of Polish and Classical Philology, Adam Mickiewicz University of Poznań, Poland. Her research interests include digital humanities, neuroaesthetics, and the anthropology of the body and the senses as new perspectives within literary studies. In particular, she explores literary synaesthesia in twentieth-century Polish poetry.

KATARZYNA LISOWSKA graduated from the University of Wrocław, Department of Polish Studies, where she currently teaches poetics. Her research interests comprise gender criticism, queer criticism, feminist literary criticism, and gay and lesbian criticism. In her doctoral thesis she considers different kinds of metaphors used in gender discourse as it functions in literary studies in Poland since 1989.

URSZULA LISOWSKA, Ph.D., is an Assistant Lecturer in the Institute of Philosophy at the University of Wrocław, Poland. She has recently defended her doctoral thesis, in which she proposes a politico-aesthetic approach to Martha Nussbaum's philosophy. She continues her research on the intersections between liberal political philosophy and aesthetics.

SABINA MACIOSZEK is a Ph.D. student at the University of Wrocław, Poland. Her research is currently focused on the strategies of interaction between bodies and technologies in present-day operas. She is also interested in the relationship between stage presence and absence, as well as in the multilayered intermingling of different kinds of visual and performative arts.

JOANNA MAJ is a Ph.D. candidate at the University of Wrocław, Poland. She has graduated from the Department of Polish Studies and the Institute of Philosophy. Currently, she is preparing her doctoral thesis, which deals with the New Genre Perspective of Polish Literary History. The areas of her academic interests include comparative literary theory, literature in a geopoetical perspective, and the ethical implications of literary studies.

GLORIA LUQUE MOYA is a doctoral candidate at the University of Málaga, Spain. She is currently writing her dissertation on John Dewey's aesthetics. She has published various articles in Spanish academic journals and has participated in international conferences, including the 19th International Congress of Aesthetics, where her paper was awarded the Young Scholar Award. Her primary research interests are in aesthetics, pragmatism, and John Dewey's philosophy.

IULIA RĂDAC is a Ph.D. candidate at the Faculty of Letters at Babeş-Bolyai University in Cluj-Napoca, Romania. In her Ph.D. research, she investigates Romanian novels with protagonists that strongly resemble their authors and examines the psychological motivations, textual consequences, and the larger concepts behind these works. She is interested in metafictional strategies, the aesthetics of reception, narratology, and postmodern studies in general.
Contact: iuliaradac@gmail.com

PAULINA TCHURZEWSKA is a Ph.D. student at the Faculty of Letters, Nicolaus Copernicus University in Toruń, Poland. She holds M.A. degrees in Philosophy (with her thesis "Walter Benjamin's and Theodor W. Adorno's Aesthetic Theory and Polish Contemporary Art") and in Cultural Studies (with her thesis titled "Dialectic of Communication Process in Michael Haneke's Filmography"). She also studied at the Theater Department, Aix-Marseille University. Her research interests comprise theater, performance studies, and the role of the body in contemporary art and culture.

ALEKSANDER TROJANOWSKI is a Ph.D. candidate at the University of Wrocław, Poland, where he is currently preparing his doctoral thesis on the narratives of Roberto Bolaño, and works on Hispano-American contemporary literature in general.
Contact: aleksander.trojanowski@uwr.edu.pl

KONRAD WOJNOWSKI (b. 1987) is an assistant at the Performativity Studies Department, Jagiellonian University, Poland. He has written two books: *Pożyteczne katastrofy* (Productive catastrophes) and *Estetyka zakłócenia: kino Michaela Hanekego* (Aesthetics of disturbance: The cinema of Michael Haneke). He is interested in theories of performativity, the philosophy of communication, and various intersections between culture, science, and technology.

JAROSŁAW WOŹNIAK graduated from the University of Wrocław, Department of Polish Studies. He is currently working on his doctoral thesis devoted to the performative turn in literary theory. His research interests include performance studies, the philosophy of the body, ecocriticism, and the politics of literature.

INDEX

Eco, Umberto, 260, 264
Egginton, William, 50, 58
Ely, Roxanne, 184
embodied cognition, 156–57
embodied mind, 139, 144
emotions, 26, 37
    and aesthetic experience of
        duende, 119–20, 124–26
    and bodiliness, 27
    as judgments, 26, 43
    compassion, 29–31
    disgust, 30, 32
    grief, 41
    shame, 29–31
    wonder, 33–34, 38
empathy, 223
    and corporeality, 224–25
    and involvement, 225
    and violence, 226
    in phenomenological perspective,
        221–22
    the colloquial meaning, 226
energy, 64, 66–67, 71, 74
    and communication, 63, 69, 75–
        77, 79
    and cybernetics, 65
    and performance studies, 67–70,
        80
    and speech acts, 75
    distribution, 68–72, 75–77
Enticott, Peter G., 182
Erskine, John, 267–68, 280
exhaustion, 86, 88, 93–94
    of characters, 86, 94–96, 100
    of forms, 86, 96–100
    of themes, 99
experience, 108
    bodily, 109, 113
experience recreated in the act of
    reading, 208–9
Fairbairn, William Ronald Dodds,
    28
Falla, Manuel, de, 118–19
Fauconnier, Gilles, 157
Felman, Shoshana, 208
Ficino, Marsilio, 14, 236, 237

Filipiak, Izabela, 15, 249–53, 255–
    56
Fischer-Lichte, Erika, 63, 74, 81, 83
Fitzgibbon, Bernadette M., 182, 185
Fletcher, Phineas, 269
Foglia, Lucia, 156, 169
Forsyth, Neil, 273, 280
Foster, Hal, 94, 101
Foucault, Michel, 3, 10, 52, 55, 57,
    136, 153
Freeman, Samuel, 44
Frisch, Michael, 194–95
Friston, Karl, 66
Gadamer, Hans-Georg, 142
Gagea, Ioana, 264
Galeyev, Bulat M., 181
Garber, James, 82
gender identity, 260
    and performativity, 247–51
Gennep, Arnold, van, 63
Georgiou-Karistianis, Nellie, 182
Gibbs, Raymond, 157, 168
Gilbert, Sandra M., 253
Giordano, John, 3, 17
Giummarra, Melita J., 182
Glover, Jonathan, 44
Goffman, Erving, 31, 134
Goldstein, Kenneth S., 195
González, Susana, 207, 210
Grabuś, Łukasz, 98–99, 101
Gray, Marcus A., 182
Grimm, Jacob, 260
Grimm, Wilhelm, 260
Grishakova, Marina, 199, 210
Grotowski, Jerzy, 8, 103–5, 110
Gubar, Susan, 253, 255
Gurlui, Liliana Chicu, 262, 265
Haidt, Jonathan, 30, 45
Halberstam, Judith, 8, 85, 93, 101
Halperin, David M., 253
Hampe, Beate, 158, 168
Handtke, Ryszard, 182, 185
Harbisson, Neil, 182, 185
Harris, Thomas, 12–13, 215, 219–
    20, 226–32
Harrison, John E., 181

Laub, Dori, 208
Lem, Stanisław, 188
Leroi-Gourhan, André, 50, 58
Lévinas, Emmanuel, 142–44, 152, 216
Lewalski, Barbara, 268, 280–81
Leypoldt, Günter, 59
liminality, 63–64
Lin, Maya, 41
Lisiecka, Sława, 101
Liszka, Katarzyna, 254
literary canon
    and performativity, 199, 201, 204
    as ideology, 197–98, 201, 204
Llosa, Mario Vargas, 209, 211
Lloyd, Henry M., 171, 182
Lorca, Federico Garcia, 9, 117–29
Loughran, David K., 126, 128–29
Loxley, James, 62, 82
Luria, Alexandr R., 174, 183
Łebkowska, Anna, 173, 182, 185, 252, 254–55
Macé, Marielle, 6, 50, 55–59
Machon, Josephine, 186
Macquarrie, John, 232
Madejski, Jerzy, 251, 254, 256
Makowski, Piotr, 151
Małecki, Wojciech, 17, 58, 137–39, 152, 184
Mamet, David, 232
Markiewicz, Henryk, 183, 185
Markowski, Michał Paweł, 254
Márquez, Gabriel García, 260
Martın, William, 255
Maus, Gerrit W., 181
Maxwell, Emily C., 182
McCauley, Clark R., 30, 45
McGee, John, 82
McKenzie, Jon, 1, 17, 64, 66, 82, 93, 135, 141, 152
McLintock, David, 101
Mehlman, Jeffrey, 81
Meier, Beat, 184, 186
Melosik, Zbyszko, 254, 255
Menary, Richard, 157, 168

Merleau-Ponty, Maurice, 8, 50, 52, 103, 104–5, 107, 109, 111–14, 136–38, 143, 145, 152, 155, 164, 168, 216
Meschonnic, Henri, 183, 185
Miall, David S., 178, 183
Michaels, Walter Benn, 208
Michniewski, Wojciech, 98, 102
Miklós, Győri, 168
Mikołejko, Zbigniew, 96, 102
Milán, Emilio G., 174, 182
Millar, Susanna, 166, 168
Milton, John, 15–16, 267–69, 271–75, 280
Miłosz, Czesław, 11, 188–91, 194–96
Minati, Ludovico, 182
Mittermayer, Manfred, 85, 87–88, 90, 97, 102
Mizielińska, Joanna, 248, 254–56
moral psychology, reasonable, 21–22, 26–28, 36, 42
Morris, Christopher, 44
Morrison, Andrew, 29
Motherwell, Robert, 177
Mozart, Wolfgang Amadeus, 7, 39–40, 85, 87–88, 92–94, 99
Murat, Michel, 55
Musil, Robert, 260
Myers, Greg, 66, 82
Myers, Robert, 81
Mykietyn, Paweł, 7, 85–86, 96–100
Nabokov, Vladimir, 176, 183, 186
Nardocchio, Elaine F., 172, 183
narrative and the body, 160–61, 163, 165–67
Natalia LL (Lach-Lachowicz, Natalia), 8, 103–4, 106–10, 114
Nawrot, Teresa, 105
negative performativity, 93, 95
Nietzsche, Friedrich, 101, 136, 240
Noë, Alva, 157, 166, 169
Norton, Edward, 227
Novalis, 86, 102
Nowicki, Stanisław, 188, 195
Nussbaum, Martha, 5, 21–47